Multiple Connections in European Cooperation

International organizations are ubiquitous in contemporary Europe and the wider world. This book is the first systematic assessment of the interactions of the European Communities (EC) with other Western organizations like NATO, the OECD and the Council of Europe for the period from the late 1960s to the early 1990s. Based on fresh archival research, its various contributions explore forms of co-operation and competition between these forums and thus seek to 'provincialize' and 'de-centre' the role of the predecessors of today's European Union. Drawing on examples from a diverse set of policy fields including human rights, the environment, security, culture and regional policy, the book argues that inter-organizational dynamics are crucial to understand why the EC became increasingly hegemonic among the organizations active in governing Europe. In other words, the EU would not be what it is, were it not for the dynamics analyzed in this book.

This book was originally published as a special issue of the *European Review of History*.

Kiran Klaus Patel is Chair of European and Global History and Jean Monnet Professor at Maastricht University, The Netherlands.

Wolfram Kaiser is Professor of European Studies at the University of Portsmouth, UK, and Visiting Professor at the College of Europe in Bruges, Belgium.

Multiple Connections in European Cooperation

International Organizations, Policy Ideas, Practices and Transfers, 1967–1992

Edited by
Kiran Klaus Patel and Wolfram Kaiser

LONDON AND NEW YORK

First published 2018
by Routledge
2 Park Square, Milton Park, Abingdon, Oxon, OX14 4RN, UK

and by Routledge
711 Third Avenue, New York, NY 10017, USA

Routledge is an imprint of the Taylor & Francis Group, an informa business

© 2018 Taylor & Francis

All rights reserved. No part of this book may be reprinted or reproduced or utilised in any form or by any electronic, mechanical, or other means, now known or hereafter invented, including photocopying and recording, or in any information storage or retrieval system, without permission in writing from the publishers.

Trademark notice: Product or corporate names may be trademarks or registered trademarks, and are used only for identification and explanation without intent to infringe.

British Library Cataloguing-in-Publication Data
A catalogue record for this book is available from the British Library

ISBN13: 978-1-138-49133-5

Typeset in Minion Pro
by codeMantra

Publisher's Note
The publisher accepts responsibility for any inconsistencies that may have arisen during the conversion of this book from journal articles to book chapters, namely the possible inclusion of journal terminology.

Disclaimer
Every effort has been made to contact copyright holders for their permission to reprint material in this book. The publishers would be grateful to hear from any copyright holder who is not here acknowledged and will undertake to rectify any errors or omissions in future editions of this book.

Contents

Citation Information	vi
Notes on Contributors	viii

Introduction: Multiple connections in European co-operation: international organizations, policy ideas, practices and transfers 1967–92   1
Wolfram Kaiser and Kiran Klaus Patel

1   Facing the Greek junta: the European Community, the Council of Europe and the rise of human-rights politics in Europe   22
Víctor Fernández Soriano

2   Who should pay for pollution? The OECD, the European Communities and the emergence of environmental policy in the early 1970s   41
Jan-Henrik Meyer

3   The true 'EURESCO'? The Council of Europe, transnational networking and the emergence of European Community cultural policies, 1970–90   63
Kiran Klaus Patel and Oriane Calligaro

4   Between cooperation and competitive bargaining: the Council of Europe, local and regional networking, and the shaping of the European Community's regional policies, 1970s–90s   87
Birte Wassenberg

5   Re-designing military security in Europe: cooperation and competition between the European community and NATO during the early 1980s   109
Angela Romano

6   De-centring the European union: policy diffusion among European regional organizations – a comment   136
Thomas Risse

Index   149

Citation Information

The chapters in this book were originally published in the *European Review of History*, volume 24, issue 3 (June 2017). When citing this material, please use the original page numbering for each article, as follows:

Introduction
Multiple connections in European co-operation: international organizations, policy ideas, practices and transfers 1967–92
Wolfram Kaiser and Kiran Klaus Patel
European Review of History, volume 24, issue 3 (June 2017) pp. 337–357

Chapter 1
Facing the Greek junta: the European Community, the Council of Europe and the rise of human-rights politics in Europe
Victor Fernández Soriano
European Review of History, volume 24, issue 3 (June 2017) pp. 358–376

Chapter 2
Who should pay for pollution? The OECD, the European Communities and the emergence of environmental policy in the early 1970s
Jan-Henrik Meyer
European Review of History, volume 24, issue 3 (June 2017) pp. 377–398

Chapter 3
The true 'EURESCO'? The Council of Europe, transnational networking and the emergence of European Community cultural policies, 1970–90
Kiran Klaus Patel and Oriane Calligaro
European Review of History, volume 24, issue 3 (June 2017) pp. 399–422

Chapter 4
Between cooperation and competitive bargaining: the Council of Europe, local and regional networking, and the shaping of the European Community's regional policies, 1970s–90s
Birte Wassenberg
European Review of History, volume 24, issue 3 (June 2017) pp. 423–444

CITATION INFORMATION

Chapter 5

Re-designing military security in Europe: cooperation and competition between the European community and NATO during the early 1980s
Angela Romano
European Review of History, volume 24, issue 3 (June 2017) pp. 445–471

Chapter 6

De-centring the European union: policy diffusion among European regional organizations – a comment
Thomas Risse
European Review of History, volume 24, issue 3 (June 2017) pp. 472–483

For any permission-related enquiries please visit:
http://www.tandfonline.com/page/help/permissions

Notes on Contributors

Oriane Calligaro is a Postdoctoral Research Fellow at the Institute for European Studies, Université Libre de Bruxelles, Belgium.

Wolfram Kaiser is Professor of European Studies at the University of Portsmouth, UK, and Visiting Professor at the College of Europe in Bruges, Belgium.

Jan-Henrik Meyer is an Associate Professor at the Saxo Institute of the University of Copenhagen, Denmark, and a visiting fellow at the Center for Contemporary History, Potsdam, Germany.

Kiran Klaus Patel is Chair of European and Global History and Jean Monnet Professor at Maastricht University, The Netherlands.

Thomas Risse is Professor of International Relations at the Otto Suhr Institute of Political Science at the Freie Universität Berlin, Germany.

Angela Romano is Senior Research Fellow in the Department of History and Civilization at the European University Institute, Florence, Italy.

Victor Fernández Soriano is a fellow of the Belgian Fonds national de la Recherche scientifique (FNRS) and a member of the Centre de recherche Mondes modernes et contemporains at the Université Libre de Bruxelles, Belgium.

Birte Wassenberg is Jean Monnet Professor of European and International Relations History at the Institute for Political Studies (IEP) of the University of Strasbourg, France.

INTRODUCTION

Multiple connections in European co-operation: international organizations, policy ideas, practices and transfers 1967–92

Wolfram Kaiser and Kiran Klaus Patel

ABSTRACT

International organizations are ubiquitous in contemporary Europe and the wider world. This special issue takes a historical approach to exploring their relations with each other in Western Europe between 1967 and 1992. The authors seek to 'provincialize' and 'de-centre' the European Union's role, exploring the interactions of its predecessors with other organizations like NATO, the OECD and the Council of Europe. This article develops the new historical-research agenda of co-operation and competition among IOs and their role in European co-operation. The first section discusses the limited existing work on such questions among historians and in adjacent disciplines. The second section introduces the five articles and their main arguments. The third section goes on to elaborate common findings, especially regarding what the authors call the vectors for the development of policy ideas and practices and their transfer across different institutional platforms.

International organizations (IOs) are ubiquitous in contemporary Europe and the wider world. They are even highly active in policy fields like education that are usually seen as closely connected with sensitive issues of culture and identity and often regarded as an exclusive national, or even in federal or unevenly decentralized states, sub-national competence. Thus, to give but a few examples, the global United Nations Educational, Scientific and Cultural Organization promotes Holocaust education in co-operation with the formally international, but European-dominated, International Holocaust Remembrance Alliance.[1] The equally global Organization for Economic Co-operation and Development (OECD) seeks to compare the success of different education systems, co-ordinating member-states in joint evaluation programmes like PISA for testing the skills of 15-year-old pupils in mathematics, reading and the natural sciences.[2] The pan-European Council of Europe in turn fosters the comparison and convergence of history-teaching methods and content and the development of European school textbooks.[3] Finally, the European Union (EU), with its smaller membership and only subsidiary competences in education, nevertheless runs multiple programmes for strengthening transnational co-operation and mobility, such as the Erasmus student exchanges, launched in 1987.[4]

Thus, despite the strong inclination of European states to protect their competences in this policy field, as in some others, IOs are heavily involved in developing policy ideas, shaping practices and facilitating the transfer of ideas and solutions across borders. Clearly, the activism of IOs is even more marked in policy fields with a long history of technical or economic regulation and integration like transport, telecommunication and trade. As in the case of education, their spatial, regulatory and thematic scope frequently varies, often resulting in overlapping competences, initiatives and activities. It seems, as Karen Alter and Sophie Meunier have put it, 'that every policy issue is nowadays the subject of multiple transborder agreements' resulting in a high degree of 'density and complexity of international governance';[5] or in what Kal Raustiala and David G. Victor in their study of the international regulatory conflict over plant genetic resources first termed international 'regime complexity'.[6]

Based on fresh archival research, this special issue adopts a historical approach to exploring co-operation and competition among IOs in Europe. The articles seek to understand overlapping IO activities, the development of new policy ideas and practices in such forums, and, most importantly, their transfer among IOs. Together, they will create a strong conceptual and empirical basis for developing the historiography of IOs with a particular focus on exploring the exchange relations among them and the role of multiple actors in such processes – ranging from IO secretariats to experts, international non-governmental organizations (INGOs), and, of course, member-state governments and agencies. The resulting research on the history of the EU and a set of IOs with a (not necessarily exclusive) focus on Europe is not just relevant to analysing IOs and their history, or European co-operation and integration. Instead, it is also crucially important for understanding their larger impact on the history of Europe in the twentieth century and beyond, as states have been more and more penetrated by international rules and working practices even when they have formally retained exclusive competence over a particular issue or policy area.

The special issue's geographical focus is on Western Europe. With its peculiar combination of supranational institutional features, wide-ranging competences, legal integration and financial resources the EU has become increasingly hegemonic among IOs active in governing Europe since the end of the Cold War. The articles in this special issue seek to contribute to 'provincializing'[7] or 'de-centring'[8] the EU's role in post-war European co-operation, however. They aim to contextualize the EU's predecessors, especially the European Economic Community (EEC) created in 1957–8 and usually referred to as the European Communities (EC) after the 1967 institutional merger, in their exchange relations with other IOs like the North Atlantic Treaty Organization (NATO), the OECD and the Council of Europe, for example.

This contextualization is not just relevant for historians of the EU and its predecessors who for a long time focused too exclusively on this organization as the apparent focal point of all co-operation or integration efforts in post-war (Western) Europe. It is also crucially important for contemporary historians of Europe more generally who sometimes still narrate national histories without systematic reference to the international interdependence of societies and the role of IOs including the EC. Finally, it carries broad implications for the interdisciplinary field of European Studies, particularly for the work of political scientists who normally also only examine one IO at a time and mostly concentrate on today's European Union.

The history of IOs in Eastern Europe and in East–West relations is of course an equally relevant topic, but distinct from this special issue's core concern. Given our focus on transfers of ideas, concepts and policy solutions among IOs, it seems legitimate to concentrate on Western Europe, where the overlap of membership and the similarity of institutional set-up and political orientation made such exchange relations much more likely. Moreover, it is interesting to explore to what extent the Western post-war 'script' about Western Europe as a laboratory of international policy ideas from human rights to the environment is corroborated or needs to be revised by historical research – the more so as the more recent Cold War historiography in an attempt to develop a more global perspective has de-centred Western Europe to the extent of neglecting such questions.[9]

In other words, this special issue aims at understanding the present-day EU in its post-war development as part of a web of international organizations in the Western world. In fact, the EC was often a latecomer to new policy fields like culture and the environment precisely because its initial focus was the creation of a common market.[10] The EC frequently adopted and assimilated institutional rules and practices from member-states. However, it also imported them from other IOs with an interest in governing Europe, adjusting them to its political and institutional setting, even where their spatial scope extended beyond Europe, as in the case of the OECD after its reform in 1961–2. Actually, it is perhaps surprising quite how many ideas and policy solutions the EC more or less copy-pasted from other IOs to adjust them to its own institutional framework and political objectives.

Eventually, we hope that the new research agenda of co-operation and competition among IOs in dealing with transnational issues will allow a more fine-grained analysis of how, when and why the present-day EU has indeed become hegemonic in governing Europe. We contend that the dominant literature that highlights intra-organizational dynamics – most importantly the bargaining processes among member-states – misses an important dimension. This also holds true for the research – less developed in history, and more prominent in political science – that focuses on inter-institutional dynamics or the interplay between the various institutions *within* the EU, such as the European Parliament, the Commission and so on.[11] Instead, inter-organizational links need more attention, since important developments in the history of the EU can only be explained through this lens.

The agenda of this special issue thus transcends disciplinary boundaries and particularly speaks to debates in political science about today's European Union and the role of other IOs. To foster this kind of interdisciplinary dialogue, the editors have invited Thomas Risse, one of the most distinguished political scientists in his field, to comment on the findings of this special issue from his perspective. His contribution underlines the interdisciplinary basis that this special issue builds on as well as the fruitfulness of such a conversation across disciplinary divides.

For the purpose of this special issue we concentrate on the period from 1967, when the EC's institutional merger took place, new social movements advanced new policy agendas, globalization took off and the economic crisis after 1973 troubled Western Europe, through to 1992, when the end of the Cold War and the Maastricht Treaty transformed the role of the EC/EU quite fundamentally.

Introducing the special issue, this article will develop the new historical research agenda of co-operation and competition among IOs and their role in European co-operation. The first section will situate the special issue within the limited existing work on such questions among historians and in adjacent disciplines, especially International Relations. The second section will then introduce the five articles and their main arguments. The third section will go on to elaborate common findings from the empirical research, especially concerning the nature of and motives for co-operation and competition among IOs and what we call the vectors for the development of policy ideas and practices and their transfer across different institutional platforms. In conclusion, we will develop some ideas for future research on the role of IOs in governing Europe.

Understanding co-operation and competition among International Organizations

Co-operation and competition among IOs (and among transnational business organizations for setting technical standards or dividing up markets in cartels, for example) has been widespread since their origins around the middle of the nineteenth century. At the start of the First World War, 37 IOs and 466 transnational organizations already existed in Europe.[12] One particularly pertinent example of co-operation and competition is the case of rail transport.[13] This sector, like others using new technologies with transnational scope, was already characterized by inter-organizational dynamics in the nineteenth century and in inter-war Europe.

Co-operation and competition among IOs and transnational voluntary organizations continued unabated in post-war Western Europe, when the region turned into the world's most crowded space for IOs. In fact, the growing number of IOs with horizontal functions across a number of different policy areas created even more overlap than between the League of Nations and the technical organizations of the 1920s. Some, like the Council of Europe, were set up in the first instance because of competing visions for European co-operation and integration which European states had failed to resolve in other organizations – in the case of the Council of Europe this was the virulent conflict between France and the United Kingdom over whether to limit the Organization for European Economic Co-operation (OEEC), the predecessor of the OECD created in 1948, to trade liberalization, as the British government preferred, or to use it as a platform for more far-reaching economic and, ultimately, political integration.[14] The Western European Union (WEU) is another example: evolving from the 1948 Treaty of Brussels originally signed by Belgium, France, Luxembourg, the Netherlands and the United Kingdom, this IO with a strong focus on military co-operation soon had to coordinate with and delimit itself from NATO, created one year later. But the WEU also rubbed shoulders with other IOs. As early as the 1950s, it delegated some of its tasks in the field of cultural policy to the Council of Europe, and the meetings in these IOs were full of talk about the need to rationalize their work in order to avoid overlap and duplication.[15]

Researchers of Western European co-operation and integration after 1945 will intuitively recognize the importance of such co-operation and competition. Thus, when the European Coal and Steel Community (ECSC) was founded in 1951–2, its High Authority under the leadership of Jean Monnet immediately set out to establish formal relations with existing IOs not least to buttress its own role in coordinating the member-states and shaping the new organization's external relations. Similarly, the setting up of the EEC impacted strongly on existing IOs and new ones created shortly afterwards. National administrations carefully reassessed the scope and limits of the Council of Europe, for instance, rethinking its future role on the ever more crowded stage of IOs in Western Europe.[16]

The European Free Trade Association (EFTA) is another example. Founded by seven states in 1959–60, it sought to provide an alternative focus and to build bridges with the EEC after French President Charles de Gaulle's 1958 veto against a larger Western European free-trade zone in line with the 1956 British initiative in the OEEC.[17] After de Gaulle's 1963 veto against British EEC membership, the EEC and EFTA competed over accelerating their timetables for tariff reductions. Moreover, the Danish government leveraged de Gaulle's offer of separate EEC membership to demand (albeit without success) a kind of EFTA common agricultural policy to replicate the evolving EEC policy. Finally, in response to the 1964 surcharge crisis, when the new British Labour government illegally increased tariffs by 15% across the board to reduce its balance-of-payments deficit, EFTA instituted an Economic Policy Committee to deal with similar disputes in the future, which was based on the OECD template and largely duplicated its activities.[18]

Nonetheless, despite sometimes touching upon the theme in passing, contemporary historians of Western Europe so far have not systematically explored co-operation and competition among IOs and their impact on ideas, practices and the transfer of policy solutions in European co-operation. Two conceptual and two more practical reasons appear to account for this. The first conceptual reason seems to lie in the character of European 'integration' history as a research field which, from its inception in the late 1970s, remained a rather small, tightly organized field, largely focused on the history of the present-day EU.[19] Moreover, much of the early research on integration history was characterized by federalist undercurrents and teleological notions (also influenced by neo-functionalist political-science literature) of integration as a continuous 'process' towards ever-greater 'deepening' and 'widening', ultimately resulting in the present-day EU.[20] This literature normally assumed that their alleged 'supranationality' made the ECSC and the EEC creatures *sui generis*, and, as a result, they were not placed in relation to other IOs or compared to them. The allegedly 'advanced' character of ECSC/EEC integration seemed to make it unnecessary to identify, let alone explore, exchange relations with other IOs except perhaps for the ECSC/EEC's seemingly unilateral impact on them. Paradoxically, trying to counteract this trend in the historiography, even the economic historian Alan S. Milward, while advancing his notion of European integration as the result of the intergovernmental bargaining of 'national interests' by member-states, still focused largely on the origins of the ECSC and the EEC.[21]

The second conceptual reason why inter-organizational relations among IOs in post-war Western European co-operation are understudied is the dominant if often implicit realist epistemological perspective of much of the European 'integration' literature. Whether interested in national governments and their bargaining or the new 'supranational' institutions and their activism, much of this literature was for a long time predominantly focused on decision-making moments: the creation of new organizations, the revision of existing treaties and, more recently, the trajectory of major policy domains such as the Common Agricultural Policy, for example.[22] In contrast, the articles in this special issue are also interested in the intellectual roots of governance practices. Our approach owes a lot to cultural and transnational history in a broad sense and to their sensitivity to a history of knowledge, representations and perceptions as well as to connections, transfers and entanglements. This research also focuses on other phases of policy-making such as agenda-setting and policy review and implementation.

The first of two more practical reasons for the lack of more systematic exploration of the exchange relations among IOs lies in the dominant focus of the literature not just on the

ECSC/EEC/EC, but also on other IOs, on the history of a *single* IO – a focus that has often been fostered by the IOs in question in an attempt to cultivate their own historical legacy. Thus, the European Commission has sponsored research based largely on oral-history interviews, into its own institutional history.[23] Similarly, the first, and so far only, edited volume on the first years of the OEEC resulted from its decision to open its archives and apply a more liberal 15-year rule (as opposed to the customary 30) for access to its sources.[24] Although the OEEC, unlike the European Commission, did not interfere in the research and publication process, it was nevertheless keenly interested in counteracting the strong pull of the EU in the early 1990s. Other IOs, including the Council of Europe, have displayed a similar interest in safeguarding their institutional memory and historical legacy.[25]

The major resources needed to study co-operation and competition among IOs more systematically constitutes the second practical reason for why the theme has largely been neglected by contemporary historians of Western Europe. Studying one IO and its activities already constitutes a challenge, especially if such organizations are treated, as in this special issue, as more than a forum for bargaining among member-states. In fact, IOs have agency of their own.[26] Secretariats seek to carve out a role for themselves and to develop new policy initiatives, experts are heavily involved in debating issues and setting agendas, and INGOs try to propagate their ideas and interests by lobbying IO secretariats as well as member-state governments and agencies. Reconstructing the interaction of multiple actors, including the governments of member-states, applicant countries and the United States as Western Europe's benign hegemon, is challenging enough for one IO alone. Tracing their networks and exchange relations across a variety of institutional venues is even more demanding. Moreover, many policy issues are interconnected, adding to the complexity of transnational governance – something that historians can perhaps only reconstruct in teamwork, which is not easily funded or compatible with the discipline's rather traditional individual mode of research and writing.

More surprisingly perhaps, research in International Relations, too, has only recently started to study inter-organizational links among IOs. Earlier research in the neo-functionalist tradition was primarily concerned with understanding incentives for IOs, especially the EC, to expand from one policy area into other, functionally connected areas.[27] It also developed the notion of geographical 'spill-over', which sought to explain why the EC began to attract new members soon after it was set up, with repercussions for other IOs like EFTA. This research was very much preoccupied with explaining 'core Europe' integration, however. It was not open towards researching imports by the EC of policy ideas, practices and solutions from other IOs.

Similarly, the so-called sociological-institutionalist Stanford School developed the notion of 'diffusion'.[28] It started from the assumption that hegemonic centres (such as the EC) could develop norms and policy ideas, and then spread them to other countries, regions and IOs, but did not actually analyse the (negotiated) transfer processes. While interested in 'diffusion' via different forms of connections, its conceptualization as a unidirectional process buttressed the notion of movement of ideas and policy solutions from one self-contained space to another, much as in the early literature on cultural transfers in the historiography of early-modern and modern Europe in the 1980s and early 1990s.[29] The unidirectional conceptualization of 'diffusion' actually impedes research on exchange relations as multi-directional processes of debate, negotiation and selective adoption, which result in new, hybrid institutional and policy outcomes.

The more recent International Relations literature tries to overcome these limitations. It seeks to conceptualize and trace the origins of the complexity of competition and co-operation among IOs either (in the neo-functional tradition) in spill-over from negotiations in one policy field to another, within or across IOs,[30] or alternatively, in the multiplication of international agreements,[31] sub-groups of member-states in IOs interested in deepening co-operation and integration,[32] packages combining different agreements that link issues or policy areas across different IOs,[33] or the deliberate creation of strategic ambiguity to allow governments and other actors space for interpretation drawing on different and competing sets of international commitments.[34]

Other International Relations research is more interested in how the resulting complexity impacts on the strategies of actors and the implementation of international agreements. Thus, Alter and Meunier have emphasized the importance of 'forum-shopping' by actors for implementing agreements in different IOs which best serve their interests.[35] Ultimately, such strategies can effect shifting an existing set of rules from one IO to another. This literature has highlighted what it calls the bounded rationality that characterizes the strategies of different actors who operate across a variety of IOs. In other words, in an assumption that most historians will likely endorse, the complexity of international co-operation and competition is so pronounced that most actors find it difficult to assess what may be in their best interest, or to formulate rational choices in line with these interests – something that makes the development of ideas and agendas as well as the identification of and the agreement on policy solutions 'more permeable', allowing for a much greater role of IO secretariats, experts and INGOs, not just national governments.[36] Thus, the role of INGOs in linking IOs and advancing policy ideas across different institutional venues is definitely one of several promising routes for future contemporary historical research in this field.

Some International Relations research has begun to utilize concepts and methods developed in other social-science disciplines to explore co-operation and competition among IOs and the resulting outcomes.[37] This research frequently draws on organization studies in economics and social-network analysis originally developed by sociologists. The analysis of networks of actors in transnational and international politics has of course also been used by historians including in the field of European integration history,[38] although they have usually employed a less formal methodology. As Rafael Biermann has found in studying European and Atlantic security institutions, inter-organizational networking is often a response to transnational challenges that 'single organizations (and states) cannot master on their own'. Biermann has also highlighted, however, that such networking faces many obstacles, which in turn could also help historians explain competition among IOs and inefficiencies of policy-making instead of synergies. He argues that such obstacles include *inter alia* a history of institutional rivalry, interest in guarding one's autonomy and fear of compromise and its potential effect on the respective IO's identity.[39]

Other disciplines have started to join the conversation. Most notably, legal scholars Bruno de Witte and Anne Thies have recently assessed the place of the EU in the architecture of international legal co-operation, stressing particularly the legal nature of the choices that nation-states make when choosing a specific IO to co-operate internationally.[40] Legal history research has also highlighted the importance of private actors, especially firms, in mobilizing EC law and fostering the organization's further legal integration through the European Court of Justice's case law – just as individuals can appeal to the European Court of Human Rights established in 1959 to protect their rights against member-state institutions.[41] In contrast,

IOs like the OECD, the General Agreement on Tariffs and Trade (GATT, today WTO) and NATO have formal and informal mechanisms for dispute resolution among member-state governments only.[42] Such legal differences, as well as the interconnections between legal orders, are often ignored by historians and other scholars. They help to explain why a certain group of actors might prefer one IO over the other; why disputes often play out simultaneously in several organizations with partly overlapping or competing competences; and why the ways they solve these issues differ markedly. For all these reasons, venue choice, overlap and dependency are so crucial.

In sum, therefore, there seems to be an increasing awareness of the need to stop analysing the history of the EU in isolation, and to stress the multiple links among IOs that have competed, co-operated, interacted with each other in a variety of other ways, all in an attempt to 'build Europe'.

Human rights, environment, security, culture and regions

This brief survey of the limited historiography and social-science research has already highlighted several key motives and reasons for co-operation and competition among IOs which the authors discuss in their articles. Their combination in this form does not just reflect the merely incipient research on this key aspect of post-war European co-operation. Rather, the articles address five distinct policy challenges that loomed large on the agenda of various European IOs between the late 1960s and the early 1990s: human-rights violations (Fernández Soriano); environmental degradation (Meyer); security threats and détente opportunities (Romano); co-operation in the cultural field (Calligaro and Patel); and the role of regions in European co-operation (Wassenberg). At the same time, the authors explore the collaboration between the EC and a variety of other IOs: the Council of Europe (Fernández Soriano, Calligaro and Patel, Wassenberg); the OECD (Meyer); and NATO (Romano). Finally, the articles also address the roles of different sets of actors who played an especially influential role in linking IOs in their particular case study: national governments (Calligaro and Patel, Romano); elected and delegated parliamentarians (Fernández Soriano, Calligaro and Patel); experts (Meyer); interest groups (Wassenberg); and policy entrepreneurs (Calligaro and Patel), thus creating a fascinating kaleidoscope of forms of co-operation and competition among IOs.

Víctor Fernández Soriano investigates how European IOs developed their policies on human rights. In the early 1960s, the issue of the possible accession of Franco's Spain already helped the EEC to debate and to clarify its conditions for membership which henceforth de facto included a democratic constitution. Greece concluded the first association agreement with the EEC in 1961, which provided for a privileged economic relationship and the prospect of eventual membership. In April 1967, however, a group of colonels seized power. Greece was a member of the Council of Europe, alongside its association with the EEC. Parliamentarians from both IOs' assemblies pushed for a strong response to human-rights violations by the colonels' regime, with the aim of imposing sanctions on the new military dictatorship.

Fernández Soriano demonstrates that the Parliamentary Assembly of the Council of Europe was the driving force in this process. Examining the inter-organizational dynamics between the two European IOs, he argues that the EC imported policy positions and normative ideas from the Council of Europe. This transfer was greatly facilitated by individual parliamentarians. It prepared the ground in the EC/EU for an emerging human-rights agenda, so-called conditionality for formalized membership conditions and its policy of foreign aid for developing countries. All the while, the protagonists in this battle were able to draw on the normative framework of the well-established United Nations Declaration on Human Rights already proclaimed by the UN General Assembly in Paris on 10 December 1948.

Environmental degradation constituted another new policy challenge for IOs.[43] By the late 1960s, specialized IOs had been dealing with environmental-protection issues for some time. Concerns about the consequences of the growing use of chemicals in agriculture, the short-term risks and long-term impact of nuclear power, and other environmental threats motivated the environmental protest movements and stirred IOs into activity. With most environmental issues like air and water pollution being transnational in character, the United Nations organized the Conference on the Human Environment in Stockholm in 1972.[44] Other IOs ranging from the Council of Europe and NATO to the OECD and the EC also became active in the new policy field.

Jan-Henrik Meyer focuses on the discussion and definition of the Polluter Pays Principle (PPP), which became enshrined into environmental policy almost simultaneously in the OECD and the EC in the early 1970s. Meyer explores the multiple avenues for the transfer of underlying policy ideas and for the definition of the PPP. He shows how experts and expertise played a key role in the selection of particular policy concepts. At the same time, the respective IO's institutional set-up and political context largely determined how the PPP was adapted. In fact, the OECD, despite its focus on economic liberalization, ended up with a more environment-oriented definition of the PPP. In contrast, the interests of businesses concerned with the possible costs of a stricter PPP definition and implementation prevailed in the EC, which initially adopted a more loosely defined approach.

While in the fields of human rights and environmental protection the EC initially received new policy ideas more than shaping and exporting them, in security of all policy areas, paradoxically, it sometimes succeeded in developing new ideas and inserting them into other IOs, as Angela Romano demonstrates. After all, within the Western world defence and security constituted core competences of NATO created in 1949. EC countries including the United Kingdom, which joined in 1973, and not just France, shared a keen interest in developing a common approach to foreign-policy challenges. Already in the process leading up to the 1975 Helsinki Final Act, this induced the EC member-states strongly to coordinate their positions.[45]

In the early 1980s, the EC expanded its co-operation to encompass disarmament issues. Romano explores how the EC's foray into disarmament provoked competition and co-operation with NATO. She reveals the EC origins of the proposal for a Conference on Disarmament in Europe and how EC member-state governments and leading politicians like the French President Valéry Giscard d'Estaing and the German Chancellor Helmut Schmidt succeeded in implanting it in NATO. In an era of new East–West confrontation following the Soviet Union's 1979 invasion of Afghanistan, and of growing transatlantic tensions in the wake of Ronald Reagan's election to the US presidency, the EC collectively sought to avoid further escalation between NATO and the Soviet bloc to protect as best as possible the notion and practices of 1970s détente.

With its strong focus on economic integration from its inception in the 1950s the EC had no formal competences in the field of culture. In contrast, cultural co-operation had been a core activity of the Council of Europe since its creation in 1949. Together with the United Nations Educational, Scientific and Cultural Organization, the Council of Europe therefore initially dominated multilateral co-operation, alongside bilateral agreements on cultural exchange as contained in the 1963 Elysée Treaty between France and Germany.[46]

In their article, Oriane Calligaro and Kiran Klaus Patel explore the incremental process through which the EC eventually became the key IO in fostering cultural co-operation by the end of the Cold War.[47] They explore two case studies: for the 1970s, the debates about cultural heritage and the European Architectural Heritage Year; and, for the 1980s, the development of a European audio-visual policy. In both cases, the Council of Europe took the lead as a laboratory for developing ideas and policies later adapted by the EC for its purposes. As Calligaro and Patel argue, its governance structure, financial resources, market integration and generally increasing competences allowed the EC to become a much more significant player in the field of culture.

Similarly, the Council of Europe also preceded the EC in promoting co-operation among local and regional authorities. It established a regular conference forum as early as 1957, where local actors and associations were represented and tried to influence emerging European regional policies.[48] Birte Wassenberg analyses the links between the Council of Europe and the EC in the development of regional policy from the 1970s through to the early 1990s. She focuses on three vectors for the transmission of ideas and policy solutions: institutional co-operation between the two IOs; competitive bargaining among a variety of local and regional groups; and intensive lobbying of the EC.

Wassenberg shows how the EC sought to buttress its strong position in inter-IO relations by strategically limiting direct dialogue with the Council of Europe. Thus, formalized co-operation between the two IOs, their committees and involved experts was not the most important transmission belt for the transfer of ideas and policy solutions. Rather, local and regional authorities worked closely together across regional and national borders. Their networking was geared towards ensuring that they would be closely associated with, and able to shape, the evolving European regional policy. From 1988 onwards, these networks shifted their attention more and more from the Council of Europe to the EC, not least because of the prospect of receiving direct funding from the European Commission.

Co-operation and competition: vectors of transfers

The five articles together with Thomas Risse's comment in this special issue provide fascinating insights into the vectors of co-operation, competition and transfer among European IOs. Three vectors are of particular importance: ideas; actors; and institutions.

The authors do not conceptualize ideas as intellectual discoveries or discourses of a general nature. Instead, they are keenly interested how ideas are connected to social, economic and political developments in Europe. More concretely, the authors inquire into how IOs have contributed to developing ideas to inform policy solutions to shared problems, and how such policy solutions have been negotiated, stabilized and implemented.

Several authors stress the importance of public debate and pressures for how IOs have identified policy issues and sought to address them. Thus, despite the fact that the European Convention for the Protection of Human Rights and Fundamental Freedoms dated from 1950, the Cold War rationale often overrode human-rights concerns in the treatment of Western authoritarian regimes. The colonels' establishment in 1967 of a new dictatorship in Greece, the apparent cradle of European democracy, however, was sharply criticized in Western Europe. As Fernández Soriano demonstrates, the resulting public pressure for counter-measures against the new regime drove and buttressed the strongly critical response by elected parliamentarians in the assemblies of the Council of Europe and the EC in the following years. Similarly, as Meyer demonstrates, the new environmental movement forcefully demanded stronger protection measures. Apocalyptic visions of the future of mankind as in the Club of Rome's 1972 report created pressures on IOs as well as their member-states to take up this new policy challenge effectively if they wanted to remain relevant.[49]

Other pressures were of a more institutional nature. Thus, the strengthening of the role of regions in the Maastricht Treaty that created the EU was at least in part induced by the lobbying of local and regional authorities, as Wassenberg shows. At the time, their preferences reflected far more widespread concerns about the future of the regions in a more integrated Europe. Based on strong identities, existing constitutional rights and public support, local and regional authorities pushed for the EU to buttress on-going decentralization processes in highly centralized member-states like France and to protect their competences in federal states like Germany. The new notion of a Europe of the regions complemented their interest in access to funding for regional development. Ultimately, this also provoked the shift in the primary focus of local and regional authorities from the Council of Europe to the EC.

In this broader societal context, politicians and experts formulated policy responses and concrete proposals for action by IOs and their member-states. In the case of the Greek human-rights violations the options were clear enough: suspension of membership in the Council of Europe, which the colonels pre-empted by leaving the organization, and the suspension of the EC's association agreement. Parliamentary fact-finding missions to Greece prepared the decisions on these issues. Other authors study the formation of broader policy principles like the Polluter Pays Principle in the case of Meyer and the proposal for a Conference on Disarmament in the case of Romano, or of concrete policy initiatives like the EC's expansion into audio-visual policy in the case of Calligaro and Patel. While these policy ideas were politically contested, IO and member-state officials and diplomats as well as external expert advisors nevertheless played an important role in developing and transferring them among IOs.

These and other actors themselves constituted a second vector for co-operation and competition among IOs and the transfer of policy ideas and solutions. Despite their limited focus on particular policy issues, the articles in this special issue underline the extraordinary diversity of actors capable of initiating such transfers. Their findings clearly contradict simplistic notions in realist International Relations theory and traditional diplomatic historiography of states and governments as the only relevant actors in international politics.

States and governments matter, of course, especially in foreign policy, as Romano shows in her article on co-operation and competition between the EC and NATO. Following the 1970 Davignon Report the EC member-states sought to enhance their foreign policy co-operation through the creation of the European Political Co-operation (EPC) mechanism,[50] which they used effectively to co-ordinate their policies in the Helsinki process during the first half of the 1970s. In the 1980s, as Romano demonstrates, the governments drew on the EPC as a vehicle for protecting the notion and practice of détente. After the opening of the Soviet Union from 1985 onwards, they finally succeeded in getting the US administration to align itself with the EC preference for a Conference on Disarmament in 1987. In the case of détente leading politicians fostered co-operation among IOs to facilitate the transfer from the EPC to the NATO context. Below the level of political decision-making, officials and experts may have played a role in advancing and transferring policy ideas between the EPC and NATO, but they are not the focus of Romano's article, which concentrates on understanding interaction among governments. Calligaro and Patel also show how member-state governments had very different priorities for developing audio-visual policies through the Council of Europe and the EC, something that impacted strongly on the institutional and policy choices.

Regarding other issues, however, multiple other actors were influential. In the case of regional policy, Wassenberg demonstrates the great importance of local and regional state actors, not national governments. Fernández Soriano shows how elected parliamentarians without a government role strongly influenced government responses in the Council of Europe and the EC to Greek human-rights violations. In environmental policy, economists and natural scientists sought to shape the definition of the PPP drawing on their expertise and public pressure for tighter environmental regulation emanating from grassroots movements and INGOs – pressure that they often generated themselves through close co-operation with these organizations to foster their vision of environmental protection. As in the case of the OECD and the EC, experts were frequently active across a variety of IO venues, which made it comparatively easy for them to pick up ideas and policy solutions in one context and transfer them to another that appeared more promising for a particular form of implementation.

It becomes clear across the articles in this special issue, moreover, that individuals with a high level of commitment to a certain cause were often important for developing a particular agenda and linking IOs. This is a finding of fine-grained historical research that is often lost on International Relations scholars who tend to prioritize structure over the agency of individuals, as they would put it. Where this literature has addressed the role of individuals it has called them 'policy' or 'norm' entrepreneurs with particular forms of social capital, to use Bourdieu's language.[51]

The authors give multiple examples of such individual entrepreneurship. Thus, Calligaro and Patel analyse the role of Duncan Sandys among others, the co-founder of the United Europe movement in Britain after the Second World War. He helped link the Council of Europe and the EC in his attempt to protect Europe's architectural heritage and to develop greater EC activism in the field of culture. As Fernández Soriano shows, parliamentarians were sometimes able to advance and implement their initiatives when they acquired executive roles, as in the case of Edoardo Martino who entered the EC Commission in 1967 or Max van der Stoel who became Dutch foreign minister in 1973.

The IOs themselves, their institutional set-up, competences and working practices constitute a third vector for co-operation, competition and transfers. Thus, their limited financial resources and formal competences induced the Council of Europe and the OECD to develop into laboratories for the discussion of new policy ideas and solutions. In the case of the OECD in particular, exporting such new ideas to other IOs and member-states was, and still is, a crucial source of its own institutional legitimacy. The Council of Europe, too, has often acted as a forum for policy deliberation. It had a more competitive relationship with the EC, however, not least because it was also a European IO without non-European membership.

To secure space for themselves in the European and global co-operation and competition, IOs normally crafted specific institutional mechanisms for establishing themselves in a new policy field. Thus, as Meyer explains, the OECD, despite its primary mission of economic liberalization, was the first IO to establish a separate environmental committee, although this choice also entailed the danger of segregating and marginalizing rather than 'mainstreaming' environmental concerns within the organization.[52] IOs frequently expanded into new policy areas without possessing a formal competence. This is true of the EC, which developed the 1973 Environmental Action Programme but only acquired formal competence for environmental policy with the 1987 Single European Act. In the peculiar case of the OECD, the collective representation of the EC by the European Commission from 1962 onwards, alongside the member-states, created another institutional vector for debate and transfer from one IO context to another. In the meantime, the Lisbon Treaty has given the EU a legal personality of its own under international law. This actually makes it more like a state (which can operate inside IOs) rather than just being an IO, with its own member-states.

Three key characteristics contributed to the EC's particular strength in its relations with other IOs during the period from 1967 to 1992: its focus on market integration; its legal integration; and its financial resources. To begin with, the EC's original focus on creating a customs union and a broad internal market created functional connections with other policy areas, or at least allowed actors to claim such connections and use them as an instrument for expanding the EC's policy remit and developing new initiatives. The European Commission pro-actively sought to identify new policy fields to strengthen the EC, but also its own institutional role within it. This was the case for the environment, for example, as Meyer shows. Here, the European Commission could claim to be in the vanguard of policy-making to protect citizens from environmental hazards like pollution. As Calligaro and Patel highlight, however, market integration also provided an opportunity for the European Commission to expand into the field of culture. With the support of the Court of Justice it claimed that cultural products could not enjoy a blanket exception from the rules of the internal market.[53]

The EC's greater legal integration enhanced the effects of its market integration. The EC had to rely on the member-state governments and administrations to implement EC law. Moreover, lacking policing powers it also depended, and largely continues to depend, on the voluntary compliance of member-states with EC/EU law and decisions by the Court of Justice. Nevertheless, the slow emergence of an EC constitutional culture with legally binding commitments and control of their implementation by an independent judiciary gave the EC a major advantage over other IOs that had to rely entirely on the willingness of member-states to transpose more general recommendations and targets into national law.[54] Moreover, individuals could appeal to the EC's court, whereas this was not the case in organizations such as the OECD and NATO. This direct connection to companies and individuals in the member-states also helps to explain why the EC sometimes managed to develop a position of hegemony. Another factor came on top: through its generally pro-integration jurisdiction until the 1990s, the Court of Justice was able to support the European Commission in expanding the EC's policy remit, especially through an extensive interpretation of the scope of economic integration. As Calligaro and Patel show, this impacted strongly on the field of culture.

At the same time, the EC's legal integration could also act as a deterrent against agreeing more binding commitments in the first instance. Thus, as Meyer demonstrates, organized industry in the EC was keen to avoid the higher costs resulting from environmental legislation. As a result, the EC ended up with a definition of the Producer Pays Principle that was less stringent than that of the OECD, conventionally seen as one of the most pro-liberalization and business-friendly IOs.

The third characteristic was the EC's much greater financial resources. Some IOs like the OECD and the equally global Food and Agriculture Organization only had funding for their own secretariats, for statistical research, fact-finding missions and expert committee work. The Council of Europe, too, had limited funds at its disposal. As Wassenberg shows, it could offer local and regional authorities a platform for the exchange of ideas, develop policy solutions and encourage their implementation. When the EC created its own regional policy, which distributed funds for the development of poorer EC regions, however, it quickly became the focal point of lobbying. When it started to foster the notion of a Europe of the regions, moreover, the EC also promised to strengthen the institutional and constitutional role and rights of localities and regions within the member-states, which made it even more attractive as an institutional site for their interests and agendas.

Conclusion

The articles in this special issue cover different IOs alongside the EC, as well as a variety of policy challenges. As a result, their findings are necessarily incomplete. Nonetheless, they have allowed the identification of three vectors – policy ideas, actors and institutional settings – as key explanatory factors for co-operation, competition and transfers among European IOs during the period from 1967 to 1992. Moreover, three characteristics help explain why and how the EC succeeded in playing a stronger role in the battle among IOs for a more prominent role in addressing common challenges, developing policy ideas and agendas and identifying and transferring policy solutions. These are: the EC's focus on market integration; its greater legal integration; and its much larger financial resources to attract multiple state and non-state actors into its orbit as the most suitable site for articulating their concerns, making demands and negotiating policy. In this way, a division of labour appears to have developed over time between the EC and other European IOs, whereby the latter mainly function as laboratories for policy ideas relevant to Europe (and other world regions) and the EC focuses on their detailed formulation, implementation and funding.

This division of labour has created a variable geometry of European integration and cooperation, where European non-EC/EU states, depending on their precise status, are more or less marginal to EC/EU policy-making and need to utilize other IOs like the Council of Europe more to have any kind of voice. The impact of this variable geometry has been relativized by the EU's expansion to 28 member-states (2016) since 1992, which has significantly increased its overlap with Europe as a geographical space. Nonetheless, it is still highly relevant to countries like Norway, which accesses the internal market through the European Economic Area, to some Balkan countries without the immediate prospect of EU membership, for example, but probably also to the United Kingdom if and when it leaves the EU after the 'Brexit' vote in the 2016 referendum.

Despite the still limited research to date on inter-organizational relations among IOs in historical perspective, Kiran Klaus Patel has developed a tentative typology of EC/EU relations with other European IOs.[55] The findings from the articles in this special issue are not systematically comparative enough to allow its testing fully. Combined with other incipient research in a similar vein, however, they facilitate some general conclusions and support his claims. Thus, in policy fields with no alternative forums and strong EC competences, like agriculture, little interaction between the EC and other IOs appears to have taken place. The EC developed the Common Agricultural Policy with strong redistributive effects, which initially made up 80% of its budget. Other IOs with a more global scope like the OECD and the Food and Agriculture Organization in turn limited themselves in this policy area to policy deliberation and statistical work. Crucially, its regulatory and fiscal powers combined helped transform the EC into an emerging polity and primary site for non-state actors, too, who increasingly sought to influence the EC's policy-making to protect their own interests. In policy areas, where it dominated policy-making, the EC could nevertheless serve as a template for third countries and other settings, as when the Danish government advocated a similar 'supranational' agricultural policy for EFTA during the 1960s.

In other areas the present-day EU overlapped heavily with existing forums. This was the case for infrastructures including the transport sector, for example, where several existing organizations were founded in inter-war Europe and often carried over practices from the nineteenth century.[56] In such fields, the EC was often ineffectual despite having competences. The mode of interaction was characterized by crowding out of other IOs over time. Especially from the 1970s onwards the EC tried to bring the existing effective organizations within its remit in some way or another, and to develop a hegemonic role in regulatory matters.

In new policy issues, and fields, other IOs frequently developed and advocated ideas and policy solutions earlier than the EC. Examples of this would be the Council of Europe in the field of culture and the UN in the field of environmental policy. These IOs' pro-active roles sometimes led to partial convergence or co-operation as modes of interaction, and inward transfers into the EC from them. Finally, the present-day EU and its member-states have become embedded in IOs like the OECD and the GATT, for example, where transfer processes take place mainly within the IO. In these cases, the EC has been able to contribute in a pan-European or global setting, rather than interacting with other IOs as a separate entity. In these cases, it has profited from its peculiar constitutional character as an IO with many state-like features with, since the Lisbon Treaty, its own legal personality under international law.

Our findings thus confirm and substantiate the claims of the first attempt to systematize the forms of interaction among IOs in post-war Western Europe. They also demonstrate that much more work remains to be done to understand fully the past and present role of organizations such as the EC/EU, the Council of Europe, the OECD and NATO and particularly the factors and forces that drive them. In his comment, Thomas Risse underscores the significance of historical work to arrive at fine-grained answers for such issues, and how much history and political science can learn from each other in pursuing this research agenda further.

Beyond the role of IOs and their work this collection of articles also sheds new light on the history of the Cold War. They demonstrate that the Cold War – often seen as the defining feature for this period of European history, and for the role of IOs particularly – impacted to a very different extent on the various forums and issues discussed here. While détente and East–West relations stood front and centre in the interaction between NATO and the EC in the debate about military security (Romano), human-rights concerns explicitly clashed with Cold War priorities in the case of the debate about the Greek junta (Fernández Soriano). Interestingly, inter-organizational dynamics were particularly strong where actors in the Council of Europe and the EC challenged the Cold War lens. In culture (Calligaro and

Patel), actors actively strove to overcome the East–West divide. Cold War concerns were largely absent from the debates about regions (Wassenberg) and the environment (Meyer). Having said this, Cold War institutions, particularly NATO, mattered for the transatlantic transfers in environmental policy.

The articles in this special issue do not support Akira Iriye's recent claim that the Cold War was but a footnote to human-rights history, and that IOs and transnational forces may serve more broadly as the core of an alternative narrative of European and global developments since 1945.[57] Nevertheless, given that for a long time the Cold War has been seen as an all-pervading reality, impacting on security and foreign-policy debates, but also on issues as diverse as sexuality, technology, popular culture, urban planning and economic policies, the articles' findings are remarkable. They help to challenge the Cold War lens that has dominated much of the historiography on post-war European history and IOs, and to confirm the idea that at least during some phases since 1945, European IOs have been able to insulate and even to de-couple some of their concerns from the East–West conflict.[58] Since several of the articles also cover the period of the 1980s, when East–West tensions reached a new climax, the findings are all the more astonishing. This special issue cannot give conclusive answers in this regard either, but it helps to break new ground and refocus the debate on the history of co-operation and integration in post-war Western Europe, the role of IOs and the Cold War in Europe.

Notes

1. Kaiser and Storeide, 'From Europe to the World'.
2. See, for example, Martens and Jacobi, eds., *Mechanisms of OECD Governance*; Jacobi and Martens, 'Diffusion durch internationale Organisationen'.
3. Stobart, 'Fifty Years of European Co-operation on History Textbooks'; Stradling, *Teaching 20th-Century European History*.
4. Cf. Feyen and Krzaklewska, *The ERASMUS Phenomenon*.
5. Alter and Meunier, 'Politics of International Regime Complexity', 13.
6. Raustiala and Victor, 'The Regime Complex for Plant Genetic Resources'.
7. Patel, 'Provincialising European Union'.
8. Kaiser and Johan Schot, *Writing the Rules for Europe*, 4.
9. Westad, *The Global Cold War*.
10. Patel, 'Provincialising European Union', 653.
11. See, e.g., Bulmer, 'The Governance of the European Union'; Kassim 'Policy Networks, Networks and European Union Policy Making'.
12. Lyons, *Internationalism in Europe 1815–1914*, 13–14.
13. Kaiser and Johan Schot, *Writing the Rules for Europe*, chapter 4.
14. Hitchcock, *France Restored*.
15. See, e.g., HAEU, CEAB 4, 114, ECSC, High Authority, Note pour les membres de la Haute Autorité, 1959; Paul Reuter, *Organisations européennes* (Paris: Presses universitaires de France, 1965), 152–4.
16. PAAA, B 20–200/95B, Vertretung der Bundesrepublik beim Europarat an Auswärtiges Amt, 'Gedanken über den Europarat', 15 May 1957.
17. Malmborg and Olesen, 'The Creation of EFTA'.
18. For this see Kaiser, 'The Successes and Limits of Industrial Market Integration'.
19. For an introduction to the historiography of the present-day EU see Kaiser and Varsori, *European Union History*.
20. See the criticism in Gilbert, 'Process'.
21. See, in particular, Milward, *The European Rescue of the Nation-State*.

MULTIPLE CONNECTIONS IN EUROPEAN COOPERATION

22. Knudsen, *Farmers on Welfare*; as attempts to transcend such a realist perspective, see, for example, Patel, *Europäisierung wider Willen*; Patel, *Fertile Ground for Europe?*
23. See, for example, Dumoulin, *The European Commission*; Bussière, *The European Commission*.
24. Griffiths, *Explorations in OEEC History*.
25. Wassenberg, *Histoire du Conseil de l'Europe*.
26. For introduction to IOs and their agency see Mackenzie, *A World Beyond Borders*.
27. Haas, *The Uniting of Europe*.
28. Didem Buhari-Gulmez, 'Stanford School'.
29. Werner and Zimmermann, 'Beyond Comparison'; Middell, 'Kulturtransfer und Historische Komparatistik'.
30. As in Haas, *Beyond the Nation-State*.
31. See e.g. Young, 'Institutional Linkages in International Society'.
32. As in Mansfield and Reinhardt, 'Multilateral Determinants of Regionalism'.
33. Aggarwal and Fogarty, 'The Limits of Interregionalism'.
34. As in Raustiala and Victor, 'The Regime Complex for Plant Genetic Resources'.
35. Alter and Meunier, 'Politics of International Regime Complexity', 16.
36. Alter and Meunier, 'Politics of International Regime Complexity', 16–19.
37. Biermann, 'Towards a Theory of Inter-Organizational Networking'.
38. For networks among political parties see Salm, *Transnational Socialist Networks in the 1970s*; Kaiser, *Christian Democracy and the Origins of European Union*; for an example from the field of culture see Faure, *Netzwerke der Kulturdiplomatie*.
39. Biermann, 'Towards a Theory of Inter-Organizational Networking', 173.
40. Witte and Thies, 'Why Choose Europe'.
41. Rasmussen and Davies, 'Towards a New History of European Law'.
42. See, for example, Weiler, ed., *The EU, the WTO, and the NAFTA*.
43. Kaiser and Meyer, *International Organizations and Environmental Protection*.
44. See Meyer, 'From Nature to Environment'.
45. Cf. Romano, 'Untying Cold War Knots'.
46. See e.g. Defrance, 'The Élysée Treaty in the Context of Franco-German Socio-cultural Relations'.
47. See also Calligaro, *Negotiating Europe*.
48. Wassenberg, *Histoire du Conseil de l'Europe*.
49. Meadows, *Limits to Growth*.
50. Cf. Smith, *Europe's Foreign and Security Policy: The Institutionalization of Cooperation*.
51. Sunstein, 'Social Norms and Social Roles'; Bourdieu, *The Field of Cultural Production*.
52. Borowy, '(Re-) Thinking Environment and Economy'; Kaiser, 'Sometimes it's the Economy, Stupid'.
53. See Littoz-Monnet, *The European Union and Culture*.
54. For the EU's legal integration in historical perspective see Vauchez, *Brokering Europe*; Davies and Rasmussen, 'Towards a New History of European Law'; Witte and Thies, 'Why Choose Europe'.
55. Patel, 'Provincialising European Union', 653.
56. Cf. Högselius, Kaijser and van der Vleuten, *Europe's Infrastructure Transition*; Patel and Schot, 'Twisted Paths to European Integration'; Badenoch and Fickers, *Materializing Europe*.
57. Iriye, 'Historicizing the Cold War'; also see, for example, Connelly, 'Taking Off the Cold War Lens'.
58. Ludlow, *European Integration and the Cold War*.

Acknowledgements

We would like to thank the FU Berlin "The Transformative Power of Europe" Research College for support for our research project on co-operation and competition among international organizations in Europe after 1945, which has resulted in this special issue. Our special thanks go to the Research College's directors Tanja Börzel and Thomas Risse for their valuable insights and friendship over the years. Kiran Klaus Patel would also like to thank the Gerda Henkel Foundation for its support as Gerda Henkel Visiting Professor at the German Historical Institute London and the London School of Economics in 2014/15.

Disclosure statement

No potential conflict of interest was reported by the authors.

Bibliography

Historical Archives of the European Union, Florence (HAEU)
Politisches Archiv des Auswärtigen Amtes der Bundesrepublik Deutschland (PAAA)

Literature

Aggarwal, Vinod K., and Edward A. Fogarty. "The Limits of Interregionalism: The EU and North America." *Journal of European Integration* 27 (2005): 327–346.

Alter, Karen J., and Sophie Meunier. "Politics of International Regime Complexity." *Perspectives on Politics* 9 (2009): 13–24.

Badenoch, Alexander, and Andreas Fickers, eds. *Materializing Europe: Transnational Infrastructures and the Project of Europe.* Basingstoke: Palgrave Macmillan, 2010.

Biermann, Rafael. "Towards a Theory of Inter-Organizational Networking: The Euro-Atlantic Security Institutions Interacting." *Review of International Organizations* 3 (2008): 151–177.

Borowy, Iris. "(Re-)Thinking Environment and Economy: The Organisation for Economic Cooperation and Development and Sustainable Development." In *International Organizations and Environmental Protection. Globalization and Conservation in the Twentieth Century*, edited by Wolfram Kaiser and Jan-Henrik Meyer, 211–240. New York: Berghahn, 2017.

Bourdieu, Pierre. *The Field of Cultural Production: Essays on Art and Literature.* New York: Columbia University Press, 1993.

Buhari-Gulmez, Didem. "Stanford School on Sociological Institutionalism: A Global Cultural Approach." *International Political Sociology* 4 (2010): 253–270.

Bulmer, Simon. "The Governance of the European Union: A New Institutionalist Approach." *Journal of Public Policy* 13 (1993): 351–380.

Bussière Eric, Vincent Dujardin, Michel Dumoulin, Piers Ludlow, Jan Willem Brouwer, and Elisabeth Palmero, eds. *The European Commission 1973–86: History and Memories of an Institution.* Luxembourg: Publications Office of the European Union, 2014.

Calligaro, Oriane. *Negotiating Europe: EU Promotion of Europeanness since the 1950s.* New York: Palgrave Macmillan, 2013.

Connelly, Matthew. "Taking off the Cold War Lens: Visions of North-South Conflict during the Algerian War for Independence." *American Historical Review* 105 (2000): 739–769.

Davies, Bill, and Morten Rasmussen. "Towards a New History of European Law: An Introduction." *Contemporary European History* 21 (2012): 305–318.

Defrance, Corine. "The Élysée Treaty in the Context of Franco-German Socio-Cultural Relations." *German Society and Politics* 31 (2013): 70–91.

Dumoulin, Michel, ed. *The European Commission 1958–72: History and Memories.* Luxembourg: Publications Office of the European Union, 2007.

Faure, Romain. *Netzwerke Der Kulturdiplomatie. Die Internationale Schulbuchrevision in Europa, 1945–1989.* Berlin: Walter de Gruyter, 2015.

Feyen, Benjamin, and Ewa Krzaklewska, eds. *The ERASMUS Phenomenon: Symbol of a New European Generation?.* Brussels: Peter Lang, 2013.

Gilbert, Mark. "Narrating the Process: Questioning the Progressive Story of European Integration." *Journal of Common Market Studies* 46 (2008): 641–662.

Griffiths, Richard T., ed. *Explorations in OEEC History.* Paris: OEEC, 1997.

Haas, Ernst. *Beyond the Nation-State: Functionalism and International Organization.* Stanford CA: Stanford University Press, 1964.

Haas, Ernst B. *The Uniting of Europe: Political, Social, and Economic Forces, 1950–1957.* Stanford CA: Stanford University Press, 1958.

Hitchcock, William. *France Restored: Cold War Diplomacy and the Quest for Leadership in Europe, 1944–1954.* Chapel Hill: University of North Carolina Press, 2000.

Högselius, Per, Arne Kaijser, and Erik Van Der Vleuten. *Europe's Infrastructure Transition: Economy, War, Nature.* Basingstoke: Palgrave Macmillan, 2016.

Iriye, Akira. "Historicizing the Cold War." In *Oxford Handbook of the Cold War*, edited by Richard H. Immerman and Petra Goedde. Oxford: Oxford University Press, 2013.

Jacobi, Anja P., and Kerstin Martens. "Diffusion Durch Internationale Organisationen: Die Bildungspolitik Der OECD." In *Transfer, Diffusion Und Konvergenz Von Politiken*, edited by Katharina Holzinger, Helge Jörgens, and Christoph Knill, 247–270. Wiesbaden: Verlag für Sozialwissenschaften, 2007.

Kaiser, Wolfram. "Sometimes It's the Economy, Stupid! International Organisations, Steel and the Environment." In *International Organizations and Environmental Protection. Globalization and Conservation in the Twentieth Century*, edited by Wolfram Kaiser and Jan-Henrik Meyer, 153–181. New York: Berghahn, 2017.

Kaiser, Wolfram. *Christian Democracy and the Origins of European Union.* Cambridge: Cambridge University Press, 2007.

Kaiser, Wolfram. "The Successes and Limits of Industrial Market Integration: The European Free Trade Association 1963–1969." In *Crises and Compromises: The European Project 1963–1969*, edited by Wilfried Loth, 371–390. Baden-Baden: Nomos, 2001.

Kaiser, Wolfram, and Anette Homlong Storeide. "From Europe to the World: International Organizations and Holocaust Remembrance." *History & Memory.* European Sociology, (forthcoming).

Kaiser, Wolfram, and Jan-Henrik Meyer, eds. *International Organizations and Environmental Protection: Globalization and Conservation in the Twentieth Century.* New York: Berghahn, 2017.

Kaiser, Wolfram, and Johan Schot. *Writing the Rules for Europe: Experts, Cartels, and International Organizations.* Basingstoke: Palgrave Macmillan, 2014.

MULTIPLE CONNECTIONS IN EUROPEAN COOPERATION

Kaiser, Wolfram, and Antonio Varsori, eds. *European Union History: Themes and Debates*. Basingstoke: Palgrave Macmillan, 2010.

Kassim, Hussein. "Policy Networks, Networks and European Union Policy Making: A Sceptical View." *West European Politics* 17 (1994): 15–27.

Knudsen, Ann-Christina L. *Farmers on Welfare: The Making of Europe's Common Agricultural Policy*. Ithaca: Cornell University Press, 2009.

Littoz-Monnet, Annabelle. *The European Union and Culture: Between Economic Regulation and Cultural Policy*. Manchester, NH: Manchester University Press, 2007.

Ludlow, N. Piers, ed. *European Integration and the Cold War: Ostpolitik—Westpolitik, 1965–1973*. London: Routledge, 2007.

Lyons, F. S. L. *Internationalism in Europe 1815–1914*. Leiden: A.W. Sythoff, 1963.

Mackenzie, David. *A World beyond Borders: An Introduction to the History of International Organizations*. Toronto: University of Toronto Press, 2010.

Malmborg, Mikael af, and Thorsten B. Olesen. "The Creation of EFTA." In *Interdependence versus Integration: Denmark, Scandinavia and Western Europe, 1945–1960.*, edited by T. B. Olesen, 197–212. Odense: Odense University Press, 1995.

Mansfield, Edward, and Eric Reinhardt. "Multilateral Determinants of Regionalism: The Effects of GATT/WTO on the Formation of Preferential Trading Arrangements." *International Organization* 57 (2003): 829–862.

Martens, Kerstin, and Anja P. Jacobi, eds. *Mechanisms of OECD Governance: International Incentives for National Policy-Making?*. Oxford: Oxford University Press, 2010.

Meadows, Donella H., et al. *Limits to Growth*. New York: New American Library, 1972.

Meyer, Jan-Henrik. "From Nature to Environment: International Organisations and Environmental Protection before Stockholm." In *International Organizations and Environmental Protection: Globalization and Conservation in the Twentieth Century*, edited by Wolfram Kaiser and Jan-Henrik Meyer, 31–73. New York: Berghahn, 2017.

Middell, Matthias. "Kulturtransfer Und Historische Komparatistik – Thesen Zu Ihrem Verhältnis." *Comparativ* 10 (2000): 7–41.

Milward, Alan S. *The European Rescue of the Nation-State*. London: Routledge, 1992.

Patel, Kiran Klaus. "Provincialising European Union: Co-Operation and Integration in Europe in Historical Perspective." *Contemporary European History* 22 (2013): 649–673.

Patel, Kiran Klaus, and Johan Schot. "Twisted Paths to European Integration: Comparing Agriculture and Transport in a Transnational Perspective." *Contemporary European History* 20 (2011): 383–403.

Patel, Kiran Klaus. *Europäisierung Wider Willen. Die Bundesrepublik Deutschland in Der Agrarintegration Der EWG 1955–1973*. Munich: Oldenbourg, 2009.

Patel, Kiran Klaus, ed. *Fertile Ground for Europe? The History European Integration and the Common Agricultural Policy since 1945*. Nomos: Baden-Baden, 2009.

Rasmussen, Morten, and Bill Davies. "Towards a New History of European Law." *Contemporary European History* 21 (2012): 305–318.

Raustiala, Kal, and David G. Victor. "The Regime Complex for Plant Genetic Resources." *International Organization* 58 (2004): 277–309.

Reuter, Paul. *Organisations Européennes*. Paris: Presses universitaires de France, 1965.

Romano, Angela. "Untying Cold War Knots: The EEC and Eastern Europe in the Long 1970s." *Cold War History* 14 (2014): 153–173.

Salm, Christian. *Transnational Socialist Networks in the 1970s: European Community Development Aid and Southern Enlargement*. Basingstoke: Palgrave Macmillan, 2016.

Smith, Michael E. *Europe's Foreign and Security Policy: The Institutionalization of Cooperation*. Cambridge: Cambridge University Press, 2004.

Stobart, Maitland. "Fifty Years of European Co-Operation on History Textbooks: The Role and Contribution of the Council of Europe." *Internationale Schulbuchforschung* 21 (1999): 147–161.

Stradling, Robert. *Teaching 20th-Century European History*. Strasbourg: Council of Europe, 2001.

Sunstein, Cass R. "Social Norms and Social Roles." *Columbia Law Review* 96 (1996): 903–968.

Varsori, Antonio. "From Normative Impetus to Professionalization: Origins and Operation of Research Networks." In *European Union History: Themes and Debates*, edited by Wolfram Kaiser and Antonio Varsori, 6–25. Basingstoke: Palgrave Macmillan, 2010.

Vauchez, Antoine. *Brokering Europe. Euro-Lawyers and the Making of a Transnational Polity.* Cambridge: CUP, 2015.

Wassenberg, Birte. *History of the Council of Europe (1949–2009).* Brussels: P.I.E. Peter Lang, 2012.

Weiler, John H. H., ed. *The EU, the WTO, and the NAFTA: Towards a Common Law of International Trade?* Oxford: Oxford University Press, 2000.

Werner, Michael, and Bénédicte Zimmermann. "Beyond Comparison: Histoire Croisée and the Challenge of Reflexivity." *History and Theory* 45 (2006): 30–50.

Westad, Odd-Arne, and The Global Cold War. *Third World Interventions and the Making of Our Time.* Cambridge: Cambridge University Press, 2006.

Witte, Bruno de, and Anne Thies. "Why Choose Europe? The Place of the European Union in the Architecture of International Legal Cooperation." In *The EU's Role in Global Governance: The Legal Dimension*, edited by Bart Van Vooren, Steven Blockmans, and Jan Wouters, 23–38. Oxford: Oxford University Press, 2013.

Young, Oran. "Institutional Linkages in International Society: Polar Perspectives." *Global Governance* 2 (1996): 1–24.

Facing the Greek junta: the European Community, the Council of Europe and the rise of human-rights politics in Europe

Víctor Fernández Soriano

ABSTRACT

In April 1967, a group of colonels seized power in Greece. Since Greece was a member-state of the Council of Europe and held an association agreement with the European Community, both organizations had to define their positions vis-à-vis the new military regime. Very soon, politicians in the parliamentary assemblies of both organizations started to cooperate with the aim of imposing sanctions on Greece. This article examines the inter-organizational dynamics between the European Community and the Council of Europe on Greece during the colonels' regime. It argues that the European Community imported concrete policy positions and even normative ideas which had first emerged in the Council of Europe. In so doing, the Community prepared the ground for its future human-rights policies.

Introduction

In February 1968, Stylianos Pattakos, one of the members of the colonels' triumvirate which ruled Greece after the military *coup d'état* of April 1967, declared that the Council of Europe (CoE) bothered Greece no more than 'a mosquito on the horns of an ox'.[1] He made these remarks shortly after the Consultative Assembly of the CoE had approved a resolution on Greece, which urged the Greek military regime to restore democracy and to respect fundamental human rights. Otherwise, so the resolution stipulated, Greece could be excluded from the CoE. In the end, the CoE became more than a mosquito on the horns of an ox, proving Pattakos and his cynical remarks wrong. During the reign of the Greek junta, from 1967 to 1974, the CoE turned into a major forum of criticism, accusing the junta of human-rights violations. Moreover, the European Community (EC) soon emulated its comparably tough policy stance, thus adding further pressure on the Greek military government.

The CoE and the EC are particularly interesting in the history of the international crisis provoked by the Greek colonels' *coup d'état*. In a recent article, Effie G. H. Pedaliu has shown that the Western states failed to take punitive action against the Greek junta. Despite a sizeable transnational movement of anti-junta protest, they prioritized geopolitical interests.[2] The CoE and the EC were, however, exceptions to this: they undertook punitive measures against Greece. The explanation for this lies in their 'European' nature. These organizations were trapped in the rhetorical entrapment of the European integration process, traditionally associated with the defence of human rights in official speeches, declarations or the preambles of treaties. This entrapment combined with the fact that neither of the two had geopolitical power led to the use of these organizations for rebuking the colonels' regime.

Based on a wide range of documents from both organizations – mainly verbatims, notes and reports of their legal and external services – this article will argue that the Greek crisis did have an impact on European human-rights politics. Although these organizations were caught between geopolitical interests and a rhetorical entrapment, the Greek crisis led to sanctions which set an important precedent to their respective human-rights agendas.

In this context, the interplay between the CoE and the EC was crucial. This article focuses on the entangled exchanges between both organizations regarding the 'Greek case'. The EC imported political ideas and norms from the CoE. In addition, the Greek crisis was the moment in which the EC started to incorporate human rights into its political portfolio, inspired by the measures undertaken by the CoE. While today's European Union (EU) is often described as a 'normative power' with a strong commitment to human rights,[3] history holds an important lesson: policy import from another organization stood at the cradle of the EU's work in this field, and its new stance took place in the context of the rise of human rights across various forums of the Western world during the 1960s and 1970s.

The interplay between the CoE and the EC on the Greek case did not result in an official cooperation or joint action between the two organizations. Instead, the Parliamentary Assembly of the CoE led the whole process, which was then mainly driven by individual parliamentarians. Ultimately, the CoE served as a role model for the EC's human-rights politics towards the Greek junta.[4] As a result, the EC also decided to impose sanctions on Greece, thus taking up a policy stance first developed in the CoE and embracing human rights as a new, normative policy concern, significant at least rhetorically. The Greek case was therefore important for the EC to develop a rhetoric of human rights, which would eventually influence its own agenda.[5]

In the interplay between the two Western international organizations, their respective parliamentary assemblies played an important role. The Consultative Assembly of the CoE and the Parliamentary Assembly of the EC, best known as the European Parliament (EP),[6] acted as vectors of exchange, facilitating the transfer of policy proposals and norms. For this, links between some of their concrete members, the overlapping of transnational milieus and even joint institutional memberships proved central.

This article aims to explain why the Greek question was important in the development of European human-rights politics. It analyses the interplay between the CoE and the EC on this question and shows that the CoE influenced the EC's first attempts to impose sanctions for political reasons. Accordingly, this article argues that, through the Greek question, the CoE contributed to the introduction of human rights into the external agenda of the EC.

This article is divided into three main parts. The first opens with the general context and then presents the interplay between the CoE and the EC regarding the Greek question. The second part exposes the first measures undertaken by the EC against the Greek junta under the influence of the CoE. The third part explains the consequences that these actions had on the EC. The conclusion summarizes this article's main findings.

European organizations and the Greek junta

Several historians have recently argued that the 1970s saw the rise of human rights in international politics.[7] In *The Last Utopia*, Samuel Moyn has claimed that human rights only began to make sense to broad communities of people since the late 1960s, building on the ruins of earlier political utopias and thus being a new political concern at the time. Following up on Moyn's interpretation, Barbara Keys has lately made a similar claim with regard to the reactions against the Greek junta.[8] While the work of these two historians largely focuses on US politics and policy, their findings are also valid for Western Europe and its international organizations. Rhetorically, human rights played an important role in the first phase of post-war European cooperation, especially in the context of the Council of Europe, established in 1949. Practically, however, such debates had few effects up to the late 1960s.[9] Admittedly, the European Commission of Human Rights and the European Court of Human Rights had been created within the legal framework of the CoE respectively in 1954 and in 1959, as the first international judiciary institutions of this kind.[10] But the first activities and the overall profile of both the Commission and the Court remained modest. The governments of the CoE's member-states made sure to restrict its autonomy. In fact, the Commission and the Court's role was largely conditioned by the political bargaining amongst governments – by what Mikael Rask Madsen has called 'legal diplomacy'.[11]

The 1967 colonels' *coup d'état* in Greece changed all that. Debate about events in Greece flared up in many countries across the Western world. Most Western governments disliked the putsch but were not willing to change their relations with Greece. Despite the rise of an international movement of solidarities with the Greek people, governments were reluctant to change the status quo.[12] They were also reluctant to challenge Greece's status in international organizations such as the CoE or the EC.[13] Western governments were conditioned by the United States' attitude as well as by the dynamics of the Cold War, in which Greece was a key region in geostrategic terms.[14]

At the United Nations (UN), the Greek case was brought only before the Sub Commission on Prevention of Discrimination and Protection of Minorities. Events unfolded in the period prior to the ratification of the International Covenant on Civil and Political Rights (1976), which institutionalized the fundamental human rights stated in the 1948 Universal Declaration within the UN. Accordingly, the Sub Commission on the Prevention of Discrimination and Protection of Minorities simply proposed to investigate the situation in Greece. The controversy focused less on the Greek regime, but rather on the procedural dimension of putting Greece on the agenda of such an institution.[15] As the UN legal framework of the time was quite limited to treat the Greek case, attention quickly shifted to the European arena.

At the European level, the rhetorical entrapment of human rights weighed heavily.[16] The rhetoric of human rights was inherent to the process of cooperation in Western Europe since its origins. For the CoE, an organization with no political power, this was even its main *raison d'être*. As a result, the Council of Europe soon turned into a central arena of the international debates on Greece. Since at the time the CoE was the only international organization in the Western world with a huge commitment to human rights, the situation in Greece challenged the CoE's legitimacy. When it fell under military rule, Greece was a member of the CoE and a signatory of its European Convention of Human Rights. Greece was represented in all CoE institutions; a Greek judge even sat at the European Court of Human Rights and the Athens government had the same power in decision-making processes as any other member-state. The highest sanction possible in the CoE context, therefore, was exclusion from membership.

The stakes were much lower in the EC context. Despite being the pivotal organization of regional integration in Western Europe, the EC had no real commitment to human rights. The 1957 Treaties of Rome, as the EC's key legal documents, did not insist on compliance with human rights or democratic rule, neither for association nor for membership.[17] By the late 1960s, the EC still mainly defined itself through economic criteria and stipulations. Greece was not a member of the EC, but had signed an association agreement with it in 1961 which foresaw the perspective of membership in the long run.[18] This association agreement aimed at the creation of a common customs union and closer cooperation in the fields of agricultural and labour policies. Greece had no direct representation at the EC's institutions. For all these reasons, the highest conceivable sanction by the EC to Greece was the suspension of its association agreement.[19]

The parliamentary assemblies of both the CoE and the EC launched the criticism of the Greek junta. Formally, both assemblies only played a consultative role and the ministerial meetings, in charge of taking decisions, notoriously ignored their resolutions and declarations. Still, their role should not be underestimated. On a whole range of policy issues, they acted as important laboratories and sounding boards of policy-making. Through their endless series of reports, they had turned into forums of transnational cooperation amongst elite groups. Moreover, in the changing political climate of the second half of the 1960s – in which political decision-making behind closed doors met more and more resistance – the deliberations of such assemblies impacted on policy-making to a larger extent than ever before. This was also the case because debates tended to be more politicized here in comparison to other bodies, such as the EC Council of Ministers, where technical issues and the search for compromises often prevailed. The members of these assemblies were usually appointed by their national parliaments due to their pro-European credentials; across member-states, many of them happened to be members of federalist movements or other activists.

Cooperation between these parliamentary assemblies was noteworthy. Several of their members had held positions in both assemblies and became prominent voices on human-rights issues during the 1960s and 1970s. The members of both assemblies also met in an annual joint session, which, since 1959, was held in Strasbourg. The president of the Political Commission of the EP, a position held by Edoardo Martino between 1964 and 1967, also regularly exchanged views with the members of the assembly of the CoE on political issues.[20] These assemblies became, therefore, a typical venue for a web of informal networks of political cooperation, which fostered exchanges of information and positions. Institutional factors came on top: the sessions of both assemblies even took place at the same location, the Maison de l'Europe in Strasbourg, often shortly after each other. All these factors facilitated and stimulated cooperation.

The Consultative Assembly of the CoE stirred into action immediately after the *coup d'état* in Greece, and it thus came to play a pivotal role on this issue at the Council of Europe. A coincidence in timing turned into an important factor in this context. The Consultative Assembly of the CoE used to meet in four sessions per year and the second 1967 session was scheduled for 24 April. As it happens, it therefore took place a mere three days after the colonels' putsch in Athens.

The situation in Greece dominated the agenda for an obvious and sad reason: when the Assembly opened that day, its Greek members were absent, impeached by the junta and kept in custody in their home country. Such were the cases of Ioannis Zighdis, a prominent Greek politician at that time, and Achille Yerokostopoulos, who had been a member of the Consultative Assembly since 1953. Zighdis, Yerokostopoulos and many of their peers were placed under surveillance after the events of 21 April 1967.[21] For the members of the Consultative Assembly, the situation in Greece was not an abstract political problem, but a humanitarian crisis that also concerned some of their own peers, as well as the political legitimacy of their own organization. The discussion in Strasbourg therefore quickly turned into a debate about the political situation in the Mediterranean country. Most members agreed on the fact that the Assembly had to condemn publicly the putsch and should call for action against the Greek junta. The Austrian Karl Czernetz, a member of the Sozialdemokratische Partei Österreichs, introduced a project of a resolution in the name of the Socialist Group. 'One of our members has violated the fundamental principles of our community', Czernetz pointed out, and he stressed that 'as a parliamentary assembly we are obliged to take a stance'. The other groups shortly followed his lead.[22] Nevertheless, most members of the Consultative Assembly avoided calling explicitly for the expulsion of Greece: in order to keep sceptics on board, they refrained from calling for the most radical measures that the organization had at its disposal. Finally, all groups agreed on a directive and a large majority adopted it on 26 April 1967.[23] This directive, which carried the number 256, urged the Greek junta to restore democracy and to respect the terms of the European Convention on Human Rights. Although it did not mention the word 'expulsion', it implicitly referred to it by implying that compliance with the European Convention on Human Rights was a condition for CoE membership: 'As a Member of the Council of Europe, Greece must remain loyal to the Statute of the Council of Europe ... [The Assembly] protests against all measures contrary to the European Convention on Human Rights.' Directive 256 also called 'to enquire into the fate of the Greek Deputies who had been appointed members of the Assembly by the Greek Parliament'.[24] The respect of the European Convention on Human Rights and the release of political prisoners were thus the two main claims that the Consultative Assembly of the CoE lodged to the Greek government. Directive 256 was released as a press communiqué and several newspapers, amongst them the French daily *Le Monde*, published the whole text the next day.[25]

Directive 256 of the Consultative Assembly of the CoE became a role model. Governments, national parliaments and international organizations subsequently referred to it when arguing on the necessity of demanding the respect of human rights to the Greek government. On 31 May 1967, Czernetz asked the minister for foreign affairs in the Austrian Nationalrat in what way he would support the Consultative Assembly's position. In the German Bundestag, Helmut Schmidt, then the chairman of the parliamentary group of the Sozialdemokratische Partei Deutschlands (SPD) and also a member of the Consultative Assembly of the CoE, tabled a motion, which, however dismissed, asked the Federal Government to support Greece's expulsion from the CoE. In Denmark, Sweden and Norway, the Ministers of Foreign Affairs, responding to similar motions, decided that they would lodge a complaint with the European Commission of Human Rights. Shortly after, the Dutch minister of foreign affairs, Joseph Luns, announced that he would take a similar step: 'In accordance to what Mr. Luns said in his reply of 18th July to the questions put by seven Deputies on the Greek situation, the Netherlands Government have meanwhile taken the initiative of once again sounding the other Parties to the aforesaid Convention.'[26]

Directive 256 quickly gained prominence, and it helped to reaffirm the Assembly's political role as well as its institutional self-respect, given the fate of its incarcerated members. Even the Greek junta felt obliged to react. Exactly a week after it had been passed, on 3 May 1967, the military government sent a letter to the secretary-general of the CoE, in which it stressed that the new government had had to declare a state of emergency, allegedly due to an imminent communist threat. The colonels even invoked Article 15 of the European Convention on Human Rights, which allowed any member-state to derogate the Convention 'in time of war or other public emergency threatening the life of the nation'.[27] With this letter, the Greek junta implicitly admitted that it had violated the Convention. Its critics were quick to jump on this argument: the governments of the Netherlands, Sweden, Norway and Denmark used this letter as the grounds for their complaint to the European Commission of Human Rights.[28]

Directive 256 also had a direct influence on the EP. The session of the Consultative Assembly of the CoE, in which the Greek case was discussed so extensively, closed on Friday 28 April 1967 and the EP opened its own session, also at the Strasbourg Maison de l'Europe, on the following Monday. One of the main points in the agenda of this session was the Greek situation, too. There were more specific reasons for this than the *genius loci* and the fact that newspapers were full of reports on the situation in Greece. The EP was also directly involved in issues dealing with the country; hence, institutional dynamics also explain why the issue entered the agenda. More precisely, the EP played a role in the EC's association through two institutions: a Joint Parliamentary Commission EC-Greece and an EP Committee on the Association with Greece. The Joint Parliamentary Commission EC-Greece could no longer meet because its Greek members had been dismissed by the junta. However, this institution was mainly symbolic and it only met once or twice per year. The EP Committee on the Association with Greece was more important: it was due to convene during the EP's May 1967 session to discuss the latest progress of the customs union foreseen by the association agreement. This Committee was presided by the Dutch Wim Schuijt, a member of the *Katholijke Volkspartij*.[29] Instead of discussing the customs union, the Committee on the Association with Greece decided to examine the political situation in that country. On 2 May 1967, it approved a communiqué signed by Schuijt. Addressed to the EC Commission and to the Council of Ministers, the document explicitly referred to the resolution of the Consultative Assembly of the CoE and it urged stopping the European Investment Bank's financial aid to Greece. The communiqué even suggested the suspension of the association between the EC and Greece as long as democratic institutions were not restored in Athens: '[A]ny decision in accordance with the association treaty or its annexed protocols, particularly by the European Investment Bank, is not supposed to take effect until the situation in Greece will have normalised.' The communiqué also encouraged the members of the EP to send to the EC Commission and Council of Ministers as many questions on Greece as possible to pressure these bodies to stir into action against the Greek junta.[30] The EP communiqué mirrored, thus, the CoE Directive 256. As such, it was the first concrete result of the interplay of the two organizations regarding the Greek question.

European actions against the Greek junta

The 2 May 1967 EP communiqué was the starting point of a series of oral and written questions by the EP to the EC Commission and Council of Ministers, questioning the association agreement with Greece. On 8 May 1967, Wim Schuijt and Edoardo Martino, an Italian senator of the Democrazia Cristiana and at that time the president of the Political Committee, succeeded in bringing one of the vice-presidents of the EC Commission, Lionello Levi-Sandri, to the EP to discuss the situation. Procedurally, Schuijt and Martino achieved this through an oral question which, according to the legal procedure, required a swift response by the EC Commission. Levi-Sandri was a member of the *Partito Socialista Italiano* and had been the EC Commissioner for Social Affairs since 1961. A descendant of a Jewish family from Corfu and a supporter of the West European model of democracy,[31] Levi-Sandri most likely had no sympathy for the Greek colonels. Still, he used a neutral tone when speaking in the EP and did not comment on the political implications of the situation in the Mediterranean country. The EC Commission was still unready to express a real opinion on Greece and Levi-Sandri spoke in its name. Martino and Schuijt asked Levi-Sandri about the 'political nature' of the association with Greece, and other EP members went as far as demanding a suspension of the association agreement. All Levi-Sandri replied was that the EC Commission could not comment on Greece since its information about the political situation in the country was still 'incomplete'. In reality, the EC Commission seemed internally in favour of imposing some kind of sanction to the Greek junta, but as the EC Council of Ministers had not yet discussed the question and had not yet agreed on a position, it was reluctant to make a bold proposal on such a delicate issue.[32] The Committee of Permanent Representatives, where the Council of Ministers met at ambassador level, had advised the EC Commission to take this stance.[33] In the EP debate, Levi-Sandri simply did what the Committee of Permanent Representatives had advised him to do.

Levi-Sandri's lukewarm words caused outrage at the EP. The Socialist Group, referring to the resolution of the Consultative Assembly of the CoE, openly demanded the suspension of the association agreement with Greece.[34] The speaker of the Socialist Group in this affair was the German Walter Faller, a member of the SPD. It was more than a coincidence that Faller took the floor on this issue, given that he had played a prominent role in all debates about the association of Greece. He was a member of the EP Committee on the Association with Greece, where he acted as an informal speaker of the Socialist Group, too. Moreover, he was a member of the Joint Parliamentary Commission EC-Greece and as such, had recently gathered some first-hand experience with the Greek regime. Only a few days prior to the *coup d'état*, he had actually presided over, along with Wim Schuijt, a delegation of members of the EP visiting Greece on 30–31 March 1967.[35] Faller had also authored one of the written questions sent to the EC Commission in the course of the previous days. In the EP debate, he argued for a suspension of the association agreement with Greece. 'We are grateful to the Consultative Assembly of the Council of Europe for immediately having taken a position at the political level and we support the contents of the resolution it has adopted without any reservations', Faller said.[36] He was backed by several of his colleagues of the Socialist Group, who argued that the political situation in Greece did not live up to the objectives of the association agreement. They stressed that ultimately, the goal had to be the accession of Greece to the EC as a member-state. This, however, remained impossible with the colonels' regime in power, they maintained. Some members of the group, such as the Dutch Jaap Burger, member of the *Partij van de Arbeid*, even called for economic sanctions for Greece.[37]

The discontent of the members of the EP with the attitude of both the EC Commission and the Council of Ministers led them to issue their own resolution against the Greek junta.

This was quite remarkable as it implied that the EP's four main political groups reached a consensus on the Greek affair. Martino and Schuijt's oral question served as a starting point for the EP resolution but, more importantly, Directive 256 of the Consultative Assembly of the CoE formed the model upon which the EP prepared its own text. As Georges Spénale, the speaker of the Socialist Group in this question put it, the previous works of the Consultative Assembly and the EP's committees were the 'basis of the discussion'. Like in the Consultative Assembly of the CoE a few days earlier, the EP political groups built their consensus on two claims: for one, the respect of the European Convention on Human Rights; and, for the other, the release of political prisoners. The four groups stressed, during the debates, the importance of human-rights compliance, which they linked with the European Convention. The EP 'underlines the essential importance of respecting the European Convention to protect human rights and fundamental freedoms'. However, the Convention was a covenant of the CoE and did not apply in EC law. Besides, the EP argued that the association agreement with Greece could not be deemed applicable anymore as the Greek deputies could not participate in the Joint Parliamentary Commission EC-Greece: 'The practical functioning of the association treaty is stopped until a Greek parliamentary delegation will again sit in the Joint Parliamentary Commission.' [38] However, this Commission was not an official body of the agreement and the fact that it could not meet did not interfere in the functioning of the association. Regardless of its legal inaccuracies, the EP's text exerted substantial political influence on the EC Commission's attitude and basically shaped the position it announced just a few weeks later.

At first, the EC Commission's approach remained cautious, however, in line with Levi-Sandri's stance during the EP hearing. It commenced its debates about the issue right after the opening of the EP session in Strasbourg, at a confidential meeting held in Brussels on 3 May 1967. Its vice-president for External Relations, the Belgian liberal Jean Rey, emphasized his personal concern about the political situation in Greece. Rey personally was in favour of some kind of sanction to the Greek junta and sympathized with the EP's approach.[39] As a militant federalist, he was also supporting the idea that the EP should play a genuinely political role.[40] As a vice-president of the EC Commission, he frequently visited the EP, where he presented the work of his directorate-general and received feedback from the members of the assembly. He was well acquainted with the views of Faller, Schuijt and other members who, like his fellow countryman Fernand Dehousse (*Parti socialiste belge*), argued for a tough reaction to the situation in Greece.[41] In line with the EP's approach, Rey, on 3 May 1967, suggested that 'some measures should be taken regarding the application of the association agreement with Greece'.[42] Still, he did not express this view in public, staying in line with the neutral tone that the EC Council of Ministers had opted for.

However, during the next days, Rey and the EC Commission started to study how the Commission could eventually undertake actions against the Greek junta in the framework of the association agreement. More precisely, Rey intended to clarify the limits of the association agreement in international law. He first requested a memorandum from the Greek ambassador to the EC, asking to explain his government's political intentions.[43] Then, he held a series of conversations with members of the European Investment Bank (EIB), also an EC institution, which was funding several projects in Greece, and ordered a note on the Greek political situation from his own directorate-general.[44] Rey's team concluded that under international law, the association agreement with Greece could not be suspended, but that the EC could nonetheless carry out some measures against the Greek junta. Legally, the association with Greece could be restricted to the functioning of the customs union. These ideas became public when in late May 1967 Rey responded, in the name of the EC Commission, to the written questions sent a month earlier by some members of the EP. With this, he made clear that the EC Commission was already working on a solution to the Greek question in line with the demands of the EP. All this happened before the EC Council of Ministers met to discuss this issue.[45]

The EC Council of Ministers discussed Greece on 6 June 1967. The session was held in Brussels and Rey also attended. He proposed to the Council of Ministers the idea of restricting the association with Greece to its basic functioning: this is what the EC Commission now started to call 'to freeze' the association agreement. The 'freezing' would hardly change the terms of the association agreement with Greece, but it would be a clear symbol that the EC, like the CoE, reacted to the situation in the Mediterranean country. The ministers did not object: this approach had a political dimension and might help to promote the EC as an organization concerned with the principles of democracy and human rights. Still, this policy stance did not come at a high material cost as it did not change the economic status quo. For the EC Commission and for Jean Rey personally, the EC Council's approval implied a political success. The 1961 association agreement meant that the EC Commission officially represented the EC in its partnership with Greece. The EC Commission had an unusual degree of autonomy in relation to the EC Council of Ministers and a bigger say in the process of decision-making than in other policy domains. The EC Council of Ministers' acceptance of the EC Commission's policy line now reaffirmed its role on a particularly thorny issue.[46]

The EC's decision to freeze its association agreement with Greece implied that the EC had basically emulated the policy approach of the CoE. As a result, the EC introduced into its external policy a normative yardstick which up to that moment had not existed. For the first time, human-rights considerations explicitly impacted on its policy stance. The EC Commission and Council of Ministers agreed on the fact that the association with Greece was not merely an economic agreement, but had an evident political nature. For this reason, the EC could not ignore the political situation in Greece and should limit its functioning to the on-going achievement of a common customs union. Having said this, the EC Commission and Council of Ministers decided not to make any immediate official declaration on the freezing of the association to avoid upsetting the Greek government.[47] Both institutions, particularly cautious from a legal point of view, tended to avoid these terms, probably because of the implications that their use could entail over EC law.[48] Instead, it was the EP that used the concepts 'democracy', 'freedoms' and 'fundamental rights' to explain the EC's stance on Greece.[49] Hence, the turn to human rights as a normative dimension of EC policy-making was cautious. Only in the medium term did the freezing of the Greek association agreement contribute to forging a narrative according to which the EC was a promoter of human rights and democracy. It thus imported a concern that so far had mainly been associated with the CoE.

Subsequent changes within the EC then played a defining role for the next steps. In July 1967, a new EC Commission was appointed; Edoardo Martino became the new commissioner for External Relations and Jean Rey the new president. For the EC, this was the end of an important era. As one of the results of the so-called 'empty chair crisis' of 1965 and the Luxembourg Compromise of 1966, the towering first president of the EC Commission, the German Walter Hallstein, had to retire in summer 1967. Most of the literature argues that this step weakened the role of the EC Commission and strengthened the intergovernmental dimension of the EC.[50] For the Greek case, the results were distinct, however. Rey and Martino held similar views about Greece and consequently, the new EC Commission adopted a harsher tone vis-à-vis the Greek junta.[51] From this period onwards, the EC Commission seized any occasion to declare publicly that the EC kept its association agreement with Greece frozen as long as democracy was not restored. The federalist movement, trade-unions confederations and other transnational groups applauded Rey and Martino's attitude as 'the best aid that the Community could provide to the Greek people'.[52]

After freezing the association agreement, the CoE's approach continued to impact on the EC's approach to Greece. At the CoE, the Greek case reached a new level in September 1967 when four of its member-states (Sweden, Norway, Denmark and the Netherlands) filed complaints before the European Commission of Human Rights. These countries referred to the previous works of the Consultative Assembly of the CoE and accused Greece of a massive violation of the European Convention on Human Rights. On the day after these documents had been submitted to the European Commission of Human Rights, the members of both the Consultative Assembly of the CoE and the EP met jointly at the Maison de l'Europe. On this occasion, Fernand Dehousse proposed that the EC undertook a procedure against Greece similar to the one undertaken by Sweden, Norway, Denmark and the Netherlands at the CoE. The aim was to suspend Greece as a member of the CoE and as an associated country to the EC: 'anyone is free to marry', said Dehousse, 'but not necessarily whomever they like'. However, no other speaker backed his proposal during the following debates.[53]

In this context, Rey and Martino opted for a new measure which aimed to highlight the EC's political determination against the Greek junta: the EC Commission stopped the EC's financial aids to Greece. Greece had been receiving loans from the EIB since 1961; in fact, Greece and Turkey were the only non-EC countries that had access to the funds of the EIB. A protocol added to the association agreement set the management of these financial aids and this protocol was due to expire on 31 October 1967. The EIB did not oppose renewing the financial aids to the Mediterranean country, but thanks to the initiative of Martino and Rey, the Commission vetoed the renewal on 27 September 1967.[54]

Coordination continued to shape the relationship between the EP and the Consultative Assembly of the CoE in their respective initiatives against the Greek junta for several years to come. The political stakes remained dissimilar, however. In the CoE, the complaint before the European Commission of Human Rights could lead to a Greek exit from the CoE, thus justifying further debates and action in the Consultative Assembly of CoE. In the EC, the situation was different. A legal deadlock had been reached after the freezing of the association and the suspension of financial aids. Because of its economic nature, the association agreement with Greece was not bound to political considerations or human rights. From the perspective of international law, a full-fledged suspension of the association agreement was impossible to justify. For that, Greece would have had to violate specific terms of the agreement, which it did not do. This led to tensions between the EP and the EC Commission. Many members of the EC regularly called for a suspension, while Rey and Martino and later their successors tried to convince them that the freezing was as far as the EC could legally go.[55]

The Consultative Assembly of the CoE opened a parallel investigation on Greece to the one of the European Commission of Human Rights, thus creating a new channel to influence the CoE's overall direction and to impact on international debates on the Greek case. This investigation was heavily influenced by the previous works of the *Guardian* journalist

Cedric Thornberry[56] and the Amnesty International lawyers James Becket and Anthony Marreco.[57] In February 1968, the Consultative Assembly appointed the Dutch Max van der Stoel (*Partij van de Arbeid*) as its special rapporteur on the situation in Greece. Van der Stoel was, not coincidentally, a citizen of one of the countries that had filed the complaint against a Greek and a member of the Socialist Group; by choosing him, it was already clear that the Consultative Assembly wanted to adopt a tough stance. In 1968, the Dutch politician travelled to Greece twice, and he even met some prominent figures in the Greek junta, including its leader, Prime Minister Giorgos Papadopoulos. Van der Stoel wrote several reports on the political situation in Greece, which gained some publicity and managed to irritate the junta. Again, the CoE showed that it was much more than the 'mosquito on the horns of an ox' about which Pattakos had spoken so disdainfully the year before.[58]

Although not a member of the EP, Van der Stoel's work set the pace for the debate of the Greek case at the EP, too. When Van der Stoel's first report was published in May 1968, after his first trip to Greece, Schuijt asked the Greek ambassador for permission for an EP delegation to travel to Greece on the same conditions as Van der Stoel's, so that they could also visit some political prisoners. The Greek government refused this request,[59] and the EC Commission ignored the issue.[60] In September 1968, the Greek junta banned Van der Stoel from entering the country again. Against this backdrop, the European Socialist Group decided to demand an immediate suspension of the association agreement from the EC Commission.[61] Not only did the Socialists now demand a tougher stance; the EP's Committee on the Association with Greece officially submitted a petition to the EC Commission urging the suspension of the association agreement. Rey and Martino sent this petition to the EC Commission's Legal Service and asked for its advice. The Legal Service was very clear in its conclusion: to suspend the association agreement without the consent of the Greek government would constitute a violation of international law.[62] For the EC, this door remained closed, regardless of the demands emanating from the EP.

On 12 December 1969, Greece withdrew from the CoE. This event had an impact on the EC's politics and ended the Greek controversy until the downfall of the colonels' regime during the summer of 1974. The whole series of events started in November 1969, when the European Commission of Human Rights ruled against Greece; it confirmed that the junta was violating the European Convention on Human Rights. The CoE Committee of Ministers consequently proceeded to vote for Greece's expulsion. Most of the member governments seemed eager to vote against Greece. The governments of Sweden, Denmark, the Netherlands, Luxembourg, Iceland, Britain and Switzerland were openly in favour of expelling Greece.[63] In Britain, Prime Minister Harold Wilson had even previously announced to the Parliament that he would back Greece's expulsion.[64] However, before the vote could take place, the Greek government announced its official withdrawal. Due to this face-saving operation, Greece ceased to be a member of the CoE.

From there, debates quickly moved to the EC. Shortly after these events, the EP Committee on the Association with Greece asked the EC Council of Ministers whether it considered that Greece's breakup with the CoE should also entail a suspension of its relations with the EC.[65] The EC Council of Ministers met on 9 January 1970, but maintained that the freezing of the association was the EC's only possible reaction.[66] At the EC Commission, Martino hesitated about his position on Greece. During the time, he regularly met with the EP Committee on the Association with Greece.[67] Moreover, he ordered a new study from the Legal Service in order to know whether, in light of the recent events at the CoE, the

EC's association of Greece could be disputed in any way. Once again, the conclusion of the Legal Service was negative.[68] In spite of this, Martino and Rey, along with the other commissioners, decided in April 1970 to publish a press communiqué. They strongly criticized the Greek junta government but, again, they did not bring up the issue of suspending the association agreement.[69]

The EC Commission's 1970 press communiqué is still of great importance. For the first time, an EC institution other than the EP publicly used the term 'human rights' when referring to the EC's external relations: 'The repeated violations of the rights of man and of citizens lead the Commission to rethink the functioning of the association treaty, which is already now facing major difficulties.' The Commission then affirmed that the EC was ready to change the terms of the association as long as the Greek government continued to violate basic human rights.[70] Although it did not specify what exactly it intended, the Commission explicitly linked the EC's relations with a third country to the respect of human rights by the country in question.

However, after this press communiqué, the EC did not modify its relations with Greece in any way. It held on to the status quo established in 1967, as there were no legal grounds for a suspension. Therefore, relations with Greece remained 'frozen', but not suspended, until the end of the dictatorship in 1974.[71]

The setting of a European human-rights agenda

Building on the experience of the Greek case, the EC would soon expand its human-rights agenda. In 1970, the member-states of the EC launched the European Political Cooperation (EPC) to coordinate on foreign-policy issues. Respect for human rights became one important element, at least formally, in this new instrument.[72] The document which gave birth to the EPC, the so-called Davignon Report that the ministers of foreign affairs adopted in October 1970, stated that 'a united Europe should be based on a common heritage of respect for the liberty and rights of man and bring together democratic States with freely elected parliaments'.[73] This statement reflects clearly the experience of the Greek question, for instance, the wording of the EC Commission's press communiqué just a few months earlier. The Greek affair opened, thus, the way for an appropriation of human rights by the EC as an international actor.

A major next step was the EC's stance during the negotiations of the Helsinki Final Act, when its member-states supported the inclusion of an article on the respect for human rights.[74] Moreover, the Greek affair had an influence on the EC's enlargement policy. Not surprisingly, human-rights promotion would play a defining role in the accession negotiations with Greece, Spain and Portugal, which the EC opened in the late 1970s after the downfall of dictatorial regimes in these three countries. In all three cases, the EC put forward the consolidation of democracy as the condition sine qua non for membership. As Greece was the first of these countries to negotiate its accession, its case also established the pattern for future action. At the end of the negotiations, the contents of which revolved essentially around economic technicalities,[75] the EC Commission stressed that human-rights compliance counted more than any technical consideration.[76] This document set an important precedent for all later enlargement negotiations.

Finally, the Greek case in the long term also influenced the EC's relationship to developing countries. The idea of sanctioning states that failed to comply with fundamental human rights became a key factor in the granting of aid to developing countries. In other words, the Greek case had an influence on what scholars have called 'political conditionality' for developing countries. Although political conditionality is often related to cooperation on development policies from the 1980s onwards, it had its first echoes in the EC policy of the late 1970s, when the EC partially suspended development aid to states like Uganda and the Central African Republic because of 'a denial of basic human rights to their people'.[77]

From the broader perspective of international relations, the Cold War dimension hung over the Greek affair at these European organizations. The support of human rights could hardly match geostrategic considerations. To confront the colonels also meant to challenge the government of an allied state that was key in the Cold War alliance located in a central area for the allies' strategies in both the Balkans and the Middle East. The supporters of international sanctions against Greece did not want the Western allies to show any goodwill to the colonels, even if the Greek junta was a reliable ally against Eastern communism. As geostrategic assumptions impacted the position of most Western European governments towards Greece, European organizations became the ideal arena to play the democracy and human-rights promotion card. Pro-European politicians had pushed for these values as a core dimension of the European integration process for a long time. The Greek case therefore became the occasion when these concerns clashed with Cold War priorities.

Taking these factors into consideration, it was no surprise that the interplay between the CoE and the EC had an echo in NATO, too. This is an issue which has been analysed by Effie G. H. Pedaliu[78] and Konstantina Maragkou,[79] who have argued that conflict over Greece was contained at NATO without much difficulty in the name of the Alliance's geo-strategic interest. After the Greek affair started to play such a prominent role in the CoE and the EC, the governments of Norway, Denmark and the Netherlands tried to introduce this human-rights dimension into the debates of the Atlantic Council. They claimed that NATO also had to consider sanctions against the colonels. In this forum, the United States blocked the debate, insisting on a geostrategic vantage point and prioritizing the security perspective of NATO's vulnerable southeastern flank in Europe.[80] Debates within Western Europe, and not so much in the North Atlantic sphere, therefore explain why the EC started to become a factor in this field.

Conclusion

Human-rights politics and policies is one of many examples in which policy ideas and, in this case, even normative concepts, travelled from the CoE to the EC. For quite a long time, whilst the CoE promoted itself as a guardian of human rights in Europe, human rights were a marginal issue for the EC. In this context, it seems even logical that the CoE, which gave impulse to European debates on human rights, represented a role model for the EC. The Greek question of the late 1960s marks the starting point in the transfer of the interest in human rights from the CoE to the EC. As such, it constitutes a sort of prehistory of the EU's concerns with human rights today.

Informal networks of cooperation and political exchanges, particularly between the members of the European parliamentary assemblies and to some extent the EC Commission, were central for this transfer, similarly as in the case of cultural policy, as shown in Oriane Calligaro's and Kiran Klaus Patel's contribution to this special section. On human rights, actors such as Wim Schuijt, Edoardo Martino, Fernand Dehousse and Max van der Stoel deserve particular credit. However, more than in the field of cultural policies, public debate about the Greek case in the turbulent political and cultural climate of the late 1960s, sensitive to human-rights violations and reluctant to accept realpolitik along with geostrategic priorities, impacted on the trajectory of the exchange between the CoE and the EC. These wider public debates thus served as a point of reference and a support for the efforts in the parliamentary assemblies, and even gave public recognition to these bodies. These assemblies were, therefore, crucial in linking the national political spheres and in creating a new level of European politics.

The late 1960s and the debate about human rights were also important to promote a novel kind of politician. Morally grounded arguments and strong European credentials gained in importance. It is more than a coincidence that some of the parliamentarians mentioned here later landed even more important jobs, for instance Edoardo Martino, who moved from the EP to the EC Commission in 1967, and Max van der Stoel, who became the Dutch minister for foreign affairs in 1973. In both the CoE and the EC, the representations of the member-states' governments remained more hesitant to prioritize human rights, showing that the growing attention paid to this concern never remained uncontroversial.

Notes

1. Woodhouse, *The Rise and Fall of the Greek Colonels*, 52.
2. Pedaliu, 'Human Rights and International Security'.
3. Manners, 'Normative Power Europe: A Contradiction in Terms?'
4. This set of events might be considered an important episode in the process of what Frank Schimmelfenning calls 'constitutionalization of the EU', meaning 'the institutionalization of human rights in the framework of the EC/EU'. Rittberger and Schimmelfenning, 2.
5. Hebel and Lenz, 'The Identity/Policy Nexus in European Foreign Policy'.
6. The official name of the European Parliament was at the time the 'European Parliamentary Assembly'. We shall use, however, the term 'European Parliament' (EP), with which the members of the assembly already referred to it.
7. Moyn, *The Last Utopia*, 212–27.
8. Keys, 'Anti-Torture Politics'.
9. This fact leads Andrew Moravcsik to affirm that the main use of human rights in European integration was to serve as a means of democratic mutual recognition amongst the Western European governments: Moravcsik, 'The Origins of Human Rights Regimes'.
10. The European Commission of Human Rights was, within the CoE jurisdiction, the tribunal which took cases for first consideration before they could go to the European Court of Human Rights. It was abolished in 1998.
11. Madsen, 'Legal Diplomacy'.
12. Pedaliu, 'Human Rights and International Security'.
13. Pedaliu, 'Human Rights and Foreign Policy'.
14. Maragkou, 'The Foreign Factor;' Klarevas, 'Were the Eagle and the Phoenix?'
15. Pedaliu, 'Human Rights and International Security', 1024–5.
16. Schimmelfenning, *The EU, NATO and the integration of Europe*, 222.
17. De Angelis and Karamouzi, 'Enlargement and the Historical Origins of European Community's Democratic Identity'.
18. Agreement establishing an association between the EEC and Greece (1961), Article 72.
19. Treaty of Rome (1957), Preamble and Articles 237 and 238.
20. Edoardo Martino's papers on international cooperation (1964–1967), EM-53, HAEU.
21. CoE, Consultative Assembly: *Adopted texts*, 19th Session, resolution No. 351 (Strasbourg, 26 September 1967).
22. CoE, Consultative Assembly, *Working Documents*, doc. 2202, doc. 2203 (Strasbourg, 25 April 1967).

MULTIPLE CONNECTIONS IN EUROPEAN COOPERATION

23. CoE, Consultative Assembly, *Official Report of Debates*, 19th Session (Strasbourg, 24–28 April 1967), t. I, 5–11, 44–88.
24. CoE, Consultative Assembly: *Adopted texts*, 19th Session, directive No. 256 (Strasbourg, 26 April 1967).
25. 'L'Assemblée consultative du Conseil de l'Europe déplore la suspension de la légalité constitutionnelle en Grèce', *Le Monde*, 28 April 1967, 6.
26. *Yearbook of the European Convention on Human Rights 1967* (The Hague, Martinus Nijhoff, 1969), 716–92 (782).
27. *Ibid.*, 26–7.
28. CoE, Le Danemark, la Norvège, la Suède et les Pays-Bas contre la Grèce, première décision de la Commission européenne des Droits de l'Homme sur la recevabilité (Strasbourg, 24 January 1968).
29. 'Dr. W. J. (Wim) Schuijt', *Parlement & Politiek* (https://www.parlement.com/id/vg09ll89fjve/w_j_wim_schuijt; last accessed February 1, 2016).
30. EP, communiqué of the Committee on Association with Greece (Strasbourg, 3 May 1967), BAC 173/1995 1430, HAEUCOM (own translation).
31. 'Sulla esigenza di un ordinamento democratico delle Comunità Europee' (14 April 1967), LLS-8, HAEU.
32. Jean Rey's personal archive, notes on Greece (1967–1969), HAULB.
33. Confidential note to the attention of the vice-president of the Commission Lionello Levi-Sandri about the COREPER meeting of 3 May 1967 (Brussels, 5 May 1967), BAC 173/1995 1430, HAEUCOM.
34. EP, *Débats, Comptes rendus in extenso*, 91 (Strasbourg, 8 May 1967): 11–20.
35. EP, communiqué of the Joint Parliamentary Commission EEC-Greece (Salonika, 31 March 1967), BAC 3/1978 275/5, HAEUCOM.
36. There was no English version of the EP's verbatim at the time; own translation.
37. EP, *Débats, Comptes rendus in extenso*, 91 (9–10 May 1967): 21–77; Faller's quote on p. 15.
38. *Ibid.* (11 May 1967): 114–116 (own translation).
39. Jean Rey's personal archive, notes on Greece (1967–1969), HAULB 126 PP 24.
40. Jean Rey, *Discours prononcé par Jean Rey, membre de la Commission de la Communauté économique européenne, le 23 juin 1964 à Rome, devant l'Assemblée de l'Union européenne occidentale* (Brussels, Services des Communautés européennes, 1964).
41. EP, Emilio Battista, Fernand Dehousse, Maurice Faure, Wim Schuijt, W.J. and Ludwig Metzger. *Rapport fait au nom la commission des affairs politiques et des questions institutionnelles sur l'election de l'Assemblee parlementaire europeenne au suffrage universel direct* (30 April 1960).
42. EC Commission, special verbatim 401 (Brussels, 3 May 1967), BAC 209.1980, HAEUCOM.
43. Greek government's memorandum to the European Commission (Athens, 17 May 1967), BAC 173/1995 1430, HAEUCOM.
44. EC Commission, note on the political situation in Greece (Brussels, 29 May 1967), BAC 3/1978 275/4, HAEUCOM.
45. Rey's responses to the questions of the European Parliament (Brussels, 22 and 27 May 1967), BAC 26/1969 696/3, HAEUCOM.
46. EC Commission, Note on Jean Rey's intervention at the 6 June 1967 meeting of the EC Council of Ministers, BAC 3/1978 275/5, HAEUCOM.
47. EC Council of Ministers, verbatim of a confidential meeting (Brussels, 6 June 1967), CM2 1967/39, HAEUCOUN.
48. EC Commission's note on the Greek political situation's impact upon the association agreement (9 June 1967), BAC 173/1995 1490, HAEUCOM.
49. A good example of this is a report signed by Carlo Scarascia Mugnozza and approved by the EP on 5 May 1969. This report explained the measures undertaken by the EC as a means to defend human rights: EP, *Documents de séance* 1969–1970, No. 33, 'Rapport fait au nom de la Commission de l'association avec la Grèce sur les répercussions de la situation politique actuelle en Grèce et sur le fonctionnement de l'association C.E.E.-Grèce' (Strasbourg, 5 May 1969).

MULTIPLE CONNECTIONS IN EUROPEAN COOPERATION

50. Golub, 'Did the Luxembourg Compromise'; Ludlow, The European Community, 68–93.
51. Edoardo Martino's notes on Greece (Brussels, July 1967), EM-76, HAEU.
52. EC, Letter from the European Federalist Movement to the EC Commission (Bologna, 13 December 1967), EM-77, HAEU; letter of the *Secrétariat syndical européen* to the European Commission (Brussels, 14 June 1968), BAC 173/1995 1430, HAEUCOM.
53. Verbatim of the 9th joint meeting of the Consultative Assembly of the CoE and the EP (Strasbourg, 21 September 1967), PE0 AP PV/PE-AC PEAC 19670921, HAEU; Dehousse's quote on pages 20–1 (own translation).
54. Note to Edoardo Martino on EBI loan to Greece (Brussels, 26 September 1967), EM-76, HAEU; EC Commission, final verbatim 8 (Brussels, 27 September 1967), BAC 209.1980, HAEUCOM.
55. Ralf Dahrendorf, a member of the German Freie Demokratische Partei, replaced Martino in January 1970. He was followed by Lord Christopher Soames (Winston Churchill's son-in-law) in 1973. Both Dahrendorf and Soames kept a stance on Greece equivalent to Martino's. In October 1970, Dahrendorf even affirmed that this stance had strongly contributed to prevent violence in Greece, see EC Commission, Ralf Dahrendorf's communication on EC–Greece relations (Brussels, 8 October 1970), BAC 50/1982 27/1, HAEUCOM.
56. Cedric Thornberry, 'Greek Prisoners Speak of Police Torture', the *Guardian* (24 November 1967): 15.
57. Becket and Marreco, Torture of Political Prisoners.
58. Leuprecht, 'Max van der Stoel'.
59. *Η Συμμετοχή της Ελλάδας*, 161–3.
60. EC Commission, verbatim 1968, BAC 259.80 PV 35–9, HAEUCOM.
61. Notes on the meeting of the European Socialist Group (26 September 1967), EM-79, HAEU.
62. EC Commission, report of the Legal Service on the suspension of the association agreement with Greece (Brussels, 6 November 1968), BAC 173/1995 1431, HAEUCOM.
63. CoE, Conclusion de la 185ᵉ réunion des délégués des ministres tenue à Paris du 9 au 11 décembre 1969.
64. House of Commons debates, Foreign Affairs (London, 8 December 1969), Hansard.
65. EP, Committee on the Association with Greece (Strasbourg, 11 December 1969), PE0 AP QP/QO-0015/69, HAEU.
66. EC Council of Ministers, verbatim of a confidential meeting (Brussels, 26 January 1970), CM2 1970/2ac, HAEUCOUN.
67. Edoardo Martino's meeting with the Committee on the Association with Greece (Brussels, 13 March 1970), BAC 3/1978 280/1, HAEUCOM.
68. EC Commission, note of the Commission Legal Service (Brussels, 11 May 1970), EM-82, HAEU.
69. EC Commission, press release (Brussels, 16 April 1970), Jean Rey's archive, HAULB 126 PP 24.
70. EC Commission, press communiqué (Brussels, 16 April 1970), BAC 50/1982 19/1, HAEUCOM (own translation).
71. Verney and Panos, 'Linkage Politics'.
72. Patel, 'Who Was Saving Whom?'
73. Davignon Report (Luxembourg, 27 October 1970), Centre Virtuel de Connaissance sur l'Europe (CVCE).
74. Thomas, *The Helsinki Effect*, 39–54.
75. Karamouzi, *Greece, the EEC and the Cold War.*
76. EC Commission's opinion on the Hellenic Republic's application for accession (Brussels, 23 May 1979), CVCE.
77. *The EU's Approach to Human Rights Conditionality*, 42–7.
78. Pedaliu, 'A Discordant Note'.
79. Maragkou, 'Favouritism in NATO'.
80. North Atlantic Council meeting (Rome, 26 May 1970), CVR(70)28 part II, HANATO.

Disclosure statement

No potential conflict of interest was reported by the author.

Bibliography

Archival material
Historical Archive of the EU, Florence (HAEU).
Historical Archive of the EU Commission, Brussels (HAEUCOM).
Historical Archive of the EU Council, Brussels (HAEUCOUN).
Historical Archive of NATO, Brussels (HANATO).
Historical Archive of the Université Libre de Bruxelles, Brussels (HAULB).

Grey literature
Council of Europe (CoE), Committee of Ministers, resolution (69)18, *Situation in Greece* (6 May 1969).
CoE, Committee of Ministers, resolution (69)18, *Situation in Greece* (6 May 1969).
CoE, Committee of Ministers, *Conclusion de la 185ᵉ réunion des délégués des ministres tenue à Paris du 9 au 11 décembre 1969*.
CoE, Consultative Assembly, *Adopted texts*, 19th Session, directive no. 256 (Strasbourg, 26 April 1967).
CoE, Consultative Assembly, *Adopted texts*, 19th Session, directive no. 262 (Strasbourg, 23 June 1967).
CoE, Consultative Assembly, *Adopted texts*, 19th Session, resolution no. 351 (Strasbourg, 25 June 1967).
CoE, Consultative Assembly, *Adopted texts*, 19th Session, resolution no. 361 (Strasbourg, 31 January 1967).
CoE, Consultative Assembly, *Official Report of Debates*, 19th Session, t. I (Strasbourg, 24-28 April 1967).
CoE, Consultative Assembly, *Official Report of Debates*, 19th Session, t. III (Strasbourg, 29 January-2 February 1968).
CoE, Consultative Assembly, *Working Documents*, doc. 2202 (Strasbourg, 25 April 1967).
Council of Europe, Consultative Assembly, *Working Documents*, doc. 2203 (Strasbourg, 25 April 1967).
CoE, Consultative Assembly, *Working Documents*, doc. 2283 (Strasbourg, 25 September 1967).
CoE, Consultative Assembly, *Working Documents*, doc. 2322 (Strasbourg, 22 January 1968).
CoE, Consultative Assembly, *Working Documents*, doc. 2348 (Strasbourg, 7 May 1968).
CoE, Consultative Assembly, *Working Documents*, doc. 2467 (Strasbourg, September 25 1968).
CoE, Consultative Assembly, *Working Documents*, doc. 2525 (Strasbourg, January 28 1969)
CoE, European Convention on Human Rights (4 November 1950).
CoE, European Court of Human Rights, *The Greek Case : Report of the Sub-Commission* (Strasbourg, November 5 1969).
European Community (EC), Agreement establishing an association between the EEC and Greece (1961).
EC, Commission Opinion on the Hellenic Republic's application for accession (Brussels, 23 May1979).
EC, Davignon Report (Luxembourg, 27 October 1970).
EC, European Parliament, communiqué of the Joint Parliamentary Commission EEC-Greece (Salonika, 31 March 1967), BAC 3/1978 275/5, HAEU.

MULTIPLE CONNECTIONS IN EUROPEAN COOPERATION

EC, European Parliament, *Débats, Comptes rendus in extenso*, 91: 1967-1968 (Strasbourg, 8-11 May 1967).

EC, Treaty of Rome (1957).

Europeana, *"Άφιξη του Υπουργού Εξωτερικών της Ολλανδίας Μαξ βαν ντερ Στουλ στην Αθήνα", Ελληνικά Επίκαιρα* 197722 (9 June 1977).

Η Συμμετοχή της Ελλάδας στην πορεία προς την Ευρωπαϊκή ολοκλήρωση, vol. II, Από το πάγωμα της συμφωνίας σύνδεσης στην ένταξη στις Ευρωπαϊκές Κοινότητες (1968-1981) (Athens: Ministry for Foreign Affairs, Historical and Diplomatic Archive, 2006).

House of Commons, Debates, Greek Political Prisoners (London, 11 April 1968), Hansard.

House of Commons, Debates, Foreign Affairs (London, 8 December 1969), Hansard.

The Participation of Greece in the Process towards European Integration, vol. I, The Crucial Twenty Years 1948-1968 (Athens, Ministry for Foreign Affairs, Historical and Diplomatic Archive, 2003).

Yearbook of the European Convention on Human Rights 1967 (The Hague, Martinus Nijhoff, 1969).

Yearbook of the European Convention on Human Rights. *1969, The Greek Case*. The Hague: Martinus Nijhoff, 1972.

Newspaper Articles

"Greek junta has created a 'slaughterhouse'", *The Guardian*, (1 May 1970).

"L'Assemblée consultative du Conseil de l'Europe déplore la suspension de la légalité constitutionnelle en Grèce". *Le Monde*, (April 28 1967), 6.

"Mit Falanga". *Der Spiegel*, (9 December 1968).

"MPs send a telegram of protest". *The Times*, (22 April 1967), 1.

"Protestations dans de nombreuses capitales européennes". *Le Monde*, (23-24 April 1967), 2.

Secondary literature

Becket, James and Marreco, Anthony. *Torture of Political Prisoners in Greece*. London: Amnesty International, 1968.

Conispoliatis, Helen. "Facing the Colonels: How the British Government dealt with the Military Coup in Greece in April 1967." *History* 92, no. 308 (October 2007): 515–535.

Coufoudakis, Van. "The European Community and the 'Freezing' of the Greek Association, 1967-1974." *Journal of Common Market Studies* 16, no. 2 (1977): 114–131.

De Angelis, Emma and Eirini, Karamouzi. "Enlargement and the Historical Origins of EC's Democratic Identity, 1961-1978", *Contemporary European History Journal*, forthcoming (2016).

Doulis, Thomas. *The Iron Storm. The Impact on Greek Culture of the Military Junta, 1967-1974*. Bloomington: Xlibris, 2011.

Fernández Soriano, Victor. *Le fusil et l'olivier: Les droits de l'Homme en Europe face aux dictatures méditerranéennes (1949-1977)*. Brussels: Éditions de l'Université de Bruxelles, 2015.

Fierro, Elena. *The EU's Approach to Human Rights Conditionality in Practice*. The Hague: Kluwer Law International, 2003.

Golub, Jonathan. "Did the Luxembourg Compromise have any Consequences?", In *Visions, Votes and Vetoes: The Empty Chair Crisis and the Luxembourg Compromise Forty Years On*, edited by Jean-Marie Palayret, Helen Wallace, and Pascaline Winand. Brussels: Peter Lang, 2006: 279–300.

Hebel, Kai and Tobias Lenz. "The Identity/Policy Nexus in European Foreign Policy", *Journal of European Public Policy*, forthcoming (2016).

Karamouzi, Eirini. *Greece, The EEC and the Cold War 1974–1979: The Second Enlargement*. London: Palgrave Macmillan, 2014.

Kemp, Walter. "Talking to a Sphinx: An Interview with Max van der Stoel." *Security and Human Rights* 22, no. 3 (2011): 315–324.

Keys, Barbara. "Anti-Torture Politics: Amnesty International, the Greek Junta and the Origins of Human Rights "Boom" in the United States", In *The Human Rights Revolution: An International History*, edited by Akira Iriye, Petra Goedde and William I. Hitchcock. Oxford: University Press, 2012: 201-221.

Klarevas, Louis. "Were the Eagle and the Phoenix Birds of a Feather? The United States and the Greek Coup of 1967." *Diplomatic History* 30, no. 3 (2006): 471–508.

Leuprecht, Peter. "Max van der Stoel: a tireless defender of Greek democracy." *Security and Human Rights* 22, no. 3 (2011): 183–185.

Ludlow, N. Piers. *The European Community and the Crises of the 1960s: Negotiating the Gaullist Challenge.* London: Routledge, 2006.

Madsen, Mikael Rask. "Legal Diplomacy: Law, Politics and the Genesis of Postwar European Human Rights". In *Human Rights in the Twentieth Century*, edited by Stefan-Ludwig Hoffmann, 62-81. Cambridge: University Press, 2011.

Manners, Ian. "Normative Power Europe: A Contradiction in Terms?" *Journal of Community Market Studies* 40, no. 2 (2002): 235–258.

Maragkou, Konstantina. "The Foreign Factor and the Greek Colonels' Coming to Power on 21 April 1967." *Southeast European and Black Sea Studies* 6, no. 4 (2006): 427–443.

Maragkou, Konstantina. "Favouritism in NATO's Southeastern Flank: The Case of the Greek Colonels, 1967-74." *Cold War History* 9, no. 3 (2009): 347–366.

Maragkou, Konstantina. "The Wilson Government's Responses to 'The Rape of Greek Democracy'", *Journal of Contemporary History* 45/I (2010): 162-180.

Moravcsik, Andrew. "The Origins of Human Rights Regimes: Democratic Delegation in Postwar Europe." *International Organization* 54, no. 2 (2000): 217–252.

Moyn, Samuel. *The Last Utopia: Human Rights in History.* Cambridge (MA): Harvard University Press, 2010.

Patel, Kiran Klaus. "Provincialising European Union: Co-operation and Integration in Europe in a Historical Perspective", *Contemporary European History* 22 (2013): 649-673.

Patel, Kiran Klaus. "Who was saving whom? The European Community and the Cold War", *The British Journal of Politics and International Relations* (29 Dec. 2016): 1-19.

Papandreou, Nikos. *The Council of Europe fights for Democracy in Greece, 1967–1969.* Athens: Andreas Papandreou Foundation, 1998.

Pedaliu, Effie G. H. "Human Rights and Foreign Policy: Wilson and the Greek Dictators, 1967-1970", *Diplomacy and Statecraft* 18 (2011): 101-120.

Pedaliu, Effie G. H. "A Discordant Note: NATO and the Greek Junta, 1967-1974", *Diplomacy and Statecraft* 22 (2007): 185-214.

Pedaliu, Effie G. H. "Human Rights and International Security: The International Community and the Greek Dictators", *The International History Review* 38/5 (2016): 1014-1039.

Rittberger, Berthold and Schimmelfenning, Frank. "Explaining the Constitutionalization of the European Union". In *The Constitutionalization of the European Union*, edited by Berthold Rittberger and Frank Schimmelfenning, 1-20. London and New York: Routledge, 2007.

Roger, Ludwig. "Exporter la démocratie?: La Commission face aux Juntes grecque et turque." *Les Cahiers IRICE* 12 (2014): 59–73.

Schimmelfenning, Frank. *The EU, NATO and the integration of Europe.* Cambridge: Cambridge University Press, 2003.

Seidel, Katja. *The Process of Politics in Europe: The Rise of European Elites and Supranational Institutions.* London: IB Tauris, 2010.

Thomas, Daniel C. *The Helsinki Effect: International norms, Human Rights, and the Demise of Communism.* Princeton, NJ: Princeton University Press, 2001.

Vardabasso, Valentina. "Échec aux colonels: La diplomatie parlementaire et la crise grecque." *Revue d'histoire diplomatique* 2, no. 2013 (2013): 179–199.

Varsori, Antonio. "L'Occidente e la Grecia: dal colpo di Stato militare alla transizione alla democrazia (1967-1976)". In *Democrazie: L'Europa meridionale e la fine delle dittature*, edited by Mario del Pero, Víctor Gavín, Fernando Guirao and Antonio Varsori, 5-94. Milan: Le Monnier, 2012.

Verney, Susannah, and Panos Tsakaloyannis. "Linkage Politics: The Role of the European Community in Greek Politics in 1973." *Byzantine and Modern Greek Studies* 10, no. 1 (1986): 179–194.

Woodhouse, Christopher. *The Rise and Fall of the Greek Colonels.* London: Granada, 1985.

Who should pay for pollution? The OECD, the European Communities and the emergence of environmental policy in the early 1970s

Jan-Henrik Meyer

ABSTRACT

Environmental policy emerged as a new European and global policy field within a very brief period of time during the early 1970s. Notably in Europe, international organizations played a central role in defining core principles for this new policy domain. This article argues that inter-organizational connections were crucial in this context: the exchange and transfer of policy ideas facilitated the rise of environmental policy across different international organizations. Focusing on the co-evolution of the polluter-pays principle enshrined almost simultaneously both at the OECD and the European Communities, the article assesses the multiple routes along which policy ideas travelled, the role inter-organizational competition played and the selective nature of transfers. While expertise played a key role in determining which policy concepts were selected, institutional conditions and the politics of the recipient institution determined how they were adapted to the respective new context.

In a speech in the European Parliament (EP) on 15 September 1970, the then new President of the European Commission, the Italian Christian Democrat Franco Maria Malfatti (1970–72) officially addressed the issue of the environment as a new policy objective of the European Communities (EC) for the first time. He placed great emphasis on the 'heavy and unexpected costs' of 'economic and industrial progress', such as the 'destruction of natural assets by industry'. Furthermore, he argued that purely national measures to fight environmental degradation were insufficient: the 'Community provide[d] the minimum scale for effective action'.[1] Nine months later, in July 1971, the Commission in fact issued a 'First Communication ... about the Community's Policy on the Environment', which was the first step towards designing an EC environmental policy.[2]

About two months after this speech, on 24 November 1970, Emiel van Lennep, the new Dutch Secretary-General of the Organisation of Economic Cooperation and Development (OECD), held a 'welcoming address' for the OECD's newly established Environmental Committee. Like the EC Commission president, van Lennep emphasized the importance of his international organization's (IO) contribution to the new policy area. However, the speech highlighted a very different understanding of what constituted 'costs'. Instead of criticizing the – often unquantifiable – cost of pollution to citizens and societies, van Lennep pointed to the cost of pollution-control programmes to businesses that had measurable consequences for their profitability and economic performance. Van Lennep demanded introducing the most cost-effective measures and policy instruments that did not have a negative impact on trade and economic growth.[3]

These two episodes are illustrative of two issues that are at the core of this article. First, when the environment emerged as a new political concern in the late 1960s, which integrated previously separate issues such as nature protection, resource conservation and pollution control into the new comprehensive political concept of the environment,[4] IOs quickly started taking an active interest in this new area and sought to shape policy contents. IOs seemed ideally suited to deal with environmental problems that often cut across national borders and apparently required international solutions and the setting of new international norms, notably in the area of pollution control. Fighting pollution was the most pressing issue in the early 1970s. The massive economic growth of the post-war period – accompanied by the rise of mass consumerism – had caused unprecedented local, but increasingly also cross-border, pollution problems. Moreover, some of these problems were caused by manufactured products, notably vehicles, which were traded internationally. Various IOs could also build on some of their earlier work in nature protection and scientific cooperation, as activities that had contributed to placing this new issue on the international political agenda in the first place.[5]

In the early 1970s both the OECD and the EC started to address the new political issue of the environment almost simultaneously. With its Environmental Committee, the OECD was the first IO worldwide to set up a separate institutional forum to discuss environmental concerns.[6] Despite lacking the formal legal basis within its founding treaties, the EC devised a comprehensive policy programme, the Environmental Action Programme of November 1973, which laid the basis for subsequent policy-making, until the policy area was officially included in the Single European Act of 1987.[7] Moreover, both IOs developed normative principles for the field in order to ensure a cohesive approach to the difficult, often very technical, issues of environmental policy. For instance, the principle of precaution states that under conditions of scientific insecurity about environmental hazards, citizens should not be exposed to excessive risks, whereas the principle of prevention seeks to avoid pollution already at its source. Among these principles, the polluter-pays principle (PPP) was most prominently discussed, as it not only had moral implications, by clarifying who should bear the cost of pollution and pay for remedies. Economists in particular also found the principle attractive as a policy instrument, because they expected that making the polluter pay would steer citizens and business in the desired direction of environmentally friendly behaviour. Moreover, its application was to encourage the most cost-effective instruments of pollution control, just as van Lennep demanded in 1970.[8] Almost concomitantly, both IOs issued recommendations defining their respective views of this principle in the short period between 1972 and 1975.[9] Both IOs positioned themselves in the emerging debate. This air of competition also contributed to the rise of environmental policy as an international concern.

Secondly, Malfatti's and van Lennep's speeches suggest that the two IOs differed in their perception of the environmental problem. More precisely, they diverged in their understanding of what actually constituted the most relevant aspect of the cost of pollution: the harm it did to humans and nature, or the cost of remedying this harm. Their respective positions seem well in line with present-day stereotypes about both IOs that are reflected in the academic literature, too. Researchers have often accepted the – to some extent self-styled – public image of the European Union, the EC's successor, as an 'environmental leader',[10] for instance, as the driving force in climate change negotiations vis-à-vis the more hesitant United States. This perception has only been challenged very recently.[11] In contrast to the EC, the OECD has always been viewed as an economic organization. As a think-tank of the developed countries, it has not just been committed to promoting trade, business and economic growth, but was also central to establishing the 'growth paradigm', the expectation of ever-increasing economic expansion as the normative point of reference in post-war economic and political debates.[12] Environmental policy, in contrast, today plays no prominent role in the OECD's public image, even though – as recent research has highlighted – for a brief period in the early 1970s, the OECD was among the first IOs to address such issues as 'problems of modern society'. However, after the oil crisis, by 1977–79, the OECD turned into a leading promoter of neoliberal economic growth policies.[13] Against this backdrop, this article suggests that this contrast might be exaggerated, at least with a view to the early 1970s. Clearly, both organizations were committed to economic growth, but were also increasingly aware of its negative side effects. Both drew on the insights of environmental economics in order to reconcile environmental objectives and economic growth, rather than buying into the Club of Rome's critique of continued exponential growth (*Limits to Growth*, 1972), a critique that many environmentalists shared, however.[14]

This article analyses how both the OECD and the EC approached environmental policy during its formative period in the early 1970s, to what extent they borrowed ideas from other IOs, such as the Council of Europe, and from each other, and which role institutional linkages played in this respect. Focusing on the PPP enshrined almost simultaneously both at the OECD and the EC, the article will assess the routes along which policy ideas travelled. It will discuss the importance of experts and expertise, the role of inter-organizational competition and the selective nature of transfers.[15] The article argues that the differing definitions of the principle were due to political considerations, including the balance of member-state interests and the 'fit' with existing institutional conditions and policies of the recipient organization.

To examine these inter-organizational links, the article first provides an overview of the emergence of environmental policy in the late 1960s and early 1970s. During this period several IOs, including NATO and the Council of Europe, came to play an important role as agenda-setters and mediators of new ideas concerning the environment. Part two will outline the emergence and the varying definitions of the PPP between and across IOs until the mid-1970s. Part three will then analyse the role of transfers between the OECD and the EC in the definition of the polluter-pays principle, before the conclusion will summarize and generalize the article's findings. Empirically, the interpretation is based on newly accessible sources from the archives of the different EU institutions in Brussels and Luxembourg and the OECD Archives in Paris, the National Archives of the United Kingdom in Kew, as well as oral-history interviews. On this basis, this analysis shows that inter-organizational links mattered, and that the emergence of environmental policy in the EC and across IOs in Western Europe at the time cannot be understood if organizations are studied in isolation.

This article seeks to advance the state of the art in three areas of scholarship. First, it contributes to the literature in international history and politics. Research so far has mainly highlighted the role of key member-states, non-governmental organizations (NGOs) and experts as core shapers of ideas and agendas.[16] Relations between IOs have been curiously underplayed. Secondly, this article contributes to the politics and history of European integration. By stressing the importance of policy imports from other IOs, the article not only attempts to de-centre the EC,[17] it also turns the conventional Europeanization narrative on its head. The EC has not always been the primary factor impacting on member-states, neighbouring countries and other actors, but has itself been influenced by other IOs.[18] Finally, the article contributes to environmental history, which has long been pre-occupied with environmental ideas and perceptions of the environment and their policy relevance, including key concepts such as wilderness, biodiversity or ecological modernization.[19] The importance of IOs as sites of negotiating such concepts has frequently been mentioned,[20] but rarely studied in detail.[21]

The emergence of environmental policy and international organizations

When the environment emerged as a new area of policy-making during the late 1960s and early 1970s, the global and regional IOs created in the aftermath of the Second World War played an active role in defining its core principles. Debates extended across IOs, and policy ideas travelled from pioneering IOs to those joining the conversation slightly later. Four Western and Western European IOs became the most prominent places for international cooperation on environmental issues at the time, namely the Council of Europe, NATO, the OECD and the EC, along with the United Nations (UN) as the world organization. The UN Stockholm Conference on the Human Environment of 1972 signalled the international breakthrough of environmental policy, but multiple IOs remained engaged in shaping it.[22]

Already in the mid-1960s, the Strasbourg-based Council of Europe pioneered environmental issues and principles. Founded in 1949, the Council of Europe included the democratic European countries west of the Iron Curtain.[23] Well-known for its activism concerning human rights, the Council of Europe also dealt with issues of nature conservation, the most traditional aspect of environmental protection. In the course of the 1960s, it took up pollution, the second major component of the emergent international environmental agenda. Addressing cross-border air and water pollution, it issued a Resolution on Air Pollution Control and a European Water Charter in 1968.[24] By declaring the year 1970 the European Conservation Year,[25] and by organizing a major conference in Strasbourg in February 1970, where many of those experts and officials who shaped environmental policy at the national and international levels met and learnt from each other, the Council of Europe contributed to the breakthrough of environmental debates in Western Europe.[26]

NATO's pioneering role in early international environmental policy is largely forgotten. On the initiative of the Nixon administration, involved in establishing an ambitious environmental policy within the United States, the Western defence organization set up a Committee for the Challenges of Modern Society (CCMS) in 1969. Among these challenges the environment featured prominently. CCMS remained largely limited to research cooperation and exchange of technical standards. However, it was initially an important avenue to spread new American policy concepts across the Atlantic.[27]

One year after NATO, the OECD started to discuss environmental policy. The Paris-based OECD had emerged from the Organisation for European Economic Cooperation in 1961. It had been established to administer the European Recovery Programme from

1948 onwards with the intention to rebuild Western Europe economically and to foster trade. By the 1970s, the OECD had turned into an increasingly global IO. Alongside the EC member-states it included Australia, Austria, Canada, Finland, Greece, Iceland, Japan, New Zealand, Norway, Portugal, Spain, Sweden, Switzerland, Turkey and the United States. It aimed at coordinating Western industrialized countries' economic policies, based on the exchange of policy-relevant information.

The OECD's route to environmental policy was informed by two different, but converging, concerns. First, this new interest emerged from the OECD's focus on research cooperation. Since the 1960s, this work had included research on pollution.[28] Secondly, as the organization was committed to economic growth, it came to be concerned with the economic impact of environmental policies. To pre-empt negative effects, the OECD first set up an 'ad hoc preparatory Committee' 'on activities concerning environmental problems linked to economic growth' in early 1970. Its purpose was to 'identify non-desirable consequences of economic growth' and 'promote measures nationally and internationally to eliminate these'. While it thus addressed the costs that Malfatti highlighted in his speech, the committee was also set up to 'evaluate the impact of these measures on economic growth' – that is, those costs that van Lennep had talked about.[29] In November 1970, the OECD established a full-fledged Environmental Committee. Here, NATO served as a point of reference, which is not surprising due to a largely overlapping membership, and a strong role for the United States within the OECD. Early OECD discussions framed the environmental problem in the language NATO had introduced, notably with an emphasis on 'problems of modern society' and the need to cooperate with NATO along with other IOs 'active in the field of the CCMS', such as the EC.[30]

In an increasingly crowded field, as in so many other policy domains, the EC was a latecomer rather than a pioneer.[31] Like the OECD, the EC had been established to reconstruct Western Europe economically. Beyond abolishing trade restrictions, EC member-states set up a common market to foster growth. While the OECD only focused on economic policy coordination and trade promotion, the EC also created some supranational governance structures. Its policy-makers did not consider the market as a panacea for all social ills. The EC therefore established some redistributive policies, such as the Common Agricultural Policy and the Regional Policy, involving substantial subsidies.[32] Unlike the OECD, the EC remained a regional Western European IO. After its first enlargement in 1973, its nine member-states constituted a strong bloc within the OECD. Moreover, the European Commission represented the EC externally in all trade-related matters; hence, the EC aimed at speaking with one voice in the OECD. In the OECD's committees on the various policies, such as research, or from 1970 the environment, national experts (and also EC Commission representatives) conducted the IO's day-to-day work. This provided an important institutional connection and avenue for transfers between both IOs.

From early 1970 onwards European Commission officials began collecting information about practices and concepts for a future EC environmental policy. NATO's CCMS with its various events, publications and other activities served as a central point of reference. The Washington-based policy think-tank Atlantic Council and its journal *Atlantic Community Quarterly* also acted as an important mediator in NATO.[33] A memorandum of 1970 by the American economist and Senate Finance Committee advisor Harald Malmgren to the Atlantic Council's editor and policy officer Joseph Harned made its way to the relevant Commission official Vladimiro Mandl. It was amongst the first documents to alert the

Commission to the trade implications of environmental policy. Malmgren advocated international coordination, a ban of discriminatory practices and the introduction of 'general principles for governments to follow'. This prescription outlined the main elements of the subsequent debate about the PPP.[34] In January 1971, the Atlantic Council – together with another think tank, the Batelle Institute – organized a major conference in Washington D.C. to promote these issues, and Harned was one the three editors of the book emerging from the event.[35] Leading EC officials attended, most importantly from the European Commission. Director-General for Industry Robert Toulemon, who was put in charge of developing environmental policy by Commissioner Altiero Spinelli,[36] presented insights on the European situation.[37] The EC was starting to get involved in international debates about environmental policies.

But NATO was not the only reference point in the nascent EC debate. The aforementioned Stockholm UN conference induced EC member-state governments to live up to their previously largely rhetorical commitments and finally move ahead on EC environmental action. At their Paris summit of September 1972, the heads of state and government agreed on establishing an EC environmental policy. Explicitly drawing on the debates and results from Stockholm, the EC member-states laid down core principles of an Environmental Action Programme during a meeting in Bonn in October 1972.[38] In November 1973, when the Oil Crisis had started to hit Western economies, the First Environmental Action Programme was formally published. At a time when most of their European member-states were still developing environmental policies, both the OECD and the EC started to formulate concepts relating to the economic implications of environmental policy. No single IO had the lead in this field; instead, many of these ideas and policy lines were developed and mediated in the framework of various IOs. These linkages became even more important with a view to the concrete contents of policy-making, as will be demonstrated for the case of the PPP.

The polluter-pays principle and international organizations

What is the PPP, and how did the IOs active in this field define it during the 1960s and 1970s? The notion that those causing harm to someone else – for instance by spoiling the water or polluting the air – should be held responsible for the damage, is an old legal principle dating back to the Romans. In the nineteenth century, those affected by pollution occasionally took industrialists to court and forced them to pay compensation.[39] During the second half of the twentieth century, debates reached a new level of sophistication, informed by the development of post-war neoclassical, rational-choice based economics. Economists modelled economic actors as rational-interest maximizers, who would always select the most advantageous option. Economists did not just argue that they were able to predict, but also to guide actors' behaviour. If policy-makers offered the right kind of incentive, like the carrot for the donkey, businesses and consumers would behave in the fashion desired. This assumption also formed the basis for the field of environmental economics, which started booming in the late 1960s.

Environmental economics reframed the problem of the allocation of the cost of pollution to those who caused it from a fairness issue to an issue of economic efficiency.[40] The Canadian economist John Dales, who is widely recognized as the inventor of emissions trading,[41] demanded in his much-quoted book *Pollution, Property and Prices* of 1968 that the costs of negative externalities (such as pollution) should be internalized into the cost of production.[42] Such an approach had two important advantages, at least from the viewpoint of the advocates of market-based policy solutions. First, the PPP created a level playing field and fair competition. If all participants in the market had to include the cost of pollution, nobody would benefit from the undue subsidy that the continued externalization of costs effectively meant. Secondly, and more importantly, the PPP would quasi-automatically lead to the most efficient solution to the environmental problem. If pollution was given a price tag, this created incentives to avoid and reduce it. Market forces would advance the search for the cheapest – and thus most efficient – remedy to the pollution problem.[43] Hence, environmental economists with their pro-market leanings argued that such a market-based instrument would be more effective than the comparatively inflexible method of command-and-control. However, in order to function fairly and efficiently, the principle needed to be applied without exemptions, such as state subsidies for anti-pollution measures.[44] This persuasive economic rationale clearly appealed to the many economists working for the OECD and the EC. Hence, it did not remain an abstract part of academic reasoning, but was repeatedly spelt out to legitimate OECD and EC recommendations.

Although it is routinely associated with the EC and the OECD,[45] it was another IO that initially flagged the PPP before it arrived to these two IOs. The Council of Europe was the first IO to include officially the PPP in its Declaration of Principles on Air Pollution control in a resolution in 1968. This non-binding text only appealed to member-states to include these goals in their own legislation, to 'give the Declaration the widest possible publicity', and to report about progress every three years. The PPP was listed as one of the Principles and did not even go by the name 'polluter-pays principle', but remained slightly hidden under the headline 'Financing' of anti-pollution action: 'The cost incurred in preventing or abating pollution should be borne by whoever causes the pollution.' The wording was rather lenient on exemptions from the principle: 'This does not preclude aid from Public Authorities.'[46] Unlike later, more sophisticated definitions, it did not spell out the economic rationale and the potential consequences. All this limited the Council of Europe's impact on the subsequent debate, despite its pioneering role.

Indeed, during the early 1970s, the OECD became the primary IO to define and push for the PPP. The OECD advanced this agenda in a series of recommendations. Just like the Council of Europe's declaration, these non-binding legal instruments only called upon member-states to consider the PPP in national law-making and encouraged cooperation. Many of the areas of priority action the new OECD Environmental Committee dealt with were carried over from OECD's Committee on Research Cooperation. Since the mid-1960s, the OECD had been involved in exchanging research findings and facilitating cooperation on air and water pollution, pesticides and solid waste with other IOs. These issues mark the transition to the more comprehensive environmental policy agenda.[47]

However, as an economic organization the OECD did not intend to leave the power to define environmental issues to the natural scientists. Already the ad hoc preparatory committee for the Environmental Committee stressed the need for complementing natural science expertise with that of lawyers and economists.[48] Indeed, economic expertise dominated the debate on environmental issues. Thus the PPP, which reflected the state of the art in environmental economics and addressed economic and legal issues of international trade, immediately became an issue of priority of action within the new Environmental Committee.

Not surprisingly, the OECD's first definition of the PPP in the recommendation of May 1972 clearly outlined the economic rationale: the need to internalize universally environmental costs in the price of goods, in order to induce environmentally friendly behaviour and avoid trade distortions. Consequently, with a view to exemptions, it was much more restrictive than the Council of Europe. It maintained that the costs of measures

> to ensure that the environment is in an acceptable state ... should be reflected in the cost of goods and services which cause pollution in production and/or consumption. Such measures should not be accompanied by subsidies that would create significant distortions in international trade and investment.

Beyond defining the economic rationale of the principle, the OECD also demanded its implementation by its member-states: this '[p]rinciple should be an objective of Member countries'. However, while asserting the principle, the text reflects a certain degree of flexibility, adding that 'there may be exceptions or special arrangements, particularly for the transitional periods'.[49]

In order to ensure the appropriate implementation of the PPP, the OECD issued a second recommendation in November 1974. In it, the OECD 'reaffirm[ed]' the ambition of a 'uniform application of this principle, through the adoption of a common basis for Member states' environmental policies'. Legitimating this demand, it referred again to the two key aspects of the economic rationale: not only would this policy 'encourage the rational use and the better allocation of scarce environmental resources'. It would also 'prevent ... distortions in international trade and investment'.[50]

Anticipating implementation problems, the recommendation accepted three reasons for exemptions. First, it recognized that the cost of rapidly introducing environmental measures could lead to significant 'socio-economic problems'. Secondly, it accepted that innovation might require subsidies, such as 'experimentation with new pollution control technologies'. Thirdly, the principle was not supposed to thwart states' capacity to engage in social and regional policies, where subsidies were routinely used to act upon 'serious interregional imbalances'. However, exemptions were to be applied in a 'selective and restricted' manner, to sectors in economic distress, and limited in time.[51]

In order to ensure the actual implementation of the recommendation, the OECD relied on a strategy of 'naming and shaming', a common instrument IOs have been using until today, given their lack of formal powers to make binding decisions.[52] The recommendation thus introduced a notification and consultation procedure: member-states introducing state aids or tax breaks were required to notify the OECD secretariat in advance; other member-states had the right to be consulted.[53] All in all, the OECD did not just contribute to a more fine-grained definition of the principle, based on the state of the art in economics, in comparison to the ethical approach of the Council of Europe. The OECD also developed a more sophisticated strategy to induce member-states to actually implement it.

'The polluter pays principle ... has been invented by the Commission', Michel Carpentier, the first and long-time director of the Commission's Service for the Environment and Consumer Protection (SEPC), an economist by training and an activist promoter of environmental policy, claimed in a recent oral-history interview.[54] In actual fact, however, the EC institutions imported the principle, mainly from the OECD, and Carpentier was himself involved in this transfer process. Apart from directly drawing on debates in environmental economics and existing national laws, EC institutions, notably the European Parliament and the European Commission, borrowed from the work of several IOs.[55]

While it lacked decision-making powers at the time, the European Parliament was an important agenda-setter and mediator.[56] From 1970 onwards, parliamentary committees authored reports to demand EC action on environmental issues, starting with water and air pollution. Already in the first such report of November 1970 on water pollution, rapporteur Adriaan Pieter Oele,[57] a Dutch socialist, advocated economic instruments of pollution control, including the PPP.[58] Even though he was an engineer by training, Oele was well familiar with the critical writings of relevant economists, such as Ezra Mishan from the London School of Economics.[59] Mishan's book *The Cost of Economic Growth* of 1967 was a best-selling economic critique of the undesirable side effects of prosperity, quoted also by expert economists consulting the OECD.[60]

IOs also did not feature prominently as a source of the PPP in the subsequent parliamentary report on air pollution of December 1971. It referred mostly to economic experts' models of national and subnational legislation, for instance from the West German state of North Rhine Westphalia, and only mentioned the Council of Europe in passing. The OECD did not appear at all.[61]

The PPP clearly mattered to the European Parliament. The report on the Commission's First Communication of 1971 openly criticized the European Commission for not including the PPP.[62] Only with its Second Communication of March 1972 did the European Commission fully embrace the principle.[63] Indeed the Commission's initial oversight seems curious given that the officials in charge of drawing up both Communications, namely Carpentier and his superior, Toulemon, had repeatedly been confronted with debates about the PPP. The OECD's Environmental Committee is only one example: Carpentier and Toulemon attended its sessions in 1971–2, representing the EC. Moreover, Carpentier had participated in earlier OECD debates on environmental issues since the 1960s as a member of the OECD Committee on Research Cooperation. Hence it does not come as a surprise that the Second Communication extensively discussed the model of the OECD.[64] The main reason for the lack of attention to the PPP in the First Communication was probably simply its timing. When the Commission drafted it in early 1971, the OECD's work on the PPP was still in its preparatory phase.

The EC's definition of the PPP in its 1975 Recommendation for this reason closely mirrored the OECD's framing. Like the OECD, EC lawmakers legitimated the principle on the basis of its fairness and economic efficiency, as it incentivized the 'rational use of resources'.[65] However, the EC did not simply copy-paste OECD practices. Reflecting demands for a flexible application in various parliamentary reports and business interest group statements,[66] the Recommendation specified a large number of exemptions, notably regarding subsidies within a number of the EC policy areas, such as the 'investment affecting environmental protection benefit from aid intended to solve certain industrial, agricultural or regional structural problems'.[67] All in all, however, the EC thus entered the debate rather late and its eventual course of action was strongly inspired by other IOs, most notably the OECD.

The PPP in the OECD and the EC

When defining the PPP, which had come to be framed as an issue of environmental economics, both the OECD and the EC heavily relied on economic expertise. Experts also helped connect the debates between institutions. However, the two IOs organized their expert consultation in slightly different ways, which contributed to different policy outcomes, notably regarding the politically contentious issue of exemptions to the PPP.

The OECD's committees did not just provide expertise; in fact, they frequently pre-determined decisions. Very often, their recommendations – such as the one on the PPP – were basically rubber-stamped at ministerial level. The Environmental Committee and its subcommittees were composed of officials from the relevant ministries and agencies, notably those responsible for the environment as well as trade and industry, and of govern-ment-appointed experts. These included scientists, planners and business representatives, for instance, a representative of the German subsidiary of the multinational oil company BP.[68] The experts' dual role was to provide scientific, economic, legal and business expertise and experience, but also to represent their respective national governments or relevant business interests.

In order to address environmental issues with economic implications more adequately, the OECD's Environmental Committee in 1971 established a Subcommittee of Economic Experts.[69] When this subcommittee dealt with the PPP as one of its first issues, the experts unanimously praised its economic efficiency, 'providing for a pollution control policy at the least cost'. Nonetheless, the experts were not ignorant about its policy implications. Indeed, 'some delegates' stressed the need for exceptions, too, as policy-makers had to account for 'competing objectives', including 'employment policy, regional policy' and local concerns.[70]

The subcommittee did not only rely on its own members' expertise, but organized a broad consultation process to get an overview of the field. In the summer of 1971 it organized a seminar on 'Problems of Environmental Economics' at the OECD, which brought together a large number of economists discussing questions of cost allocation and trade.[71] On the basis of this very broad process of gathering economic expertise, the OECD developed its first, rather general, Recommendation of May 1972.

For its 1974 Recommendation on the Implementation of the Polluter-Pays Principle the OECD did not simply rely on the theoretical debate in economics, but studied concrete reports from various member countries, only to realize that actual policies in place routinely deviated from the PPP. In order to gain acceptance and to offset the cost of new anti-pol-lution measures, environmental-policy makers frequently relied on aids and subsidies.[72]

After lengthy negotiations, the Environmental Committee in late 1973 agreed on those exemptions that made it to the final Recommendation: namely 'transitional arrangements', if environmental-measures policy were rapidly introduced, and in cases 'when socio-economic policy objectives and the employment in a certain region would be adversely affected'. It also clarified that '[a]id to promote research and development' was not considered 'inconsistent with PPP'.[73] This result was a clear departure from the rigour of the economic rationale. Instead, it was the effect of political negotiations. Notably the Italian representatives had repeatedly stressed the need to grant assistance to new plants in 'regions with heavy dise-conomies'.[74] After the Environmental Committee discussion, the PPP thus started to look like a Swiss Emmental cheese – hollowed out by numerous exceptions.

When the European Commission proposed a recommendation on the PPP, its work was connected to the OECD's experience in more than one way. Clearly, it drew on the example the OECD had set, as the Italian commissioner responsible for environmental affairs, Carlo Scarascia-Mugnozza, liberally acknowledged in a speech in front of the OECD ministers in November 1974.[75]

Like the OECD Environmental Committee, the Commission sought to base its proposal on external economic expertise, but it opted for a different procedure. Instead of a broad consultation of experts, the European Commission only commissioned two expert reports.[76] The choice of the two experts was revealing. The author of the first report was Achille Hannequart, a Belgian economist and senior advisor to the Belgian economic programming office. Hannequart was also the Belgian representative in the OECD's Subcommittee of Economic Experts, thus creating a strong link to OECD debates.[77] By contrast, the other expert, Harald Jürgensen, was a Keynesian economics professor from Hamburg and an academic entrepreneur with a long-time connection to the EC. Jürgensen had worked on EC-related issues since his PhD research in the 1950s on the German steel industry and the European Coal and Steel Community. In 1961, as a young professor, he had established an institute for European economic policy to provide policy advice. Even though he was not formally connected to the OECD, Jürgensen was also familiar with the relevant OECD's Subcommittee and their work. In November 1972, he attended an expert conference at the Centre for Nuclear Research in Karlsruhe on the PPP in water-pollution control. The event was sponsored by the West German Ministry of the Interior, the main promoter of the incipient federal-level environmental policy in West Germany at the time, in which the PPP also featured prominently, notably in the environmental programme published in the autumn of 1971.[78] The West German government had not only invited the OECD Subcommittee and the relevant officials from the OECD secretariat Jean-Philippe Barde and Michel Potier, the Commission official working on the PPP Vladimiro Mandl, but also domestic and international experts, such as Allen V. Kneese, an environmental economist, expert on water pollution and economic instruments from the Washington D.C.-based think tank Resources for the Future. Along with Harned, Kneese had been involved in the 1971 event organized by the Atlantic Council and had co-edited its proceedings.[79] In drafting the report for the Commission, Jürgensen drew on the support of his PhD student, Kai-Peter Jaeschke.[80] Despite Jürgensen's clear awareness of the OECD debate, Commission officials considered his report inferior to similar work prepared by the OECD, which provides further indication of the prestige and concomitant influence of the OECD's expertise.[81]

Like the OECD Environmental Committee, the Commission's SEPC consulted its own group of national economic experts on environmental issues. This group discussed a first draft recommendation on the PPP in May 1973, and continued to work on the issue subsequently.[82] Both Hannecart and Jaeschke, Jürgensen's collaborator, attended as experts. The group also included some of the members of the OECD's Subcommittee: the British official from the Department of Trade and Industry David Allen and the Dutch official from the Ministry of Public Health and the Environment J.M. Corbijn. This clearly contributed to a transfer of expertise: at one of the Commission group meetings Allen for instance recommended utilizing certain OECD methods for assessing the cost of pollution.[83]

Despite these various connections to the OECD, the precedent it set and similar practices of gathering economic expertise, the Commission developed its own approach to the PPP already in the proposal that emerged from the experts' consultation. This approach was adapted to the EC's existing institutional and policy framework. It also took account of the balance of member-state preferences. Against that backdrop, the reference to the OECD in the introduction of the SEPC's proposal is revealing. It states that the Commission had recommended the inclusion of the PPP already in the proposal for an Environmental Action Programme in 1972 'in accordance with the guiding principles of the OECD'. Referring to the OECD the Commission seems to have been trying to benefit from the OECD's prestige in this area. At the same time, the wording makes it very clear that the Commission was trying to demonstrate that it was acting independently.[84]

Indeed, the Commission's PPP proposal included many more exemptions than the OECD's definition. As such, it reflected important political considerations: for one, the interest of member-states who did not want any interference with their regional policies, notably Italy; for another, the EC's interest to prevent any limitation of existing EC redistributive EC policies, such as social and regional policies, which were expanding in the course of the 1970s.[85] The EC approach was more lenient than that of the OECD, allowing for exemptions for three types of reasons: first, difficulties in adapting to environmental policy rules, be it for economic, technical or social reasons. In this case, exceptions should be temporary. Secondly, a blanket exception was granted where other EC policy objectives ('regional, social, research, industrial, conjunctural') interfered with environmental objectives. The wording ensured that the application of the principle remained secondary to regional policy. Thirdly, costs of services in the general public interest, such as local waste-treatment plants, were exempt from the PPP. It remained permissible to finance the operation of such installations via taxes.[86] Similar to the direction taken at the level of its expert committees, the Commission's proposal was full of exceptions. This is clearly contrary to the widespread belief that the EC and the EU stand for prioritizing environmental policy and thus the application of its fundamental principles, whereas the OECD embodies a pro-business approach less concerned with its environmental implications.

The negotiation of PPP became even more politicized when it moved from the economic experts and the Commission to the stage of decision-making in the Council of Ministers in 1974. The positions of the member-states differed strongly, according to their attitude towards EC policy-making more generally and with a view to the contents of the Recommendation. In fact, a number of pro-integration minded delegations, including the Belgian, Dutch and West German (as well as the relevant EP committee) demanded enshrining the principle in a binding directive. The choice of this legal instrument would have forced the member-state governments to transpose the PPP into national law. Less Euro-enthusiastic governments such as the ones of Denmark, France, Ireland and the United Kingdom preferred a non-binding recommendation, along the lines of the practice in other IOs.[87]

Usually a pro-integration country, Italy was also against a binding directive, because the Italian government feared that a strict implementation of the PPP would threaten the Italian policy practice, namely granting massive subsidies for the economically depressed South. Like they had done in the OECD, the Italians insisted on a more generous interpretation of the PPP. In July 1974, they even proposed not to consider the list of exemptions exhaustive. Such a proposal would have rendered the EC's version of the PPP meaningless.[88]

Conversely, the idea of the PPP seemed to have particular appeal in the Netherlands. It was the Dutch parliamentary rapporteur Oele who had placed the concept on the EC agenda. Moreover, due to its geography on the lower Rhine, Meuse and Scheldt, the country suffered from massive water pollution, while their neighbours upstream caused most of the damage. In any case, the Dutch delegation took a particularly strict position on exemptions to the PPP. Referring explicitly to the OECD and emphasizing the need to cooperate with this IO, the Dutch representatives argued not to go beyond the OECD's list of exemptions, and were particularly critical of the blanket exemptions for certain EC policy areas.[89]

Although the processes of establishing the PPP in the OECD and the EC shared a surprising number of common features and were interlinked in multiple ways, notably through the involvement of experts, both IOs arrived at different conclusions. The OECD remained much closer to the rigour of its economist advisers, while a political logic mattered more in the EC context. Institutional differences equally played a role for the selective appropriation of the concept. As OECD recommendations were non-binding, accepting stricter rules posed less of a problem to national negotiators, who could point to their superiors in national capitals that technically the implementation of IO recommendations was voluntary. The political stakes and the level of commitment was different in the EC, given that it was capable of making binding rules, and indeed a substantial number of governments would have preferred a binding directive. Against the backdrop of this 'shadow' of binding rules, the EC allowed for more generous exemptions.[90] Institutional differences also played a role in a further respect. The principle did not ideally 'fit' with existing national and EC policies, which relied heavily on subsidies. Those, however, were anathema to the environmental-economics view of the PPP. Such a lack of fit frequently limits the acceptability of policies, as scholars of policy implementation have highlighted. This may also explain the reluctance of EC policy-makers to implement the PPP more strictly.[91]

Conclusions

Research on IOs usually tends to treat these institutions and their respective policies in isolation, at best considering IOs' internal politics and the role of their leading member-states. Textbook overviews for instance routinely mention the founding of the Council of Europe and the OECD along with the creation of the European Coal and Steel Community in their early chapters, but these 'other' (regional) IOs then quickly drop out of the picture. However, as this article demonstrates, these 'other' IOs indeed continued to exist, and played an important role in placing environmental policy on the European agenda.

This article traced the maze of the multiple connections between IOs in the emergent debate about environmental policy – involving NATO, the Council of Europe, the OECD and the EC. Obviously, connections are not limited to these IOs. Public and academic debates in Western Europe – including relevant publications, such as Mishan's much-quoted book – contributed to the rise of EC environmental policy and the PPP, as did the views of governments and experts outside of Europe, notably ideas and policies first formulated and promoted by academics and think tanks in the United States. Having said this, the link to the OECD proved to be particularly influential for the EC.

In general, the EC was more often a receiver of policy approaches formulated elsewhere than a pioneer. Moreover, the relations between the EC and other IOs were not necessarily only cooperative, but at times competitive.[92] In fact, the OECD and other IOs had started dealing with environmental challenges earlier than the EC. This also holds true for the PPP as the main focus of this article. And there is a second area in which views of the EC's role in international policy-making are often distorted. Advocates of EC action – such as the authors of the first EP reports on the new policy domain – often referred to the EC's superiority thanks to its capacity to make binding laws. For the PPP, however, member-states opted for a non-binding recommendation, exactly because many of them feared an all too strict application of the principle. Hence, the EC did not always take binding decisions. And since the legal and political stakes tended to be higher in this forum than in other IOs, it sometimes opted for a more lenient approach. The PPP is a perfect example: here, the OECD adopted a much stricter application of the insights of environmental economics in order to achieve a cleaner environment, falsifying the idea that this IO stands for a pro-business line, while the EC was more concerned with environmental issues. Indeed, the fundamental difference between the OECD and the EC concerning the PPP was not premised on the familiar conflict between ecology vs. economy, as the speeches by Malfatti and van Lennep seem to suggest, but on different perceptions of the role of the state and the market: while the OECD was more committed to market-based instruments already in the 1970s, the EC only converted to this agenda in the 1990s. Again models from the United States played an important role, as did policy experiments that had been undertaken in some of the member-states, notably in the Netherlands. These insights and ideas were mediated by leading Dutch officials in the Commission's Environment directorate general in the 1990s.[93]

Overlapping membership clearly plays a role in explaining the exchanges and the different paths the various IOs eventually chose: most EC member-states were members of NATO, and all of them also of the Council of Europe and the OECD. The representation of the Commission in the OECD provided an important vector facilitating exchange at various levels: at the level of the Commissioners, at the level of Commission officials, and most likely even with a view to recruiting economic experts. Individuals like Carpentier did matter here, too, with their multiple memberships and connections. This also held true for experts such as Hannequart. However, this factor and the role of policy entrepreneurs active in several forms appears less important than in the other contributions to this special section, for instance in comparison to the role of Duncan Sandys in cultural policy, as discussed in the article by Oriane Calligaro and Kiran Klaus Patel.

At the beginning of the debate, other IOs also played an important role, for Western Europe particularly the Council of Europe. In fact, it had a pioneering role in environmental policy amongst the various IOs and also with regard to the PPP. Very soon, however, the Council of Europe was marginalized – as in several of the other policy domains covered in this special section. The international debate concerning the PPP was increasingly driven by an economic rationale – a logic that did not fit the competences of the Council of Europe. Thus the Council of Europe soon lost in importance, leaving the pride of place to organizations with strong economic credentials, most importantly the OECD and the EC. As early as 1972, the Council of Europe even encouraged its member-states to actually use the OECD to help avoid new trade barriers due to environmental regulation.[94] Thus, within the course of a few years, the OECD and the EC became the central IOs in Western Europe in this field, and the main points of reference for the principle in international law.[95] Cooperation, competition and crowding out thus led to a new division of labour between various IOs in Western Europe. This also helps to explain why by today, the EU has crowded out all other European IOs in the areas of environmental policy, as it did in many other policy fields. As this article has shown, this was a rather unlikely perspective when the whole debate started in the early 1970s, and the EU's eventual rise to prominence owes a lot to the inter-organizational links to a whole host of other IOs.

Notes

1. Malfatti, 'Statement to the European Parliament'.
2. European Commission, 'First Communication'.

MULTIPLE CONNECTIONS IN EUROPEAN COOPERATION

3. OECD Environment Committee, 'Summary Record of the 1st Session held at the Chateau de la Muette, Paris, on 24 and 25th November 1970, ENV/M (70) 1', OECD Archives, Paris (OECDA) Film 390 (1970): 15–19.
4. Engels, 'Modern Environmentalism', 124f.
5. For an overview: Meyer, 'From Nature to Environment'.
6. OECD, 'Celebrating 40 Years'.
7. Council of the European Communities, 'Declaration on the Programme of Action'.
8. Beder, 'The Polluter Pays Principle'; Sadeleer, *Environmental Principles.*
9. OECD, 'Recommendation on the Implementation of the Polluter-Pays Principle, 14 November 1974'; 'Recommendation on Guiding Principles concerning International Economic Aspects of Environmental Policies, 26 May 1972'; European Community, 'Council Recommendation of 3 March 1975 regarding Cost Allocation'.
10. Zito, 'The European Union as an Environmental Leader'.
11. Lenschow and Sprungk, 'The Myth of a Green Europe'.
12. Schmelzer, *The Hegemony of Growth*; idem, 'Expandiere oder stirb'. See also: Mitzner, *Research for Growth?*
13. Schmelzer, 'The Crisis before the Crisis', 1011.
14. Borowy, *Defining Sustainable Development*; Biedenkopf, 'Emissions Trading'; Meadows, *Limits to Growth.*
15. Kirchhof and Meyer, 'Global Protest Against Nuclear Power'; Kaelble, 'Between Comparison and Transfers'.
16. Wöbse, 'Oil on Troubled Waters?'; Iriye, 'Environmental History and International History'; Haas, *Saving the Mediterranean.*
17. Patel, 'Provincialising European Union'.
18. For the increasingly self-critical debate in political science: Börzel and Risse, 'From Europeanisation to Diffusion'.
19. Cronon, 'The Trouble with Wilderness'; Turner, 'The Promise of Wilderness'; Bemmann, Metzger, and von Detten, *Ökologische Modernisierung*; Robin, 'The Rise of the Idea of Biodiversity'.
20. Hünemörder, *Die Frühgeschichte der globalen Umweltkrise*; McCormick, *The Global Environmental Movement.*
21. With the exception of Borowy, *Defining Sustainable Development* and contributions in Kaiser and Meyer, *International Organizations and Environmental Protection.*
22. For a more extensive treatment: Macekura, *Of Limits and Growth,* 91–133.
23. By the early 1970s, apart from its founding members in 1949, Belgium, Denmark, France, Ireland, Italy, Luxembourg, Netherlands, Norway and Sweden, the following countries had joined: Greece, Turkey, West Germany, Iceland, Austria, Cyprus, Switzerland and Malta.
24. Council of Europe, *Resolution (68)4; idem, European Water Charter, 6 May 1968.*
25. Schulz, 'Das Europäische Naturschutzjahr 1970'.
26. Meyer, 'Appropriating the Environment'; Johnson, *Politics of the Environment.*
27. Hamblin, 'Environmentalism for the Atlantic Alliance'; Schulz, 'Transatlantic Environmental Security'; Risso, 'Nato and the Environment'.
28. Kaiser, 'Sometimes it's the Economy'.
29. A. de Baerdemaeker, Permanent Representation to OECD to European Commission, DG External Relations, Rapport 458, 3 Feb 1970, including OECD C(70) 20, draft resolution to set up ad hoc preparatory committee on environment, 'Historical Archives of the European Commission' (HAEC), BAC 3/1978 No. 572 (1970): 3. Here and in the following: My translation from the French original.
30. *Ibid*; Schmelzer, "The Crisis before the Crisis', 1003–5.
31. Patel, 'Provincialising European Union'.
32. Patel, *Fertile Ground for Europe*; Knudsen, *Farmers on Welfare*; Dinan, *Europe Recast,* 28–51.
33. For example, Livingston Hartley, 'Some International Implications on Environmental Challenges'. *The Atlantic Community Quarterly,* 1970, 234–41. (handwritten note: M. Mandl),

MULTIPLE CONNECTIONS IN EUROPEAN COOPERATION

HAEC, BAC 68/1984, No. 199. Commission official Vladimiro Mandl worked on these environmental issues at the time.

34. H[arald] Malmgren to Joseph Harned [Atlantic Council]: Memorandum: International Approach to Environmental Control, 9/2/70, *ibid.*

35. Kneese, Rolfe, and Harned, *Managing the Environment.*

36. Bossuat, Bussière and Legendre, 'Entretien avec Robert Toulemon, Paris, 17 décembre 2003', 38f.

37. d'Arge and Kneese, 'Environmental Quality and International Trade', 421; European Commission, Political and Institutional Aspects of Environmental Management (summary), Washington, 15 January 1971 [presented at Atlantic Council and Battelle Institute Joint Conference on Goals and Strategy for Environmental Quality in the Seventies, 15–17 January 1971], HAEC, BAC 35/1980, No. 199. In The National Archives (TNA) (FCO 55/661 No. 21) the text is attributed to Robert Toulemon.

38. European Commission, 'Aims and Underlying Principles of a Common Environmental Policy Draw[n] up by the Member and Acceding States, SEC (1972) 3901, 7 November 1972, [R/2413/72 ENV 49]', Archive of the Council of Ministers (ACM), CM 2.1973 No. 24.

39. Radkau, *Nature and Power*, 240, 244; Fressoz, "Payer pour polluer".

40. Schwartz, 'The Polluter Pays Principle'; Beder, 'The Polluter Pays Principle'; de Sadeleer, *Environmental Principles.*

41. Biedenkopf, 'Emissions Trading', 6–7.

42. Dales, *Pollution, Property and Prices.*

43. Gaines, 'The Polluter-Pays Principle'.

44. d'Arge and Kneese, 'Environmental Quality', 421–2.

45. For example, Gaines, 'The Polluter-Pays Principle', 477.

46. Council of Europe, *Resolution (68)4*, 8, (§ I-III), 10 (§16).

47. OECD, 'Environment Committee. First Session to be held at the OECD Headquarters Paris, on 24th and 25th November 1970, ENV A (70) 3, 4 November 1970', OECD Archives (OECDA), Film 0390 (1970).

48. Baerdemaeker to European Commission, DG External Relations, Rapport 458, 4.

49. OECD, 'Recommendation, 26 May 1972'.

50. 'Recommendation on the Implementation, 14 November 1974', § I.3.

51. *Ibid.*

52. For example, Hartlapp, 'On Enforcement, Management and Persuasion'.

53. OECD, 'Recommendation on the Implementation', 14 November 1974, § II-III.

54. van Laer, 'Entretien avec Michel Carpentier', 4. The commonly used acronym SEPC follows the French word order.

55. For a more extensive discussion: Meyer, 'Making the Polluter Pay'.

56. *Idem*, 'Green Activism'.

57. 'Adriaan Oele'; Koerts, 'Ad Oele'.

58. Europäisches Parlament, 'Bericht im Namen des Ausschusses für Sozial- und Gesundheitsfragen über die Reinhaltung der Binnengewässer unter besonderer Berücksichtigung der Verunreinigung des Rheins, 11.11.1970, doc 161/70, Berichterstatter: Jacob Boersma', Historical Archive of the European Parliament (CARDOC) PE0 AP RP/ASOC.1967 0161/70: 19 §15.

59. *Idem*, 'Bericht im Namen des Ausschusses für Sozial- und Gesundheitsfragen über die Erste Mitteilung der Kommission der Europäischen Gemeinschaften über die Politik der Gemeinschaft auf dem Gebiet des Umweltschutzes, Berichterstatter Hans Edgar Jahn, 14.04.1972, doc 9/72', CARDOC PE0 AP RP ASOC.1967 0009/72: 7 (§16).

60. Quah, 'EJ Mishan Obituary'; OECD, 'Working Document. John H. Cumberland: A Comparative Evaluation of Alternative Environmental Models with Emphasis on Waste Matrices, 20 December 1973', OECDA, AEU ENV divers (1973).

61. Hans Edgar Jahn, 'Bericht im Auftrag des Ausschusses für Sozial- und Gesundheitsfragen über die Notwendigkeit einer Gemeinschaftsaktion zur Reinhaltung der Luft, 15.12.1971', CARDOC PE0 AP RP ASOC.1967 0181/71: 12 (§32), 15 (§44).

MULTIPLE CONNECTIONS IN EUROPEAN COOPERATION

62. Europäisches Parlament, 'Bericht über die Erste Mitteilung', 7 (§16), 59 (§80).
63. European Commission, 'Note à l'attention de MM. les membres de la Commission. Objet: Communication et projets de la Commission au Conseil sur la politique des Communautés européennes en matière d'Environnement, SEC (72) 666 (12), 20.03.1972', HAEC BAC 244/1991 No. 4: 2.
64. Communication on a European Communities' Programme on the Environment: 35–7.
65. Community, 'Council Recommendation of 3 March 1975', §1.
66. For example, Parlament, 'Bericht über die Erste Mitteilung', 7 (§16), 59 (§80); COMITEXTIL, 'Prise de Position de COMITEXTIL (Comité de Coordination des Industries Textiles de la Communauté Economique Européenne) relative au projet de recommandation du Conseil en ce que concerne l'allocation des coûts et de l'intervention des pouvoirs publiques en matière de l'environnment (Principe pollueur-payeur), 5 November 1974', HAEC BAC 68/1984, No. 201.
67. Community, 'Council Recommendation of 3 March 1975', §6b).
68. OECD, 'Environmental Committee. Subcommittee of Economic Experts Summary Record of the Exploratory Meeting on Industrial Pollution Control Cost Estimates, 12 July 1973', OECDA AEU /ENV/73.6.
69. 'Environmental Committee. Sub-Committee of Economic Experts. 1st Meeting to be held a the OECD on 15th and 16th June. Draft Agenda', OECDA AEU-ENV 1971, AEU/ENV 71.1: 3.
70. 'Environmental Committee. Sub-Committee of Economic Experts. Record of the 1st Meeting held in Paris on 15th and 16th June', OECDA AEU-ENV 1971, AEU/ENV 71.5: 4 [§11–13].
71. 'Environmental Committee. Sub-Committee of Economic Experts. Problems of Environmental Economics. Record of the Seminar held at the OECD (Summer 1971)', OECDA AEU-ENV 1971, AEU/ENV 71.19.
72. 'Note on the exceptions to the Polluter Pays Principle: the case of the pulp and paper industry, 18 December 1973', OECDA AEU /ENV/73.22; 'Practical Suggestions to be drawn from the Swedish Environmental Policy, 1 December 1973', OECDA AEU /ENV/73.23.
73. 'Environmental Committee. The Polluter-Pays Principle. Note on the Implementation of the Polluter-Pays Principle, Paris 21 January 1974', OECDA ENV (73) 32 final: 4 §7–8.
74. 'Environmental Committee. Summary Record of the 12th Session held at the OECD Headquarters in Paris on 11 and 12 September 1974', OECDA ENV M (74) 3: 7 [§10]. Similarly: 'Environmental Committee. Meeting at Ministerial Level. Minutes of the 13th Session held at the OECD Headquarters in Paris on 13 and 14 September 1974', OECDA ENV M (74) 4: 44, § 190.
75. Carlo Scarascia Mugnozza, 'Intervention de M. Scarascia-Mugnozza, Vice-Président de la Commission des Communautés européennes, à l'occasion de la session du Comité de l'Environnement réuni au niveau ministériel, OECD Paris, 13 November 1974', HAEC Speeches Collection, Box S, Scarascia-Mugnozza.
76. Harald Jürgensen and Kai-Peter Jaeschke, 'Study to Determine the Social Cost of Pollution, Hamburg, April 1973, ENV/63/73 d', HAEC BAC 58/1992, No. 319; Achille Hannequart, 'A Study of the Economic Tools for an Environmental Policy, Brussels, 24 May 1973, ENV/49/73 A', *ibid.*
77. OECD, 'Environmental Committee. Sub-Committee of Economic Experts. Record of the 1st Meeting held in Paris on 15th and 16th June'. Annex: List of Participants.
78. Bundesregierung, 'Umweltprogramm der Bundesregierung', 10.
79. Kernforschungszentrum Karlsruhe, *Durchsetzung des Verursacherprinzips*; Kneese, Rolfe, and Harned, *Managing the Environment*; 'Obituary: Allen Kneese'.
80. Bongard, 'Der fliegende Professor'.
81. John B. Richardson, SEPC, Division General Studies and Improvement of the Environment, 'Report on Mission to Paris on 22–24 January 1975 for the attention of Mr. Hammer. Re: OECD, Sub-Committee of Economic Experts, Brussels 29 January 1975', HAEC BAC 68/1984, No. 201.
82. European Commission, 'Groupe d'Experts économiques chargés des questions d'environnement. Réunion des 10 juillet et 11 juillet 1973, ENV/59/73 F', *ibid.*: 2.

83. European Commission, 'Compte-rendu. Réunion du groupe d'experts economiques spécialisés en matière d'environnement, Bruxelles, le 29 janvier 1974, ENV/43/74-F, Liste des participants', *ibid.*: 5, 8–9.
84. Service of the Environment and Consumer Protection, European Commission, 'Allocation des coûts et intervention des pouvoirs publics en matière d'environnment, Document de travail des services de la commission, 7 May 1973, ENV/23/1/73 F', HAEC BAC 58/1992, No. 319: 3.
85. *Ibid.*
86. *Ibid.*, 18 [section IV].
87. Council of the European Communities, 'Note. Draft Recommendation regarding cost allocation and action by public authorities on environmental matters (applying the polluter pays principle) Coreper 638, 24 July 1974, R/2573/74 (ENV 115)', ACM CM2 1975.651.1: Annex 1, 1, fn. 1.
88. *Ibid.*, 10f. [§ 21–2].
89. 'Note. Draft Recommendation regarding cost allocation and action by public authorities on environmental matters, applying the polluter pays principle. Minutes of the Proceedings of the Working Party held on 29 March 1974, R/970/74 (ENV 41)', ACM CM2 1975.648.1: 2. Similarly: 'Note. Draft Recommendation regarding cost allocation and action by public authorities on environmental matters (applying the polluter pays principle) Coreper 638, 24 July 1974, R/2573/74 (ENV 115)', 5f. § 9–12.
90. De Witte and Thies, 'Why Choose Europe', 23–5.
91. Börzel, 'Why There Is No Southern Problem'.
92. On these criteria, see: Patel, 'Provincialising European Union'.
93. Jordan et al., 'European Governance and the Transfer of New Policy Instruments'; Biedenkopf, 'Emissions Trading'; Meyer, 'Interview with Marius Enthoven'.
94. Council of Europe, 'Recommendation 659': Part A, Principle II; Part B, §3c.
95. For example, Gaines, 'The Polluter-Pays Principle', 467–80.

Disclosure statement

No potential conflict of interest was reported by the author.

Funding

This research was supported by the KFG 'The Transformative Power of Europe' at FU Berlin, by a Marie Curie Intra European Fellowship [220109] and a Marie Curie Reintegration Grant 268338, by the Danish Research Council for Culture and Communication (FKK) within the project 'Institutions of Democracy in Transition. Transnational Fields in Politics, Administration and Law in Denmark and Western Europe after 1945' at Aarhus University, the Rachel Carson Center in Munich and the Department of History at NTNU Trondheim.

ORCID

Jan-Henrik Meyer (iD) http://orcid.org/0000-0002-8655-0243

Bibliography

Archival material
Archive of the Council of Ministers of the European Union, Brussels (ACM)
Historical Archives of the European Parliament, Luxembourg (CARDOC)
Historical Archives of the European Commission, Brussels (HAEC)
Historical Archives of the European Union, Florence (HAEU)
OECD Archives, Paris (OECDA)
The National Archives of the UK, London (TNA)

Grey literature
Bundeskanzler der Bundesrepublik Deutschland, "Umweltprogramm der Bundesregierung". *Bundestagsdrucksache* VI/2710, 14. Oktober 1971. http://dipbt.bundestag.de/doc/btd/06/027/0602710.pdf
Council of Europe. *European Water Charter, proclaimed at Strasbourg, 6 May 1968*. Strasbourg, 1968. http://www.regjeringen.no/nb/dep/oed/dok/NOU-er/1994/nou-1994-12/40.html?id=139533.
Council of Europe. "Recommendation 659 on National Environmental Policy in Europe (including Principles on National Environmental Policy), adopted 20 January 1972." *European Yearbook* 20 (1972): 357–361.
Council of Europe. *Resolution (68)4, adopted by the Ministers' Deputies on 8 March 1968, approving the "Declaration of Principles" on Air Pollution Control*. Strasbourg, 1968.
Council of the European Communities."Declaration of the Council of the European Communities and of the representatives of the Governments of the Member States meeting in the Council of 22 November 1973 on the programme of action of the European Communities on the environment." *Official Journal of the European Communities* 16, C 112, 20 December 1973: 1–53.
European Commission. "First Communication of the Commission about the Community's Policy on the Environment. SEC (71) 2616 final, 22 July 1971." *Archive of European Integration*, http://aei.pitt.edu/3126/1/3126.pdf.
European Commission. "Communication from the Commission to the Council on a European Communities' Programme concerning the Environment (submitted on 24 March 1972)." *Bulletin of the European Communities. Supplement* 5 (1972): 1–69.
European Community. "75/436/Euratom, ECSC, EEC: Council Recommendation of 3 March 1975 regarding cost allocation and action by public authorities on environmental matters." *Official Journal of the European Communities*, L 194, 25 July 1975: 1–4.
Franco Maria Malfatti, "Statement to the European Parliament by the President of the Commission. Strasbourg, 15 September 1970," *Archive of European Integration*, http://aei.pitt.edu/14166/1/S62-S63.pdf.
Kernforschungszentrum Karlsruhe, *Durchsetzung des Verursacherprinzips im Gewässerschutz. Ergebnis der 2. Internationalen Expertengespräche am 20. und 21. November 1972. Veranstaltet vom Bundesminister des Innern in Zusammenarbeit mit dem Institut für Angewandte Systemtechnik und Reaktorphysik, KFK 1804 UF*. Karlsruhe: Kernforschungszentrum, 1972, http://bibliothek.fzk.de/zb/kfk-berichte/KFK1804UF.pdf
OECD. "Celebrating 40 years of the OECD Environment Policy Committee (1971–2011)." OECD, http://www.oecd.org/env/48943696.pdf.

OECD. "Recommendation of the Council on Guiding Principles concerning International Economic Aspects of Environmental Policies, 26 May 1972,C(72)128." http://acts.oecd.org/Instruments/ShowInstrumentView.aspx?InstrumentID=4&Lang=en&Book=False.

OECD. "Recommendation of the Council on the Implementation of the Polluter-Pays Principle, 14 November 1974, C(74)223." http://acts.oecd.org/Instruments/ShowInstrumentView.aspx?InstrumentID=11&InstrumentPID=9&Lang=en.

Interviews

Bossuat, Gérard, Eric Bussière and A. Legendre. "Entretien avec Robert Toulemon, Paris, 17 décembre 2003." Historical Archives of the European Union, http://archives.eui.eu/en/files/transcript/15194.pdf

Meyer, Jan-Henrik. "Interview with Marius Enthoven, The Hague, 27 September 2016." Historical Archives of the European Union, forthcoming.

van Laer, Arthe. "Entretien avec Michel Carpentier, Bordeaux, 22 octobre 2010. " Historical Archives of the European Union, http://archives.eui.eu/en/files/transcript/16415.pdf

Newspaper articles

Bongard, Willy. 1969. "Der fliegende Professor. Wer heute Volkswirtschaft lehrt: Harald Jürgensen." *Die Zeit*, no. 8 http://www.zeit.de/1969/08/Der-fliegende-Professor.

Koerts, Agnes. 1999. "Ad Oele, spagaat tussen ingenieurs en politici." *Binnenlands Bestuur* 20, no. 42: 20–23.

"Obituary: Allen Kneese. 2001." *The Economist*, 24 March, 101.

Quah, Euston. 2014. "EJ Mishan Obituary. Economist who Argued that Economic Growth Could Make us less Happy." *The Guardian*, 7 November.

Secondary literature

"Adriaan Oele." In *Who's Who in Europe. Dictionnaire biographique des personnalités européennes contemporaines*, edited by Edward A. de Maeijer, 2261, Brussels: Europ-élite, 1972.

Beder, Sharon. "The Polluter Pays Principle." In *Environmental Principles and Policies. An Interdisciplinary Introduction*, edited by Sharon Beder, 32–46, London: Earthscan, 2006.

Bemmann, Martin, Birgit Metzger, and Roderich von Detten, eds. *Ökologische Modernisierung. Zur Geschichte und Gegenwart eines Konzepts in Umweltpolitik und Sozialwissenschaften*. Frankfurt: Campus, 2014.

Biedenkopf, Katja. "Emissions Trading – A Transatlantic Journey for an Idea?" *KFG 'The Transformative Power of Europe' Working Paper* 45 (2012): 1–28. http://userpage.fu-berlin.de/kfgeu/kfgwp/wpseries/WorkingPaperKFG_45.pdf.

Borowy, Iris. *Defining Sustainable Development for Our Common Future. A History of the World Commission on Environment and Development (Brundtland Commission)*. Abingdon: Routledge, 2014.

Börzel, Tanja A. "Why There Is No Southern Problem. On Environmental Leaders and Laggards in the European Union." *Journal of European Public Policy* 7 (2000): 141–162.

Börzel, Tanja A., and Thomas Risse. "From Europeanisation to Diffusion: Introduction." *West European Politics* 35 (2012): 1–19.

Cronon, William. "The Trouble with Wilderness, or, Getting Back to the Wrong Nature." *Environmental History* 1 (1996): 7–55.

d'Arge, Ralph C., and Allen V. Kneese. "Environmental Quality and International Trade." *International Organization* 26 (1972): 419–465.

de Witte, Bruno, and Anne Thies. "Why choose Europe? The Place of the European Union in the Architecture of International Legal Cooperation." In *The EU's Role in Global Governance: the Legal Dimension*, edited by Jan Wouters, Bart van Vooren and Steven Blockmans, 23–38. Oxford: Oxford University Press, 2013.

Dales, John Harkness. *Pollution, Property and Prices. An Essay in Policy Making and Economics*. Toronto: University of Toronto Press, 1968.

de Sadeleer, Nicolas. *Environmental Principles. From Political Slogans to Legal Rules*. Oxford: Oxford University Press, 2002.

Dinan, Desmond. *Europe Recast. A History of European Union. Second Edition*. Basingstoke: Palgrave, 2014.

Engels, Jens Ivo. "Modern Environmentalism." In *The Turning Points of Environmental History*, edited by Frank Uekötter, 119–131. Pittsburgh, PA: University of Pittsburgh Press, 2010.

Fressoz, Jean-Baptiste. "Payer pour polluer. L'industrie chimique et compensation des dommages environmentaux, 1800–1850." *Histoire & Mesure* 28 (2013): 145–186.

Gaines, Sanford E. "The Polluter-Pays Principle: From Economic Equity to Environmental Ethos." *Texas International Law Journal* 26 (1991): 463–496.

Haas, Peter M. *Saving the Mediterranean. The Politics of International Environmental Cooperation*. New York, NY: Columbia University Press, 1990.

Hamblin, Jacob Darwin. "Environmentalism for the Atlantic Alliance: NATO's Experiment with the 'Challenges of Modern Society.'" *Environmental History* 15 (2010): 54–75.

Hartlapp, Miriam. "On Enforcement, Management and Persuasion: Different Logics of Implementation Policy in the EU and the ILO." *Journal of Common Market Studies* 45 (2007): 653–674.

Hartley, Livingston. "Some International Implications of Environmental Challenges." *Atlantic Community Quarterly* 8 (1970): 234–241.

Hünemörder, Kai F. *Die Frühgeschichte der globalen Umweltkrise und die Formierung der deutschen Umweltpolitik (1950–1973)*. Stuttgart: Franz Steiner, 2004.

Iriye, Akira. "Environmental History and International History." *Diplomatic History* 32 (2008): 643–646.

Johnson, Stanley P. *The Politics of the Environment. The British Experience*. London: Tom Stacey, 1973.

Jordan, Andrew, Rüdiger Wurzel, Anthony R. Zito, and Lars Bruckner. "European Governance and the Transfer of 'new' Environmental Policy Instruments (NEPIs) in the European Union." *Public Administration* 81 (2003): 555–574.

Kaelble, Hartmut. "Between Comparison and Transfers." In *Comparative and Transnational History. Central European Approaches and New Perspectives*, edited by Heinz-Gerhard Haupt and Jürgen Kocka, 33–38. New York: Berghahn, 2009.

Kaiser, Wolfram, and Jan-Henrik Meyer, eds. *International Organizations and Environmental Protection. Conservation and Globalization in the Twentieth Century*. Berghahn: New York, 2017.

Kaiser, Wolfram. "Sometimes it's the Economy, Stupid! International Organisations, Steel and the Environment." In *International Organizations and Environmental Protection. Conservation and Globalization in the Twentieth Century*, edited by Wolfram Kaiser and Jan-Henrik Meyer, 153–181. New York, NY: Berghahn, 2017.

Kirchhof, Astrid Mignon, and Jan-Henrik Meyer. "Global Protest Against Nuclear Power. Transfer and Transnational Exchange in the 1970s and 1980s." *Historical Social Research* 39 (2014): 165–190.

Kneese, Allen V., Sidney E. Rolfe, and Joseph W. Harned. *Managing the Environment: International Economic Cooperation for Pollution Control*. New York, NY: Praeger Publishers, 1971.

Knudsen, Ann-Christina L. *Farmers on Welfare. The Making of Europe's Common Agricultural Policy*. Ithaca: Cornell University Press, 2009.

Lenschow, Andrea, and Carina Sprungk. "The Myth of a Green Europe." *Journal of Common Market Studies* 48 (2010): 133–154.

Macekura, Stephen. *Of Limits and Growth. The Rise of Global Sustainable Development in the Twentieth Century*. Cambridge: Cambridge University Press, 2015.

Meadows, Dennis, Donella Meadows, Erich Zahn, and Peter Milling. *The Limits to Growth*. New York, NY: Universe Books, 1972.

McCormick, John. *The Global Environmental Movement*. Chichester: John Wiley, 1995.

Meyer, Jan-Henrik. "Appropriating the Environment. How the European Institutions Received the Novel Idea of the Environment and Made it Their Own." *KFG 'The Transformative Power of Europe' Working Paper* 31 (2011): 1–33. http://userpage.fu-berlin.de/kfgeu/kfgwp/wpseries/WorkingPaperKFG_31.pdf.

Meyer, Jan-Henrik. "From Nature to Environment: International Organisations and the Environment before Stockholm." In *International Organizations and Environmental Protection. Conservation and*

Globalization in the Twentieth Century, edited by Wolfram Kaiser and Jan-Henrik Meyer. New York, NY: Berghahn, 2017, 31–73.

Meyer, Jan-Henrik. "Green Activism. The European Parliament's Environmental Committee promoting a European Environmental Policy in the 1970s." *Journal of European Integration History* 17 (2011): 73–85.

Meyer, Jan-Henrik. "Making the Polluter Pay: How the European Communities Established Environmental Protection." In *International Organizations and Environmental Protection. Conservation and Globalization in the Global Twentieth Century*, edited by Wolfram Kaiser and Jan-Henrik Meyer, 182–210. New York, NY: Berghahn, 2017.

Mitzner, Veera. Research for Growth? The Contested Origins of European Union Research Policy (1963–1974). PhD thesis, Florence: European University Institute, 2013.

Patel, Kiran Klaus, ed. *Fertile Ground for Europe? The History of European Integration and the Common Agricultural Policy since 1945*. Baden-Baden: Nomos, 2009.

Patel, Kiran Klaus. "Provincialising European Union: Co-operation and Integration in Europe in a Historical Perspective." *Contemporary European History* 22 (2013): 649–673.

Radkau, Joachim. *Nature and Power. A Global History of the Environment*. Cambridge: Cambridge University Press, 2008.

Risso, Linda. "NATO and the Environment: The Committee on the Challenges of Modern Society." *Contemporary European History* 25 (2016): 505–535.

Robin, Libby. "The Rise of the Idea of Biodiversity: Crises, Responses and Expertise." *Quaderni. Communication, technologies, pouvoir* 76 (2011): 25–37.

Schmelzer, Matthias. "The Crisis before the Crisis: the 'Problems of Modern Society' and the OECD, 1968-74." *European Review of History* 19 (2012): 999–1020.

Schmelzer, Matthias. "'Expandiere oder stirb'. Wachstumsziele, die OECD und die Steigerungslogik wirtschaftlicher Expansion." *Geschichte und Gesellschaft* 41 (2015): 355–393.

Schmelzer, Matthias. *The Hegemony of Growth. The OECD and the Making of the Economic Growth Paradigm*. Cambridge: Cambridge University Press, 2016.

Schulz, Thorsten. "Das ,Europäische Naturschutzjahr 1970' – Versuch einer europaweiten Umweltkampagne." *WZB-Discussion Papers* P 2006, no. 7 (2006): 1–34. http://bibliothek.wzb.eu/pdf/2006/p06-007.pdf.

Schulz, Thorsten. "Transatlantic Environmental Security in the 1970s? NATO's 'Third Dimension' as an Early Environmental and Human Security Approach." *Historical Social Research* 35 (2010): 309–328.

Schwartz, Priscilla. "The Polluter Pays Principle." In *Research Handbook on International Environmental Law*, edited by Malgosia Fitzmaurice, P. Merkouris and David M. Ong, 243–261. Cheltenham: Edward Elgar, 2010.

Turner, James Morton. *The Promise of Wilderness. American Environmental Politics since 1964*. Seattle, WA: University of Washington Press, 2013.

Wöbse, Anna-Katharina. "Oil on Troubled Waters? Environmental Diplomacy in the League of Nations." *Diplomatic History* 32 (2008): 519–537.

Zito, Anthony R. "The European Union as an Environmental Leader in a Global Environment." In *The Globalization of Environmental Crisis*, edited by Jan Oosthoek and Barry K. Gills, 81–94. Abingdon: Routledge, 2008.

The true 'EURESCO'? The Council of Europe, transnational networking and the emergence of European Community cultural policies, 1970–90

Kiran Klaus Patel and Oriane Calligaro

ABSTRACT

The roots of EU action in the field of culture lie in the 1970s. At the time, the Council of Europe (CoE), the United Nations Education, Scientific and Cultural Organization (UNESCO) and other organizations were already established players in the field. This article analyses the incremental and often haphazard process in which the European Community (EC) became the key organization at the European level by the end of the Cold War. It stresses the role of the EC's specific governance structure, its considerable financial resources, and its objectives of market integration and expanding powers as drivers of this process, along with selective forms of adaptation of practices first tried out in other forums. Besides scrutinizing general tendencies of inter-organizational exchange during the 1970s and 1980s, the article zooms in on two concrete case studies. For the 1970s, it highlights the debates about cultural heritage and the European Architectural Heritage Year (EAHY) project: although initiated by the CoE, the EAHY became one of the first cases of EC policy import, strongly facilitated by transnational networks. The second case study, for the 1980s, deals with the development of a European audio-visual policy. Here again the CoE took the lead and worked as a laboratory for schemes later adapted by the EC.

Jean Monnet is often quoted to the effect that if he could commence European integration anew, he would start with culture. Nobody, however, has been able to find a reference for this line, which is also alien to Monnet's general approach to integration.[1] Instead, he focused most of his attention on economic policies, which came to form the core of the European Communities (EC). EC activities in the field of culture only started to evolve in the 1970s, in a process where cooperation, emulation, and conflict with other inter- and transnational platforms came to define the Community's trajectory. Other organizations started to engage in cultural policies much earlier, most notably UNESCO on a global scale and the Council of Europe (CoE) at the Western European level. As in many other policy domains, EC action can only be understood properly within this wider context.[2]

This article examines the incremental and often haphazard process in which the EC, as a relative latecomer on the stage of European cultural policy, developed into the key organization by the end of the Cold War. This development is particularly puzzling if one considers that the CoE had been in charge of cultural matters in Western Europe since the 1950s. How, then, did the EC come to play a role in this policy domain in the first place, and why did it ultimately become more significant than the Council of Europe? In order to answer these questions, it is key to analyse the interrelationship between the two organizations, this article argues. It claims that the EC's rise to prominence resulted to a great extent from its multifaceted exchanges with the CoE, in which the EC selectively adopted many CoE practices. There were three main reasons why the EC dominated the field by the end of the Cold War: its substantial financial means, with which the CoE could not compete; its legally more binding regulations in contrast to CoE rules; and, finally, the fact that EC cultural policies were first part of the Common and later of the Single Market project, as a crucial context without equivalent in the CoE. These developments, particularly at the level of inter-organizational exchange, were strongly driven by a small group of transnational policy entrepreneurs, experts and international non-governmental organizations (INGOs) who pushed for EC action in this field. Other actors, in contrast, stressed the CoE's pioneering role, but increasingly lost ground.

The Cold War always loomed in the background of these processes. Throughout the period under study, culture was presented as a seemingly apolitical instrument to bridge the East–West conflict and, ultimately, several Eastern European countries participated in some of these Western European projects. In this context, the CoE and the more politicized EC also tried to use cultural exchange to promote Western values.

It should be added that the boundaries of cultural policy – as of the term 'culture' – were notoriously porous and vague, intersecting with issues as diverse as citizenship, education, media and market integration. This article shows how both the CoE and the EC refrained from proposing a clear-cut definition of culture and a precise remit for cultural policy. Interpretations shifted according to political needs and contexts, oscillating among anthropological, civilizational and more economic connotations. Debates in both forums drew heavily on concepts proposed in other contexts; neither organization can claim to have been an innovator in this regard. Hence, this article does not start from a preconceived definition of cultural policy; its whole point is to show the *gradual* emergence of a sphere of action at the European level, eventually leading to a discernable policy domain.

Besides scrutinizing general tendencies of inter-organizational exchange, we focus on two concrete case studies chosen for their particular significance for the period under study. For the 1970s, we highlight the debates about cultural heritage and the European Architectural Heritage Year (EAHY) project, which the CoE continues to praise – in its specific English – as a 'stone mile' in its activities.[3] Initiated by the CoE, the EAHY became one of the first cases of EC policy import, strongly facilitated by transnational networks. The second case study, for the 1980s, deals with the development of a European audio-visual policy. Here again the CoE took the lead and worked as a laboratory for schemes later adapted by the EC. By the mid-1980s, the EC's cultural initiatives had gained momentum and the cooperation with the CoE became less and less fundamental and formative for EC action in the field. Having said this, some member-states continued to oppose an EC cultural policy, and preferred the CoE as an alternative arena for audio-visual issues. As a result, contrasting modes of interaction emerged between the two organizations, fluctuating among cooperation, emulation and competition, all contributing to explaining the creation of an EC audio-visual policy by the end of the decade. Together, these two case studies also reveal that this field of political action was highly fragmented during the Cold War's last two decades, so that different institutional constellations, geographies, and actor networks came to define inter-organizational relations and their effects.

The existing literature on European cultural policy has mainly focused on intra- rather than inter-organizational dynamics. Only a few works have assessed these processes on a solid archival basis.[4] Many studies are dominated by the narratives created by the institutions under study themselves,[5] which often stress harmonious and cooperative interaction and fail to reveal the multi-layered and complex forms of links and exchange. Others have shown the significance of non-governmental organizations in promoting Western culture in the Cold War context.[6] Our interpretation, in contrast, explores the inter-organizational relations as well as the links between transnational policy entrepreneurs, networks and INGOs on the one hand and international organizations on the other. It builds on fresh archival research in the Historical Archives of the European Union in Florence, the Historical Archives of the European Commission in Brussels, UNESCO's archive in Paris, various national and private archives in Germany, Great Britain and France, as well as several interviews and a vast variety of grey literature. The article is structured as follows: a first part shows how, from the 1950s until the late 1970s, the CoE emerged as the leading international organization for cultural cooperation in Europe. The second part is dedicated to the case of the EAHY and the EC's increasing involvement in the cultural field in the 1970s. The section on audio-visual policy in the 1980s examines the intensification of competition between the EC and the CoE, before the conclusion summarizes our main findings.

Emerging coexistence, 1950s to late 1960s

The Treaty of Rome did not equip the EC with any explicit competence in the realm of culture, and against this backdrop, its gradual creep into this policy field is remarkable. The Treaty treated cultural commodities and services as any other part of the economy and only allowed certain export restrictions for the 'protection of national treasures possessing artistic, historic or archaeological value'.[7] Other initiatives, such as the Commission's university information policy and its promotion of European studies, included educational and cultural dimensions.[8]

Two reasons explain why the early EC touched upon culture only marginally, and chiefly through the economic lens. For one, the member-states regarded culture as their own preserve. Given the strong role culture and cultural policies had played historically in the rise of national identities and nation-states, they were reluctant to transfer extended competences in this realm to the international level.[9] This was even more so due to the EC's supranational elements and the federalist tendencies associated with it.[10] For another, other organizations already dealt with such issues at the international tier – most notably UNESCO at the global level and the CoE in Western Europe. The latter's range of activities always challenged plans for extending the EC's functions in this field. While never being consistent about it, the member-states continuously aimed at reducing overlapping powers and duplication between international organizations.[11] While the CoE always had more members than the EC, it would be wrong to overemphasize the difference in geography, at least for the period under study in this article. During the second half of the 1960s, the CoE had 12 members more than the EEC – but four of them (the United Kingdom, Denmark, Norway and Ireland) applied to join the Communities, and most of the remaining states were small (Iceland, Malta, Cyprus, Switzerland, Austria, Sweden, Greece and Turkey). Hence, the idea of avoiding duplication was not without substance.

But what, then, did the CoE do in this field? Article 1 of its 1949 Statute declared that the CoE aimed to 'achieve a greater unity between its members', and amongst the areas in which 'agreements and common action' should be pursued, culture was mentioned prominently.[12] Partly to compensate for the failure of sweeping federalist hopes, the CoE soon developed several initiatives for culture, broadly defined. Some of its early work focused on exchange between scholars and artists, with art exhibitions figuring prominently on its agenda. There was no grand design that held the various programmes together; instead, they developed by trial and error.[13]

Having said this, the CoE soon became the most important Western European international organization dealing with cultural policy. Its 1954 European Cultural Convention, focusing on the preservation of cultural heritage, was key in this respect. It provided the first official declaration on culture by a European organization during the post-war era and put cultural heritage front and centre. The text built on a broad definition of culture, referring to its civilizational dimension while also viewing culture in its material expressions, ranging from artistic patrimony to on-going cultural production.[14] One year later, in 1955, the concept of 'European cultural policy' officially entered the CoE's vocabulary.[15] December 1961 saw the creation of the Council for Cultural Co-operation (CCC), into which actors in the Consultative Assembly (one of the CoE's two statutory organs, later renamed the Parliamentary Assembly) in particular invested great hopes. Danish Representative Ole Bjørn Kraft stressed in a 1962 report that the creation of the CCC 'has marked the beginning of a new era of cultural cooperation in Europe', hoping it would become 'what UNESCO is for the United Nations; it's probably not too bold to use the word EURESCO from now on'.[16]

Such high-flying hopes never materialized. While the CCC enjoyed enormous autonomy, EC Commission sources noted in 1962 that the 'CCC's budget was very limited', and that for this reason, the CCC's chairman was seeking to encourage the Commission 'to cooperate actively (= financially)'. While the Communities did not accept this proposal, the financial dimension came to define the CCC/CoE–EC relationship from an early stage.[17]

Moreover, information channels between the two organizations were wide open. Since the 1950s, the parliamentary assemblies of the CoE and the EC started to hold joint meetings – no comparable links existed with the other international organizations at the time.[18] On cultural issues specifically, EC actors regularly attended CCC meetings as observers.[19] Against this backdrop, the European Parliament (EP) regularly discussed the CCC's work, just as it followed UNESCO's activities.[20] From the early 1960s, the CoE and the EC cooperated on a small-scale, case-by-case basis in the cultural realm, for instance by co-organizing the Campagne d'Éducation Civique Européenne.[21] The CoE took the lead in these forms of inter-organizational cooperation and held a dominant position in European cultural matters.

Having said this, the CoE also voiced concerns. When, in 1961, the EC planned to strengthen cooperation between the universities of its member-states and discussed setting up a European university in Florence, the CoE's Consultative Assembly proposed integrating this effort into a CoE framework. It critiqued such EC initiatives and stressed the advantages of the 'greater Europe' represented by its 18 member-states.[22] In the course of

Discovering cultural heritage

During the 1970s, the conservation of Europe's cultural heritage turned into one of the main fields of interaction between the EC and other organizations. For the Community, the CoE became the central reference point, even if UNESCO deserves to be mentioned first. After Venice and Florence experienced devastating floods in 1966, UNESCO's Executive Board joined the Italian government in devising plans for their preservation and restoration.[24] More generally, the second half of the 1960s saw intense debates about protecting the world's cultural and natural heritage, culminating in UNESCO's 1972 World Heritage Convention.[25] Less well-known initiatives came on top. During the same year, UNESCO hosted a pan-European conference on culture in Helsinki.[26] Thanks to these and similar projects, questions of cultural heritage loomed large in international debates from the second half of the 1960s.

The CoE leapt into action when, in 1970, its Consultative Assembly recommended holding a European year of cultural heritage. On this basis, the CoE's Committee of Ministers decided in January 1971 to declare 1975 European Architectural Heritage Year, organized around the slogan 'A Future for our Past'. Similar to UNESCO's work, the main intellectual and political drivers of this project were the fear that urbanization, industrial growth, and an obsession with things modern jeopardized the existing architectural heritage.[27] Institutionally, this initiative was partly triggered by UNESCO's work and the need to underscore the CoE's role in this field at the European level;[28] partly, the EAHY project built on earlier CoE discussions, starting with an Assembly Recommendation of 1963 on the preservation and development of ancient buildings and other sites.[29] In concrete terms, the 1970 Assembly initiative was underlain by a CCC report which for its part built on a 1969 conference in Brussels, co-organized by the CoE, the European Conference of Local Authorities, and Europa Nostra, an INGO active in this field. While UNESCO sent an observer to the 1969 meeting, the EC was not involved in these early stages of the initiative.[30] Together with smaller and more technical organizations, UNESCO and the CoE clearly took the lead in this emerging field of political action, and national administrations once again discussed the need for a 'useful division of labour between European and international parliamentary organizations'.[31]

The CoE's EAHY initiative centred around raising awareness of architectural heritage across European societies and safeguarding existing buildings. Given its limited budget, a good part of the work focused on disseminating information: printed material, a multi-award winning film, and commemorative stamps and coins celebrating Europe's architecture and the EAHY fall into this category. National committees also organized pilot projects to restore and renovate historic monuments. A conference in Zurich in 1973 launched the preparatory campaign, followed up by a congress in Amsterdam in October 1975, at which the CoE adopted the European Charter of the Architectural Heritage.[32]

During the formative stages of the project, the European Community played no noteworthy role in this endeavour.[33] In spring 1974, however, when the CoE's activities had been well under way for three years, the conservative British MP Lady Elles officially authored a report for the EP's Committee on Cultural Affairs that suggested creating an inventory of Europe's artistic treasures and called for active support for the CoE's initiative.[34] While bearing her name, it was Robert Grégoire, a civil servant in the Commission, who actually penned the report – revealing the strong links between these two EC organs.[35] During the EP session in May 1974, in which the Elles report was discussed, Commission Vice-President Carlo Scarascia-Mugnozza took the floor to stress that: 'the Commission is in full agreement on the importance of the European Architectural Heritage Year. We shall do all in our power ... to ensure that the Year is a success.' After this endorsement, the EP adopted the Resolution supporting the EAHY.[36] Roughly half a year later, in December 1974, the Commission followed up with a Recommendation to step up efforts to preserve Europe's cultural heritage. It urged member-states to sign or ratify UNESCO's convention on the protection of world heritage and recommended to 'actively support the actions' of the EAHY.[37] Close cooperation between some members of the EP and the Commission was thus the starting point for EC action in the field.

Why did the EC finally join the bandwagon? First, the zeitgeist attributed increasing relevance to questions of cultural heritage, with criticism of the negative effects of economic growth on heritage and the environment. This compelled an aspiring organization such as the EC to position itself. Also in this phase, the EC opted to avoid a clear-cut definition of culture: the term could encompass the fine arts, a way of living, a dimension of the economy and other things. This very vagueness created space for political initiatives. In some cases, culture was also merely a strategic device to push for further integration.[38] Beyond these reasons specific to culture, the EC also had other motives to become more active in this field. The end of the Gaullist challenge to the EC, the first enlargement round, the youth protests associated with '1968' and the dramatic changes in the architecture of internationalism in the Western world in the early 1970s sparked a far-ranging debate about the role of the EC and its concept of culture. The 1972 Paris Summit declared that economic integration was not an end in itself and adopted a report (officially authored by Spinelli but in fact penned by the aforementioned Grégoire) on community action in the cultural field.[39] The following year, the Copenhagen Declaration on European identity stressed that integration was based on common values and the 'diversity of cultures within the framework of a common European civilisation'.[40] Likewise, EP debates on cultural heritage at the time hardly connected culture to economic or social issues, but mainly understood it in anthropological terms, seeking to facilitate a common identity and more solidarity amongst Europeans. A growing sense of institutional crisis and some first cracks in the permissive consensus that had carried integration thus far, along with the search for ways to inject new dynamism into the integration process, were key reasons why the EC became more active in the field, and why it imported the concept of cultural heritage from UNESCO, the CoE, and national contexts.[41]

But there were also specific links that explain the EC's sudden support for the EAHY. Elles's report built on a motion submitted by her Italian colleague Augusto Premoli on behalf of the Liberal and Allies group in the EP.[42] National and party boundaries did not hinder such transfers, given that Elles was a British conservative and Premoli an Italian liberal, and they were further facilitated by Grégoire in the Commission.[43] While the latter remained in the background, it was not just Elles herself who acknowledged Premoli's role, but also for instance the Commission. In the decisive EP session in May 1974, Scarascia-Mugnozza first congratulated Elles for her motion, but then went on to 'express my own and the Commission's gratitude to Senator Premoli whose motion for a resolution was the starting point for this debate'.[44] Premoli, however, had only joined the EP in October 1972. Previously, he had been a member of the CoE's Consultative Assembly and as such also in the CCC. What is more, in 1970 he had been the rapporteur recommending the EAHY in the Consultative Assembly.[45] From playing a key role in launching the debate in the CoE at the beginning of the decade, he came to play the same role in the EC some four years later.[46]

A thick layer of transnational networking came on top, with a preeminent British politician in the driving seat: Duncan Sandys, the staunchly pro-European (ex) son-in-law of Winston Churchill, had been involved in CoE business ever since the late 1940s. Even before Premoli's motion of 1970, Sandys had become the *spiritus rector* of the EAHY. During the period in which the Heritage Year was prepared, he authored several reports and recommendations on the programme's details.[47] Moreover, Sandys was central not just as an Assembly member and the CoE's chairman of the EAHY's International Organising Committee. He also acted as president of Europa Nostra (founded in 1963; under Sandys's presidency since 1969), the civil-society organization that played a crucial role in executing the EAHY. Many of his reports and recommendations helped assure a central role for Europa Nostra in realizing the EAHY – for instance by preparing reports or acquiring CoE funding for an EAHY film project.[48] Looking back, one leading German CoE cultural politician recently argued that Sandys 'accomplished that great job of turning Europa Nostra into a heavyweight; an index fossil for our work at the Council of Europe'.[49]

And Sandys wore even more hats. In 1957, he had founded the Civic Trust in Great Britain, which now became the key hub executing the EAHY initiatives in his own country. CoE Assembly member and chairman of the EAHY International Organising Committee, president of Europa Nostra and of the Civic Trust – it was impossible to pull more strings at the same time, and the central role of Sandys and Europa Nostra in setting up the EAHY was undisputed.[50] Not everybody liked this, of course. In December 1972, for instance, the British Treasury stressed that the Civic Trust's role in implementing a scheme partly funded by the government 'places us in a most embarrassing situation'.[51] Still, the Civic Trust came to play an important role in the EAHY's implementation.

British politicians were also key in forging the link to the EC. Elles, who took up the ball in the EP, and Sandys were direct colleagues as Conservative members of the House of Lords; both of them belonged to the strongly pro-European wing of the party in which Elles also headed the international office, working hard to strengthen the links to continental parties of similar political orientation. In a House of Lords debate in 1976, one year after the EAHY, Elles extended 'my congratulations and thanks to my noble Friend Lord Duncan-Sandys for the initiative he took in establishing 1975 as the European Architectural Heritage Year'. After returning her thanks, Sandys stressed that there was 'room for closer coordination between the activities in this sphere of the Community and the Council of Europe'. To that effect, he also spoke to Commission President Ortoli around the same time.[52]

These details shed light on the precise forms of interaction. It was not 'the' CoE that forged new links with 'the' EC, or the EC that supported a CoE initiative. Sandys was a transnational policy entrepreneur with his own agenda. While he was part of a specifically British debate about the conservation of architectural heritage,[53] he also aptly used inter- and transnational forums for his own ends. The examples of Premoli, Elles, Scarascia-Mugnozza and Ortoli demonstrate that inter-organizational linking and learning had strong supporters in the Consultative Assembly, the EP and the European Commission but much less in the EC's Council of Ministers and the CoE's Committee of Ministers. EP and Commission actors embraced CoE policies partly for content-related reasons, partly to broach new territory and win additional competences.[54]

For the CoE, money was an important argument: in 1973, CCC chairman Georg Kahn-Ackermann deplored the 'lack of resources' and the CCC's limited competences that kept it from playing a bigger role in the EAHY preparations.[55] While some, like Premoli, therefore strove to close ranks with the EC, others stressed the CoE's primacy in the field of culture.[56] In a letter to Sandys, CoE Secretary General Lujo Toncic-Sorinj for instance discussed the organization's financial problems, both with regard to the EAHY as well as more generally. He then went on to plead for a clear division of labour with the EC, rather than coopera-tion.[57] Sandys, in contrast, felt that the CoE lacked the resources to deliver properly. In an exchange with the same Kahn-Ackermann, he insisted: 'It is not enough to proclaim a Year, to set up a committee and to expect things to happen automatically. Money is required for this as for other activities.'[58] This is exactly what the EC provided in the end: on the basis of its 1974 Resolution and Recommendation on the EAHY, the Community helped to finance the so-called European Centre in Venice, set up as a CoE initiative to oversee training of craftsmen in the conservation of architectural heritage.[59]

All the same, the EC did not have a consistent, unambiguous position either. The Council of Ministers for instance stressed in late 1973 that with regard to the CoE, 'co-operation except for exchange of information was very difficult'.[60] While some national governments, such as the Irish, wanted more joint projects, others – including the British and German – remained critical, fearing unproductive overlap between the two organizations.[61] And while the Council's Tindemans report of 1975 gave legitimacy to such work by arguing that the Community 'must make itself felt in education and culture', not all member-states were prepared to go that way.[62]

The case of the EAHY also reveals that CoE actors and Sandys in particular had a clear vision of how cultural initiatives could impact East–West relations. They stressed from the beginning that the EAHY scheme was open to societies beyond the club of European democracies – as the CoE liked to describe itself.[63] Its seemingly apolitical and non-ideo-logical character – CoE civil servant and public intellectual Nicolaus Sombart even spoke of its 'para-political' qualities – also made it acceptable for non-democratic European states.[64] In 1976, Sandys stressed that eventually 'Portugal, Spain, Yugoslavia, Poland, Romania, Hungary, Czechoslovakia and the Soviet Union' had also started to cooperate in the EAHY. Cultural heritage was seen as a pan-European phenomenon, serving as a bridge between West and East, but also to the (former) dictatorships in Europe's South.[65] Since EC actors simply followed the programmatic lead of the CoE and Europa Nostra, they did not add any specific angle to this.[66] Moreover, the EC was seen as the more politicized body in Western Europe. It was therefore easier for the CoE – supported and complemented by UNESCO in this endeavour – to forge a pan-European image and stress its role as a bridge-builder between East and West.[67]

The EAHY initiative reveals several crucial aspects: the central role that a few individ-ual transnational actors played as policy entrepreneurs and in linking various forums; the leading role of the CoE; and the fact that the EC only stepped in at a late stage, primarily by emulating CoE action and ultimately also with financial support. The asymmetry of resources between the CoE and the EC became an important source for a shift of role between the two organizations. For the time being, the EC's inroads into the field remained very limited, while for the CoE in general, the 1970s was a difficult period. It did not manage to deepen or widen its field of activities in substantial ways, which would have helped to tackle the challenge of the EC during the 1980s.[68]

Audio-visual policy: CoE and EC between emulation, cooperation and competition

Despite the opposition of certain member-states, the EC continued to expand its work in the field of culture during the second half of the 1970s. The 1974 EP Resolution on European heritage, supported by another Resolution on a 'Community Action in the Cultural Sector' in March 1976, offered a legal basis from which the Commission developed its activities further. In 1977, it issued a 'Communication on the Community Action in the Cultural Sector', drafted by Grégoire.[69] This text remained cautious, approaching cultural policies primarily from the vantage point of market liberalization. However, its second part called for further action to protect architectural heritage, as a follow-up to the 1974 Resolution, and new measures like the creation of a European Youth Orchestra. The accession of Greece to the EC in 1981, and of Spain and Portugal in 1986, also gave impetus for more cultural integration. In the 1980s, describing Greece as the cradle of democracy and the EP as an heir of the Athenian parliament was a leitmotiv whenever members of the EP called for an enhanced cultural policy.[70] In the Cold War context, safeguarding Greek cultural heritage sent two messages: it presented the EC as the defender of European democratic values and highlighted North–South integration within Western Europe. While the EC continued to stress that it did not pursue cultural policy in the strict sense of the term, it thus broadened its activities in the field.[71]

Actors in the CoE quickly felt that they were losing ground. When in 1982 a report of the Commission entitled a 'Stronger Community Action in the Cultural Sector'[72] proposed increasing the budget and developing long-term measures in the cultural sector, CoE representatives sensed that the EC was challenging their organization's primacy. A Recommendation by the CoE's Parliamentary Assembly of the time referred to 'the new initiatives for extending European Community activity in the general field of culture and education', 'regretting that' EC texts 'only specifically refer to cultural co-operation at the level of this Community'.[73] The inter-organizational relationship would soon change forever.

During the 1980s, competition between the CoE and the EC in the field of culture culminated in the field of audio-visual policy. As on so many other issues, the CoE was first to develop European policies in the field, originally with a focus on television and cinema, and it eventually turned into a laboratory for the EC. The two organizations pursued competing projects for the regulation of transnational broadcasting during the 1980s, and member-states used the CoE to counter EC initiatives they considered intrusive. In this field, interactions between the two organizations oscillated among cooperation, emulation and competition. To a large extent, these quickly evolving and complex interactions with the CoE account for the incremental constitution of a powerful EC cultural policy by the end of the decade.

As in the case of heritage, the CoE had started to address audio-visual issues during the 1950s, long before the EC, which became a significant actor only in the mid-1980s.[74] In the early 1960s, the CoE proposed to intensify 'the practical film co-operation which had been going on for some years' and 'develop its television work'.[75] In the following years, it consolidated its activities in the field. In 1976, for instance, it created an administrative unit on mass media and increased the means of its expert committee on cinema and television.[76] The CoE also organized numerous international conferences dedicated to audio-visual issues.[77]

Through these initiatives, it built up the expertise that during the 1980s would turn out to be pivotal for the design of regulatory measures both in the CoE and EC.

The intensification of the CoE's activities, and the expansion of the field in general, were largely a consequence of technological change, with the development of communication satellites facilitating transfrontier broadcasting. Broadcasting now became a transnational issue and a field of harsh competition within Europe and with the United States and Japan. In 1981, the CoE's newly created permanent Steering Committee on Mass Media (SCMM) produced exploratory studies, especially on transfrontier television. In 1981, building on such work, the Parliamentary Assembly of the CoE proposed a convention on transfrontier television in order to close Europe's regulatory gap in this domain. Since satellites allowed for transnational circulation and acquisition of audio-visual programmes, the goal was to secure, through legal cooperation, the artistic independence of programme-makers vis-à-vis the state and commercial interests (especially those of advertisers), the harmonization of copyright and royalty regulations, and respect for common standards regarding programme contents.[78]

The first text adopted by the EP on audio-visual issues was to a large extent a reaction to these CoE initiatives. In 1982, an EP report (mainly dedicated to transfrontier broadcasting) started with the observation that, so far, only the CoE had been active in the field.[79] The EP stressed its intention not to leave the regulation of pan-European broadcasting to the CoE and raised the question of its own role in the field. The EP's answer to this question was twofold. For one, it recognized the validity of the CoE's project of a convention and urged the Commission to 'take account of the proposals currently being prepared by the CoE'.[80] The Commission followed this Recommendation; its first report on audio-visual issues largely built on the CoE's exploratory work and frequently referred to its texts.[81] For another, the EP emphasized the superiority of Community law because of its more binding quality – while a CoE convention would be legally enforceable its implementation would depend on each member-state's decision to ratify the text; EC legislation was directly binding throughout the Community. This superiority of the EC was stressed again in a second EP report in 1985.[82] The text argued that the Community 'must take considerably more far-reaching action than the CoE' in the audio-visual field and that 'any framework of law in this area should be produced by the European Community rather than leaving it to the less certain procedures of the Council of Europe'.[83] The EP criticized not only the regulatory weakness of the CoE but also its attempts to limit the EC's action in the audio-visual sector. The 1985 report denounced attempts by the CoE's SCMM to 'discuss initiatives called for by the European Parliament and taken by the Commission in bodies that have no authority to do so and actually to deliver opinions on such matters to Community bodies in order to hamper their activities and lead them in other directions'. From a latecomer in the audio-visual sector, emulating the CoE, the EC quickly turned into a self-confident competitor.

The CoE tried to fight this challenge by strengthening its cooperation with the EC, true to the motto 'if you can't beat them, join them.' In October 1984, the new Secretary General of the CoE, Marcelino Oreja, recognized that the extension of the EC's competences constituted a major challenge for the CoE and worked hard to improve relations between the two organizations:

> Admittedly, the coexistence in Europe of two institutional systems with a common purpose poses problems. But it would be pointless to take refuge in a chilly attitude of withdrawal: on the contrary, we must face up to the dynamism of the Community by adopting a positive attitude and devising new forms of co-operation.[84]

A few days after his nomination, Oreja met with the Secretary General of the Commission, Émile Noël, who tried to cool down his enthusiasm: 'While accepting that this cooperation could be improved, I cautioned the Secretary General to be over-ambitious. I did not think that it was possible to achieve a "qualitative jump" regarding the cooperation between the two organisations or the participation in the conventions of the Council of Europe.'[85] There was obviously a discrepancy between the CoE's and the EC's expectations. While the CoE, increasingly losing ground, searched for more cooperation, the EC's Commission, aware of its power, consciously set limits to this cooperation. In 1985, at the request of the CoE, both institutions appointed high-level contact groups 'to explore the feasibility of making further progress in co-operation'. Despite these efforts, a report by the CoE Secretary General observed that in the audio-visual field the two organizations' activities 'suffer from a lack of genuine co-ordination and complementarity', the result being 'parallel action on the same issue, sometimes leading to divergent solutions'.[86]

The EC's cultural activities gained remarkable momentum in the early 1980s and account for this discrepancy in the two organizations' attitudes. While in the mid-1970s, the EC needed to join the EAHY as a CoE activity to expand its remit, the EC's initiatives in culture now had a more independent institutional basis and legitimacy. The 1983 Solemn Declaration on European Union included a long list of actions to strengthen 'cultural cooperation'.[87] The EC's national ministers of culture started to meet regularly and, months after the Stuttgart declaration, decided to launch the European Capital of Culture programme.[88] During this period, heritage protection turned into a field of EC action and in 1984, the EP exercised its power to amend the budget and create a dedicated budget line.[89] The following year, the new Commission headed by Jacques Delors put culture high on its agenda.[90] There was now a separate Directorate-General, with an energetic Commissioner, Carlo Ripa di Meana, at the helm.[91] Finally, at a more general level, the publication of the 1985 White Paper on the completion of the Single Market by 1992 and the agreement reached with the Single European Act the following year gave market integration a lot of momentum. The objective of a common market for broadcasting was amongst the measures proposed in the White Paper.[92] In sum, by the mid-1980s, the EC had gained significant political, financial and administrative resources to develop its cultural policy. No longer did it need to cooperate with the CoE to justify its initiatives. Competition, hence, outpaced cooperation.

This rivalry was reinforced when the Commission proposed the ambitious 'Television without Frontiers' (TWF) Directive in April 1986, far superseding a first Green Paper from 1984, which had aimed mainly at deregulation, proposing an interventionist and protectionist instrument: a system of quotas for European audio-visual works.[93] Under this, 30% of the programming time of each broadcaster had to be reserved for audio-visual content produced in the EC, mainly to contain the growth of US productions. The EP and several member-states supported the Commission's plan, chiefly France and Italy as the major film producers in Europe. They had powerful allies within the Commission: the Italian Commissioner Ripa di Meana and above all President Delors, who actively supported the Directive during the final vote in the Commission.[94]

Other countries blocked the Directive. Its idea was to regulate media content in order to achieve cultural objectives, which went beyond the creation of a common market. The United Kingdom, Germany and Denmark refused the very idea of EC competence in culture, including broadcasting. Several small member-states joined this coalition, especially Ireland, Portugal, Belgium and the Netherlands. These countries had weak film industries and imported most of their programmes. European productions were significantly more expensive than American ones: European quotas would have dramatically increased their expenditures.[95] Finally, countries that were not members of the EC but members of the CoE, like Austria, Sweden and Switzerland, considered a Community-centred solution inappropriate for a wider European problem.[96] In response to the Commission's proposed Directive, the Austrian government suggested organizing the first CoE European Ministerial Conference on mass-media policy in Vienna by the end of 1986 in order to make progress towards a CoE Convention.[97] The opponents of a Directive within the EC actively supported Austria's initiative and a CoE solution to the problem. In the ad hoc Working Party established by the European Council, they brought forward three main reasons for their choice. Firstly, if the cultural dimension of broadcasting was to be taken into consideration, this had to be done in the framework of an international organization officially in charge of culture, that is, the CoE.[98] Secondly, a CoE Convention, unlike an EC Directive, was based on unanimity and less binding. In that sense, it left the member-states more room for manoeuver. In the case of an EC Directive, in contrast, member-states could be sued for non-compliance. A third reason came on top for Germany: a CoE-framed solution had the advantage of including the German-speaking neighbours Switzerland and Austria that were not part of the EC.[99]

While the Commission was therefore struggling to get its Directive adopted, the CoE Convention project made quick progress. At the Vienna conference in December 1986, the Ministers declared that the CoE, notably because of its geographical scope, was 'the most suitable institution for shaping a coherent mass media policy and for implementing such a policy'.[100] The Ministers agreed to create 'political instruments' and 'binding legal instruments' on transfrontier broadcasting, thus reacting to the EP's recurrent criticisms concerning the inefficiency of the CoE's regulations.

In the EC, the picture was very different. In 1987 and 1988, the divided European Council was unable to reach any agreement on the planned TWF Directive. Commission representatives started to fear that some countries wanted to abandon the project, considering it redundant in light of the CoE's initiative. In the EC negotiations, the Commission repeated its demand to give priority to its Directive and to assure the complementarity with the CoE's policy.[101] The Commission even tried to sabotage a meeting of the CoE's Ministers planned for April 1988 in Vienna to discuss the Convention project. It asked the EC member-states not to participate and unofficially urged the Austrian government to cancel the meeting, causing a stir amongst the representatives of the member-states in Brussels.[102] In July 1988, Ivo Schwartz, the Commission official who had drafted the Green Paper on the TWF, explained the situation to the German CDU federal committee for media policy: 'Let's not forget that the idea of the Convention came from the opponents of the creation of a common broadcasting market and is above all a manoeuvre to prevent or at least to delay the Directive.'[103] Transborder television thus became the field of a downright 'regulatory race' between the two organizations.[104]

However, the two competing projects also started to converge during 1988, not least due to the contacts between experts active in both organizations. These contacts were particularly useful to change the French government's position, initially in favour of an ambitious EC Directive and opposed to a less protectionist CoE Convention. At the time, Michel Lummaux was Vice-President of the CoE's SCMM and Bernard Blin was the official in charge of the negotiations on the CoE Convention in the French Foreign Ministry.[105]

Lummaux and Blin regularly informed their colleague Michel Berthod, member of the EC ad hoc experts committee on the TWF Directive, about the progress made within the CoE.[106] They argued that adoption of the CoE's project, while not entirely satisfactory for France, would be a good next step: 'It will not be possible to hold a maximalist position in Brussels for long. It could therefore be in our interest to reach first an agreement on minimal European regulation within the CoE, which would not exclude further progress at the Community level at a later stage.'[107]

Blin and his German counterpart discussed combining the two projects in the CoE's SCMM. Blin reported to his ministry that an agreement on the CoE Convention was probably the only way to lift the German veto on the EC Directive.[108] These discussions between experts eventually impacted on the negotiations on the member-states' representatives at the EC level, much to the regret of the European Commission. In September 1988, Delors wrote to the President of the Luxembourg Government, Jacques Santer: 'We observed that several member states try to replace certain aspects of the Commission's proposal by solutions established by experts meeting within the Council of Europe.'[109]

This manoeuvre was largely successful: in the end, the EC's European Council adapted its Directive largely along the lines of the CoE Convention on Transfrontier Television, which had been finalized in November 1988. It thus aimed at avoiding a chaotic situation in which the member-states of the CoE and the EC would have to comply with diverging regulations.[110] In December 1988, the European Council declared that it was 'important that the Community's efforts should be deployed in a manner consistent with the Council of Europe Convention' and asked the Commission to 'adapt the proposal [for the TWF Directive] in the light of the Council of Europe Convention'.[111] However, the stipulations of the Convention were less interventionist than the EC Directive. In contrast to the proposed EC Directive, the CoE Convention did not speak of quotas and instead recommended a vague 'majority proportion' of European works. Similarly, the text was more lenient on advertizing.[112] As the representative of the EP Culture Committee underlined, following the Convention on these points would be a way of watering down the most interventionist and protectionist elements of the Directive.[113] Despite the EP's attempts to reintroduce quotas, this 'soft' version of the Directive was eventually adopted on 3 October 1989.[114] The CoE's Convention had a further characteristic that was absent from the EC Directive: it could be opened to non-member countries, including the countries of the Eastern Bloc. The CoE in 1988 organized a symposium dedicated to cinema and television as a vector of exchange between East and West that brought together professionals and experts from both sides of the Iron Curtain.[115] In the following years, the CoE time and again recommended that European audio-visual policy should put special emphasis on East–West relations, both for CoE and EC programmes.[116] As during the 1970s, the CoE continued to see itself and culture as bridge-builders between East and West.

In the end, both organizations thus created regulatory frameworks. The fact that the EC Directive emulated the less binding instruments designed in the CoE could at first sight appear as a setback for the promoters of the supremacy of EC law. In the long run, however, adapting the CoE policy line proved beneficial for the EC. As predicted by the French officials mentioned above, the integration of the CoE's more consensual stipulations eventually allowed the supporters of an EC solution to 'save' the Directive and lay the foundation of an EC audio-visual policy. As the French Minister for European Affairs, Edith Cresson, declared after the European Council negotiations of April 1989: 'The compromise that we have reached is probably too timid. It represents however the starting point of a dynamic movement which will help us to save our culture and our film production.'[117] Immediately thereafter, the Commission started to formulate proposals for the development of what was now called a 'European audio-visual policy'.[118] The Treaty of Maastricht (art. 128) substantially enhanced the EC's cultural competences. On its basis, the Commission created a 'European audio-visual policy' unit, which played an active role in the GATT negotiations of 1993.[119] The official in charge of this unit considered that the 1989 TWF Directive constituted the 'legislative foundation for audio-visual regulation, which as *acquis communautaire* will contribute to strengthen the Europeans' position in the negotiations of the Uruguay Round'.[120] As a matter of fact, by the 1990s, the EC had become the main policy arena for discussing the European positions in the audio-visual sector both at the inner-European and global levels.[121] The CoE, in contrast, had become marginal.

Conclusion

Our analysis demonstrates the need to examine inter-organizational connections in order to explain the logics and dynamics underlying the emergence of an EC cultural policy, even if the bulk of the existing literature has ignored this factor. Its significance, shown here for one specific policy domain, has wide implications for the history of European integration more generally, as the introduction to this special issue demonstrates in more detail.[122] On questions of cultural heritage as well as audio-visual policies, the CoE took the lead, while the EC only stepped in at a later stage. The CoE functioned as a laboratory of ideas but also a springboard for EC initiatives. Given the CoE's pioneering role, the EC, in turn, had to justify its policies, and there were three main reasons why it eventually successfully challenged the CoE's superiority: its superior financial means; its legally more binding regulations; and the links between cultural policy and the market-integration project, to which the CoE had no equivalent.

Moreover, our analysis underlines the importance of going beyond a sheer focus on the two organizations – both of them have to be disaggregated further, but also placed into broader contexts. For the EC, for instance, the European Parliament and the Commission played important roles – hence, it is key to scrutinize the role of specific organs within an organization. Moreover, it is crucial to also transcend the scope of the CoE and the EC and examine transnational policy entrepreneurs and their networks as well as INGOs, all of which operated across several organizations and contexts. People such as Sandys, Premoli and Grégoire played an important role in connecting the various professional, institutional and political levels, and the same holds true for pressure groups such as Europa Nostra and other networks. Despite the increasing competition between the two organizations, sometimes instrumentalized by member-states opposed to an ambitious European cultural policy, individual transnational actors and INGOs represented channels for the circulation of policy ideas, especially from the CoE to the EC.

The actors who contributed to the emergence of the EC cultural policy were therefore very diverse in terms of professional and institutional positions, and shared no specific political affiliation. The geography of exchanges also varied according to the specific question at stake. In the case of heritage, the British and Italians played a particularly prominent role, while amongst the big EC and CoE member-states, the absence of France is striking.[123] On audio-visual policy, in contrast, French actors proved particularly active.

MULTIPLE CONNECTIONS IN EUROPEAN COOPERATION

Finally, while remaining a small policy field for the EC at the time, culture was highly contentious. For this reason, it has remained an ancillary policy in the EU to this day, while the CoE's activities have not gained much more momentum either. In the (late) Cold War context, cultural policy was deployed to challenge the East–West divide. In this case, the initiative lay mainly with the less politicized CoE. The Cold War first had to end – and the EC incrementally develop a cultural policy strongly inspired by the CoE – before the EC/EU managed to develop cultural-policy initiatives that truly served as bridge-builders to countries of the former East.

Notes

1. Shore, *Building Europe*, 44; Sassatelli, *Becoming Europeans*, 46.
2. For a typology of forms of interaction, see Patel, 'Provincialising European Union'.
3. CoE, *The Council of Europe and Cultural Heritage*, 8.
4. See, for example, Brunner, 'Le Conseil de l'Europe', 29–46; Calligaro, 'From "European Cultural Heritage"'.
5. See, as the most recent example, many of the contributions in Falser and Lipp, eds., *A Future for Our Past*.
6. See, for example, Berghahn, *America and the Intellectual Cold Wars*.
7. EC, *Treaty Establishing the European Economic Community*, Article 36.
8. Calligaro, *Negotiating Europe*, 19–25.
9. Patel, 'Introduction'.
10. See on differences in governance mechanisms and their consequences for this field Witte, 'Cultural Linkages'.
11. As examples for this concern, see, for example, from the British perspective FCO 41/1091, The National Archives of the UK (TNA) and from the German perspective Auswärtiges Amt, Vermerk IA1, 23 September 1971, B 21/102271, Politisches Archiv des Auswärtigen Amtes, Berlin (PAAA); avoiding overlap as a dimension in EC–CoE debates, see CoE, Committee of Ministers, Reports by the Commission of EEC for 1973 and 1974, 9 April 1975, B 21/111682, PAAA.
12. CoE, *Statute of the Council of Europe* (1949), see online http://conventions.coe.int/Treaty/en/treaties/Word/001.doc (last accessed December 1, 2015); on the wider context, see, for example, Trunk, *Europa*, 64–81.
13. Brunner, 'Le Conseil de l'Europe'.
14. CoE, European Cultural Convention (1954), see http://conventions.coe.int/Treaty/EN/Treaties/Html/018.htm (last accessed December 1, 2015); on the convention, also see Calligaro, *Negotiating Europe*, 82–3.
15. See CoE, Consultative Assembly, *Document 354* (1955).
16. CoE, Consultative Assembly, *Document 1502* (1962) (own translation from French).
17. Hammer, EEC Commission, Rapport de Mission, 7 June 1962, BAC 118/1986, N. 1447, Historical Archives of the European Union, Florence (HAEU) (own translation from French); this situation did not improve much over the next years, see, for example, CoE, CCC, *Projet de programme pour 1968* (CCC (68) 9/III), BAC 118/1986, N. 1449, HAEU.
18. CoE, Consultative Assembly/ ECSC, Common Assembly, *Joint Meeting*, 22 June 1953; CoE, Consultative Assembly, EC, European Parliamentary Assembly, *Sixth Joint Meeting*, 17 January 1959; on other levels of contact see, for example, EC, European Council, Note, 3 October 1973, EN 457, HAEU.
19. See, for example, Letter Staderini, Euratom, to Benvenuti, CoE, 19 February 1960, BAC 118/1986, N. 1447, HAEU.
20. See, for example, EC, EP, *Rapport intérimaire*; EP, Committee on Research and Culture, *Minutes*, 14 September 1966, PEO-18768, HAEU; BAC 3/1978–1126, HAEU. However, there were no formalized links between the EC and UNESCO on these issues, while there were

MULTIPLE CONNECTIONS IN EUROPEAN COOPERATION

joint working groups in other fields, see, for example, UNESCO, Note Maheu, 6 March 1973, UDC No. 002A8CEC, UNESCO Archives, Paris; also see UNESCO, *Report of the Director-General*, 28.

21. See, with a summary of this cooperation, Letter Toncic-Sorinj, CoE, to Malfatti, EC, 13 October 1971, BAC 3/1978, 1263, HAEU; see, for example, also Curtis, CoE to President of Euratom, 8 February 1962, BAC 118/1986, N. 1447, HAEU; Letter Sforza, CoE, to Malfatti, EC, 5 July 1971, BAC 3/1978, 1263, HAEU.

22. CoE, Parliamentary Assembly, *Recommendation 301* (1961).

23. Brossat, *La culture européenne*, 320–1.

24. UNESCO, Executive Board, *Resolutions and Decisions*, 30 September 1968.

25. Cameron and Rössler, *Many Voices*, 1–26.

26. For details, see B 30/69, PAAA; UNESCO, *Conférence intergouvernementale*; UDC No. 008(4) A06'72', UNESCO Archives.

27. CoE, Consultative Assembly, *Recommendation 589* (1970); CoE, Committee of Ministers, *Document 2880* (1971); also see CoE, Consultative Assembly, 21st Ordinary Session, 22–30 January 1970, *Official Report of Debates*, 783–98; now also Lipp and Falser, 'Thresholds of Monument Awareness', 21–60.

28. See, for example, CoE, Parliamentary Assembly, *Document 2985* (1977).

29. CoE, Consultative Assembly, *Recommendation 365* (1963); also see CoE, *The Council of Europe and Cultural Heritage*, 1–148 on other resolutions at the time as well as Fürniß, 'Die Kampagne'.

30. CoE, Consultative Assembly, *Report, Document 2714* (1970).

31. Letter Blumenfeld, CoE, to Scheel, German Foreign Minister, 7 December 1972, B 4/52, PAAA (own translation from German); see, for example, also German Foreign Ministry, Note, 16 March 1970, B 90/1186, PAAA.

32. CoE, EAHY 1975, *European Programme of Pilot Projects: Launching Conference, Zürich, 4–7 July 1973* (Strasbourg: CoE, 1973) in AR 1/76, TNA; *Aims, Organisation & Activities* (Strasbourg: CoE, 1973) in *ibid*; also see F. Notter, 'Premier aperçu de l'Année européenne du patrimoine architectural 1975 en Suisse', *Patrimoine* 68 (1973): 20–5.

33. UNESCO, the Commission and several INGOs were represented in the preparatory committee, however. UNESCO's Director-General even gave a speech in Zurich: Address Maheu, 4 July 1973, DG/73/11, UNESCO Archives, and UDC, No. 069:72A8CE, *ibid*.

34. EC, EP, *Document 54* (1974); also see 'Baroness Elles', in: *Telegraph*, 29 October 2009.

35. Grégoire, *Vers une Europe*, 205–6; Calligaro, *Negotiating Europe*, 84–5.

36. EC, EP, *Debates of the EP*, 13–15 May 1974, 13–4; also see C 62/5, 30 May 1974.

37. *Official Journal of the EC* (OJ), 75/65/EEC.

38. In 1972, the Club of Rome's *Limits to Growth* report provoked a heated debate. The same year the United Nations contributed to a global discussion of the issue by organizing an international conference on 'human environment' in Stockholm. As another initiative, UNESCO adopted its Convention for the Protection of the World Cultural and Natural Heritage; for the EC's reasons to engage in this field at the time, also see Patel, 'Introduction'; Staiger, 'The European Capitals'.

39. EC, European Commission, *Memorandum 'Pour une action communautaire dans le domaine de la culture'*, 11 September 1972, EN 664, HAEU, and EC, Letter Mercereau to Noël, 16 October 1972, *ibid*.

40. 'Document on European Identity' (1973), published in Hill and Smith, eds., *European Foreign Policy*, 94.

41. Calligaro, 'European Cultural Heritage'.

42. EC, EP, *Document 73* (1973); on his role of linking the two forums, also see CoE, Parliamentary Assembly, *Document 421* (1979).

43. On this dimension of CoE/EC cultural policy-making during the 1970s and 1980s, see also Interview with Olaf Schwencke, Berlin, 1 July 2015; another indication is the fact that many recommendations in the Consultative Assembly were accepted unanimously.

MULTIPLE CONNECTIONS IN EUROPEAN COOPERATION

44. EC, EP, *Debates of the EP, Report of the Proceedings,* 13–15 May 1974, *OJ* 13–4; also see C 62/5, 30 May 1974.

45. CoE, Consultative Assembly, *Document* 2714 (1970).

46. Premoli and Elles were both present at the 20th joint meeting of the CoE's Consultative Assembly and the EP in 1973, as a space of direct CoE–EC interaction Consultative Assembly of the CoE/EP, *20th Joint Meeting, Attendance List,* 14 November 1973, FCO 41/1094, TNA.

47. See, for example, CoE, Consultative Assembly, *Recommendation 532* (1972); CoE, Consultative Assembly, *Recommendation 681* (1972); CoE, Consultative Assembly, *Document 3183* (1972); CoE, Parliamentary Assembly, *Document 3522* (1975).

48. CoE, Consultative Assembly, *Recommendation 589* (1970); CoE, Consultative Assembly, *Recommendation 681* (1972); CoE, Committee of Ministers, *Document 198* (1970); also see Europa Nostra, London Conference: Resolutions, 6–8 July 1972, UDC No. 327.394A01CE06'68', UNESCO Archives.

49. Interview with Schwencke.

50. Very clearly in the statement by the CCC's chairman: CoE, Consultative Assembly, 14th Sitting, 23 September 1973, 446. Technically, Sandys was only a substitute at the Assembly at the time, but he had served as a Representative from 1965 to 1972.

51. Letter Evans, Treasury, to Warburton, DOE, 11 December 1972, T 227/4131, TNA, also see Letter Rippon, DOE, to Patterson, FCO, 24 July 1974, FCO 13/763, TNA; on the Civic Trust, see Aitchison, MacLeod and Shaw, *Leisure and Tourism,* 146–8; on the EAHY in the UK, see also the uncritical description in Burman and Rodwell, 'The Contribution', 262–75.

52. House of Lords, vol. 370, *Lords Sitting of 12 May 1976,* where Sandys also mentions his discussion with Ortoli; on that, also see CoE, Parliamentary Assembly, 28th Ordinary Session, 3–7 May 1976, *Orders of the Day: Minutes of Proceedings, Sitting 6 May 1976.* Strasbourg: CoE, 1976, 45–7; on his pleas to strengthen the links to the EC, see, for example, also CoE, Parliamentary Assembly, 22–29 January 1975, vol. VII, *Document 3522* (1975).

53. On the wider context, see Mandler, *Fall,* 388–418.

54. Staiger, 'The European Capitals', 19–38.

55. CoE, Consultative Assembly, 14th Sitting, 23 September 1973, 446.

56. CoE, Consultative Assembly Assembly, *Document 3017* (1971); CoE, Consultative Assembly, *Recommendation 704* (1973), see also, for example, CoE, Parliamentary Assembly, *Recommendation 607* (1975); CoE, Parliamentary Assembly, *Recommendation 940* (1982).

57. Letter Toncic-Sorinj to Sandys, 24 July 1972, GBR/0014/DSND, 9/14, Churchill Archives Centre (CAC), Cambridge; this has to be seen in the context of Toncic's reform plans for the CoE, see, for example, Slatcher, FCO to Steward, FCO, 24 August 1971, FCO 13/471, TNA; more generally, FCO 41/1091 & 1092, TNA.

58. CoE, Consultative Assembly, 23 September 1973, 446; also see CoE, Parliamentary Assembly, 30 September 1974.

59. CoE, Parliamentary Assembly, *Document 4214* (1979); UDC No. 069:72A8CE/06, UNESCO Archives.

60. EC, European Council, *Aide Mémoire,* 10 October 1973, FCO 41/1095, TNA.

61. EPC, *Meeting of Directors of Cultural Affairs,* 27 Mai 1974, FCO 13/763, TNA; on Germany: German Permanent Representation, Brussels, to German Foreign Ministry, 11 October 1976, B 90/1237, PAAA.

62. EC, Leo Tindemans, *Report on European Union, Bulletin of the European Communities,* Supplement 1/76, 12; in general, also see Calligaro, *Negotiating Europe,* 82–7.

63. TNA, AR 1/76, CoE, EAHY 1975, *Aims, Organisation & Activities* (Strasbourg: CoE, 1973); Except Discussion CoE, Committee of Ministers, 1973, B 21/1123186, PAAA.

64. Nicolaus Sombart, 'Paradigma Europarat': Speech CoE March 1975, in NL 405/130 (Nicolaus Sombart), Staatsbibliothek zu Berlin (SBB); on the CoE as club of democracies, see, for example, Nicolaus Sombart, 'Die Aktualität der Europäischen Kulturkonvention': Speech CoE July 1982, in NL 405/148.

65. House of Lords, vol. 370, *Lords Sitting of 12 May 1976*; see, for example, also CoE, Parliamentary Assembly, 26th Ordinary Session, 22–29 January 1975, vol. VII, *Document 3522*; and the contributions in Falser and Lipp, eds., *A Future for Our Past,* 349–99.

MULTIPLE CONNECTIONS IN EUROPEAN COOPERATION

66. Even if they also saw the Cold War relevance of cultural policy, see, for example, TNA, FCO 13/763, Italian Foreign Ministry, Circular Letter, 23 December 1975.
67. On UNESCO's role in this and on the pan-European dimension of the 1972 Helsinki conference, see UDC No. 008A10/53(4)5; UDC No. 008(4)A06'72' and UDC, No. 069:72A8CE, all in UNESCO Archives.
68. Brunner, 'Le Conseil de l'Europe', 44; on the CoE more generally during this period, see Wassenberg, *Histoire*, 217–301.
69. EC, European Commission, COM(77)560 final, 2 December 1977. *Bulletin of the European Communities*, Supplement 6/77 and Grégoire, *Vers une Europe,* 211.
70. See, for example, EC, EP, *Motion for a resolution presented by Mr. Beyer de Ryke on the necessity of an intervention aiming at the protection of the site and monuments of the Acropolis in Athens,* 1 October 1981, Doc 1–557/81.
71. Staiger, 'The European Capitals'; Smith, 'The Evolution', 869–95.
72. EC, European Commission, '*Stronger Community Action*'.
73. CoE, Parliamentary Assembly, *Recommendation 940* (1982); also see the debate in CoE, Parliamentary Assembly, *Document 4868* (1982).
74. CoE, Committee of Ministers, CM(58)135; CoE, Committee of Ministers, CCC/Ad hoc(62).
75. CoE, Committee of Ministers, CM (62)113, 21–2.
76. CoE, Parliamentary Assembly, *Recommendation 834* (1978).
77. CoE, Parliamentary Assembly, *Working papers,* 7–11 May 1979.
78. CoE, Parliamentary Assembly, *Recommendation 926* (1981); CoE, Committee of Ministers, 70th Session, 29 April 1982, *Droits de propriété intellectuelle et distribution par câble de programmes de télévision, Conseil de l'Europe,* Dossiers sur les Mass Media, n° 5–1983.
79. EC, EP, Working Documents 1981–82, Document 1–1013/81, 23 February 1982.
80. *Ibid.*
81. EC, European Commission, COM(83)229 final, Brussels, 25 May 1983, Annex 6, 81–4.
82. EC, EP, COM(84)300 final. Working Documents 1985–86, Document A2–75/85, 5 July 1985; more generally on this point: Witte and Thies, 'Why Choose Europe'.
83. *Ibid.*
84. CoE, Parliamentary Assembly, *36th Ordinary Session*, Official Report, *20th Sitting,* 3 October 1984, Speech Oreja, 582.
85. EC, European Commission, Émile Noël, Note de Dossier, 26 October 1984, Entretien avec Monsieur Oreja, Secrétraire Général du Conseil de l'Europe, 9 October 1984 (own translation from French), EN 874, HAEU.
86. CoE, Committee of Ministers, *Resolution (85)5,* Appendix II, 1985, 20.
87. EC, European Council, *Solemn Declaration on European Union,* Stuttgart, 19 June 1983, *Bulletin of the European Communities*, 6/1983, 24–9.
88. See Patel, *Cultural Politics.*
89. Calligaro, *Negotiating Europe,* 88.
90. EC, European Commission, *Programme of the Commission for 1985.* Statement by Jacques Delors, President of the Commission, to the EP, Strasbourg, 12 March 1985. *Bulletin of the European Communities*, Supplement 4/85, 52.
91. Calligaro, 'Florence', 95–113.
92. EC, European Commission, COM/85/0310 final, points 115–17.
93. EC, European Commission, COM(84)300 final/Part 2, 14 June 1984; EC, European Commission, COM(86)146 final, *Bulletin of the European Communities*, Supplement 5/86.
94. Agence Europe n° 2934, 20 March 1986.
95. EC, European Council, Ad hoc Working Party on Economic Questions (broadcasting) on 2, 19 and 20 June 1986, 31 October 1986, 14 and 15 May 1987, CM2 CEE, CEEA – 1.858.17, ACEU.
96. CoE, Steering Committee on the Mass Media, *Rapport Comité Directeur sur les moyens de communication de masse relatif à l'audiovisuel et au cinema,* 3 May 1986, 19920214/19, ANF.
97. CoE, Secretariat General, Note du Secrétariat Général 'Préparation de la première conférence ministérielle sur la politique des communications de masse' (Vienne, 9–10 décembre 1986), 19920214/19, ANF.

MULTIPLE CONNECTIONS IN EUROPEAN COOPERATION

98. EC, European Council, Ad hoc Working Party on Economic Questions (broadcasting) on 26 November 1986, CM2 CEE, CEEA – 1.858.17, ACEU.

99. EC, European Council, Ad hoc Working Party on Economic Questions (broadcasting) on 21 October 1987, CM2 CEE, CEEA – 1.858.17, ACEU.

100. CoE, Committee of Ministers, CM(86) 255, 11.

101. EC, European Council, Permanent Representatives Committee, *Summary Record of the 1318th Meeting Held in Brussels on 10, 11, 12 and 13 November 1987*, CM2 CEE, CEEA – 1.858.17, ACEU; Agence Europe, n° 4708, 26 January 1988, 9.

102. Telex of François Scheer, French Representative at the COREPER, to the French Minister of Foreign Affairs, 'COREPER du 20 janvier 1988', 21 January 1988, 19900634/206, SGCI 10494, ANF.

103. Schwartz, 'Fernsehen', here 8 (own translation from German).

104. Krebber, *Europeanisation*, 104.

105. See, for example, 'Réunion informelle des ministres européens chargés de la politique des communications de masse, Vienne, 12–13/04/88: programme de la réunion, délégation française', 19920214/21, ANF; 'Radiodiffusion (Télévision sans frontière) et élaboration de directives', File 521. 5 R, 19900634/206, SGCI 10494, ANF.

106. See, for example, Michel Lummaux, 'Note à l'attention de Monsieur Berthod. Réunion jointe du Comité Directeur sur les moyens de communication de masse, 25 février 1988, Strasbourg', 3 March 1988; Bernard Blin, 'Note sur la réunion informelle des ministres européens sur la politique des communications de masse. Vienne 12–13 avril 1988. Projet de Convention européenne', 14 April 1988; Telex of Bernard Blin to Michel Berthod, 'Conseil de l'Europe, 421ème réunion des délégués des ministres. Projet de Convention européenne sur la télévision transfrontière, 7 novembre 1988, Strasbourg', 8 November 1988, 19920214/21, ANF.

107. Bernard Blin, 'Note sur la réunion informelle des ministres européens sur la politique des communications de masse. Vienne 12–13 avril 1988. Projet de Convention européenne', 14 April 1988, 19920214/21, ANF. The French interministerial Secretariat for European Affairs (SGCI) almost literally reproduced Blin's analysis in a note of July 1988 addressed to Berthod, 'Directive communautaire sur la radiodiffusion et Convention du Conseil de l'Europe sur le même thème', 6 juillet 1988. 19900634/206, SGCI 10494, ANF.

108. Telex of Bernard Blin to Michel Berthod, 'Projet de Convention relatif à la télévision sans frontière'. 16 September 1988, 19920214/22, ANF.

109. Letter of Jacques Delors to Jacques Santer, 10 September 1988, 19900634/206, SGCI 10494, ANF.

110. Krebber, *Europeanisation*, 10.

111. EC, European Council, *Conclusions of the European Council of Rhodes* (2–3 December 1988), *Bulletin of the European Communities*, 12/1988, 10.

112. CoE, Treaty n°132, 5 May 1989.

113. EC, EP, *Debates of the EP*, *Report of the Proceedings*, 22–26 May 1989, OJ/C 158, 139.

114. EC, European Council, OJ L 298, 17 October 1989, 23–30.

115. CoE, Parliamentary Assembly, Committee On Culture And Education, 0AS/Cult (40) 45.

116. CoE, Parliamentary Assembly, 40th Session, *Recommendation 1098 (1989) on the East-West audio-visual co-operation*, 2 February 1989.

117. *Le Monde*, 15 April 1989, 2.

118. EC, European Commission, Note d'information de M. Dondelinger, 'La politique audiovisuelle entre Rhodes et Strasbourg. Résultats et perspectives (communication de M. Dondelinger en accord avec M. Pandolfi et M. Bangemann)', SEC(89)2017, 23 November 1989, FDE 286, HAEU; 'Un an de politique audiovisuelle communautaire. Bilan et perspectives pour l'avenir, communication de M. Dondelinger en accord avec les membres du groupe Audiovisuel', SEC(91)52, 31 January 1991, *ibid*.

119. Humphreys, 'EU Audiovisual Policy', 239.

120. Baer, 'L'exception culturelle', 5 (own translation from French).

121. Humphreys, 'EU Audiovisual Policy', 239.

122. Kaiser and Patel, 'Multiple Connections in European Cooperation'.
123. Simultaneously, France was very active on related issues in UNESCO, see UNESCO, Note de La Rochefoucauld to Pouchpa Dass, 1 February 1974, UDC No. 008A10/53(4)5, UNESCO Archives.

Disclosure statement

No potential conflict of interest was reported by the authors.

Bibliography

Archival material
Archives of the Council of the European Union, Brussels (ACEU)
Archives Nationales Françaises, Pierrefitte-sur-Seine (ANF)
Churchill Archives Centre, Cambridge (CAC)
Historical Archives of the European Union, Florence (HAEU)
Politisches Archiv des Auswärtigen Amtes, Berlin (PAAA)
Staatsbibliothek zu Berlin (SBB)
The National Archives of the UK, London (TNA)
UNESCO Archives, Paris, UDC

Grey literature
CoE, *European Cultural Convention* (1954) http://conventions.coe.int/Treaty/EN/Treaties/Html/018. htm
CoE, *European Convention on Transfrontier Television, Treaty Open for Signature by the Member States and by the Other States Parties to the European Cultural Convention and by the European Union*, Strasbourg, 5 May 1989, Treaty n°132.
CoE, *The Council of Europe and Cultural Heritage, 1954–2000*. Strasbourg: CoE, 2001.

MULTIPLE CONNECTIONS IN EUROPEAN COOPERATION

CoE, Committee of Ministers, *Agreement Concerning Programme Exchanges by Means of Television Films*, 1958, CM(58)135.

CoE, Committee of Ministers, *Resolution of the Council for Cultural Cooperation*, 1962, Ad hoc conference of film and television experts. CCC/Ad hoc(62).

CoE, Committee of Ministers, *Report of the Second Session of the Council for Cultural Co-operation*, 16 July 1962, CM (62)113.

CoE, Committee of Ministers, *Document 198* (1970).

CoE, Committee of Ministers, *Document 2880* (1971).

CoE, Committee of Ministers, *Reports by the Commission of EEC for 1973 and 1974*, 9 April 1975.

CoE, Committee of Ministers, 70th Session, 29 April 1982, *Droits de propriété intellectuelle et distribution par câble de programmes de télévision, Conseil de l'Europe*, Dossiers sur les Mass Media, n° 5 (1983).

CoE, Committee of Ministers, *Resolution (85)5, Co-operation between the Council of Europe and the European Community, Report by the Secretary General*, Appendix II. 1985.

CoE, Committee of Ministers, *Conclusions of the First European Ministerial Conference on Mass Media Policy* (Vienna, 9 and 10 December 1986), CM(86) 255.

CoE, Consultative Assembly/ECSC, Common Assembly, *Joint Meeting, Official Report of the Debate*, 22 June 1953.

CoE, Consultative Assembly, *Document 354* (1955).

CoE, Consultative Assembly, EC, European Parliamentary Assembly, *Sixth Joint Meeting*, 17 January 1959.

CoE, Consultative Assembly, *Recommendation 301* (1961).

CoE, Consultative Assembly, *Rapport Kraft sur la situation nouvelle en matière de coopération culturelle européenne, Document 1502* (1962).

CoE, Consultative Assembly, *Recommendation 365* (1963).

CoE, Consultative Assembly, *Recommendation 589* (1970).

CoE, Consultative Assembly, 21st Ordinary Session, 22–30 January 1970, *Official Report of Debates*, 783–98.

CoE, Consultative Assembly, *Report by Augusto Premoli, "Conference of Ministers Chiefly Responsible for the Preservation and Rehabilitation of Groups and Areas of Buildings of Historical or Artistic Interest", Document 2714* (1970).

CoE, Consultative Assembly, *Recommendation 589* (1970).

CoE, Consultative Assembly, 23rd Session, 12th Sitting, *Document 3017* (1971).

CoE, Consultative Assembly, *Recommendation 532* (1972).

CoE, Consultative Assembly, *Recommendation 681* (1972).

CoE, Consultative Assembly, *Document 3183* (1972).

CoE, Consultative Assembly, 14th Sitting, 23 September 1973.

CoE, Consultative Assembly, *Recommendation 704* (1973).

CoE, Parliamentary Assembly, 26th Ordinary Session, 22–29 January 1975, vol. VII, *Document 3522* (1975).

CoE, Parliamentary Assembly, *Document 3522* (1975).

CoE, Parliamentary Assembly, *Recommendation 607* (1975).

CoE, Parliamentary Assembly, 26th Ordinary Session, 22–29 January 1975, vol. VII, *Document 3522.*

CoE, Parliamentary Assembly, *Information Report: Document 2985* (1977).

CoE, Parliamentary Assembly, 28th Ordinary Session, 3–7 May 1976, *Orders of the Day: Minutes of Proceedings, Sitting 6 May 1976.* Strasbourg: CoE, 1976.

CoE, Parliamentary Assembly, *Recommendation 834* (1978), *Threats to the Freedom of the Press and Television*, 28 April 1978.

CoE, Parliamentary Assembly, *Working papers, "The Cinema and the State."* 31st ordinary session, 7–11 May 1979.

CoE, Parliamentary Assembly, *Document 421* (1979).

CoE, Parliamentary Assembly, *Report on European Cultural Co-operation, Document 4214* (1979).

MULTIPLE CONNECTIONS IN EUROPEAN COOPERATION

CoE, Parliamentary Assembly, 17th Sitting, *Recommendation 926* (1981) *on questions raised by cable and television and by direct satellite broadcasts*, Doc. 4756, Report of the Legal Affairs Committee, 7 October 1981.

CoE, Parliamentary Assembly, *Recommendation 940* (1982).

CoE, Parliamentary Assembly, 34th Ordinary Session, 3rd sitting, 27 April 1982, *Document 4868.*

CoE, Parliamentary Assembly, *Official Report,* 36th Ordinary Session, 20th Sitting, 3 October 1984, Speech Oreja, 582.

CoE, Parliamentary Assembly, Committee On Culture And Education, *Colloque on "Cinema and Television: The Audio-Visual Field as a Vector of Communication between Eastern and Western Europe",* (Orvieto, Italy, 26–28 October 1988), 9 January 1989, 0AS/Cult (40) 45.

CoE, Parliamentary Assembly, 40th Session, Third part, *Recommendation 1098 (1989) on the East-West audio-visual co-operation,* 2 February 1989.

EC, *Treaty Establishing the European Economic Community,* Article 36.

EC, European Commission, *Memorandum "Pour une action communautaire dans le domaine de la culture",* 11 September 1972.

EC, European Commission, *Communication to the Council on the Community Action in the Cultural Sector.* 22 November 1977. COM(77)560 final, 2 December 1977. *Bulletin of the European Communities,* Supplement 6/77.

EC, European Commission, *"Stronger Community Action in the Cultural Sector." Communication from the Commission to the Council and the Parliament,* 12 October 1982, *Bulletin of the European Communities,* Supplement 6/82.

EC, European Commission, *Interim Report "Realities and Tendencies in European Television: Perspectives and Options",* COM(83)229 final, Brussels, 25 May 1983, Annex 6.

EC, European Commission, *Programme of the Commission for 1985.* Statement by Jacques Delors, President of the Commission, to the EP, Strasbourg, 12 March 1985. *Bulletin of the European Communities,* Supplement 4/85, 52.

EC, European Commission, *Television without Frontiers: Green Paper on the Establishment of the Common Market for Broadcasting, especially by Satellite and Cable.* COM(84)300 final/Part 2, 14 June 1984.

EC, European Commission, *Completing the Internal Market: White Paper from the Commission to the European Council,* Milan, 28–29 June 1985, COM/85/0310 final.

EC, European Commission, *Proposal for a Council Directive on the Coordination of Certain Provisions Laid Down by Law, Regulation or Administrative Action in Member States Concerning the Pursuit of Broadcasting Activities,* COM(86)146 final, *Bulletin of the European Communities,* Supplement 5/86.

EC, European Council, *Solemn Declaration on European Union,* Stuttgart, 19 June 1983, *Bulletin of the European Communities,* 6/1983, 24–29.

EC, European Council, *Conclusions of the European Council of Rhodes* (2–3 December 1988), *Bulletin of the European Communities,* 12/1988.

EC, European Council, *Directive 89/552/EEC of 3 October 1989 on the Coordination of Certain Provisions Laid down by Law, Regulation or Administrative Action in Member States Concerning the Pursuit of Television Broadcasting Activities,* OJ L 298, 17 October 1989, 23–30.

EC, EP, *Rapport intérimaire sur les problèmes de coopération culturelle entre les États membres de la Communauté européenne.* Brussels: European Communities, 1963.

EC, EP, *Report drafted by Lady Elles, 3 May 1974, Document 54* (1974).

EC, EP, *Debates of the EP, Report of the Proceedings,* 13–15 May 1974.

EC, EP, *Motion for a Resolution submitted by Mr Premoli on Behalf of the Liberal and Allies Group on Measures, Document 73* (1973).

EC, EP, *Report drafted by W. Hahn on behalf of the Committee on Youth, Culture, Education, Information and Sport on radio and television broadcasting in the European Community.* Working Documents 1981–82, Document 1–1013/81, 23 February 1982.

EC, EP, *Report drafted by W. Hahn on behalf of the Committee on Youth, Culture, Education, Information and Sport on a framework for a European media policy based on the Commission's Green Paper on the establishment of the common market for broadcasting, especially by satellite and cable,* COM(84)300 final. Working Documents 1985–86, Document A2–75/85, 5 July 1985.

MULTIPLE CONNECTIONS IN EUROPEAN COOPERATION

EC, EP, *Debates of the EP, Report of the Proceedings*, 22–26 May 1989, OJ/C 158, 139.

House of Lords, vol. 370, *Lords Sitting of 12 May 1976*.

UNESCO, Executive Board, *Resolutions and Decisions*, 79th Session, 30 September 1968.

UNESCO, *Report of the Director-General on the Activities of the Organization, 1972*. Paris: UNESCO, 1973.

UNESCO, *Conférence intergouvernementale sur les politiques culturelles en Europe, Helsinki, Rapport final*, 19–28 June 1972. Paris: UNESCO, 1972.

Newspaper articles

Le Monde, 15 April 1989, 2.

"Baroness Elles." In *Telegraph*, 29 October 2009.

Secondary literature

Aitchison, Cara, Nicola E. MacLeod, and Stephen J. Shaw. *Leisure and Tourism: Social and Cultural Geographies*. London: Routledge, 2000.

Baer, Jean-Michel. "L'exception culturelle. Une règle en quête de contenus [The Cultural Exception: A Rule in Search of Content]", *En Temps Réel*, 11 (2003).

Berghahn, Volker. *America and the Intellectual Cold Wars in Europe: Shepard Stone Between. Philanthropy, Academy, and Diplomacy*. Princeton: Princeton University Press, 2002.

Brossat, Caroline. *La culture européenne: définitions et enjeux* [European Culture: Definitions and Challenges]. Brussels: Bruylant, 1999.

Brunner, Joséphine. "Le Conseil de l'Europe à la recherche d'une politique culturelle (1949–1968) [The Council of Europe in Search of a Cultural Policy (1949–1968)]." In *Les lucarnes de l'Europe. Télévisions, cultures, identités, 1945–2005* [Broadcasting Europe: Televisions, Cultures and Identities,1945–2005]. edited by Marie-Françoise Lévy and Marie-Noële Sicard, 29–46. Paris: Publications de la Sorbonne, 2008.

Burman, Peter, and Dennis Rodwell. "The Contribution of the United Kingdom to European Architectural Heritage Year 1975." In *A Future for Our Past: The 40th Anniversary of European Architectural Heritage Year (1975–2015)*, edited by Michael Falser and Wilfried Lipp, 262–275. Berlin: Henrik Bäßler Verlag, 2015.

Calligaro, Oriane. "Florence European Capital of Culture 1986 and the Legitimization of an EEC Cultural Policy." In *The Cultural Politics of Europe: European Capitals of Culture and European Union since the 1980s*, edited by Kiran Klaus Patel, 95–113. London: Routledge, 2013.

Calligaro, Oriane. "From 'European Cultural Heritage' to 'Cultural Diversity'? The Changing Concepts of European Cultural Policy." *Politique Européenne* 45 (2014): 60–85.

Calligaro, Oriane. *Negotiating Europe: EU Promotion of Europeanness since the 1950s*. New York: Palgrave Macmillan, 2013.

Cameron, Christina, and Mechtild Rössler. *Many Voices, One Vision: The Early Years of the World Heritage Convention*. Farnham: Ashgate, 2013.

Falser, Michael, and Wilfried Lipp, eds. *A Future for Our Past: The 40th Anniversary of European Architectural Heritage Year (1975–2015)*. Berlin: Henrik Bäßler Verlag, 2015.

Falser, Michael, and Wilfried Lipp. "Thresholds of Monument Awareness in the Mirror of the European Architectural Heritage Year 1975: An Introduction." In *A Future for Our Past: The 40th Anniversary of European Architectural Heritage Year (1975–2015)*, edited by Michael Falser and Wilfried Lipp, 21–60. Berlin: Henrik Bäßler Verlag, 2015.

Fürniß, Maren. "Die Kampagne des Europarats für das europäische Denkmalschutzjahr 1975— Entstehungsgeschichte, Ziele und Umsetzung [The Council of Europe's Campaign for the 1975 European Year of Architectural Heritage? Origins, Goals and Implementation]." In *A Future for Our Past: The 40th Anniversary of European Architectural Heritage Year (1975–2015)*, edited by Michael Falser and Wilfried Lipp, 73–85. Berlin: Henrik Bäßler Verlag, 2015.

Grégoire, Robert. *Vers une Europe de la Culture* [Towards a Europe of Culture]. Paris: L'Harmattan, 2000.

Hill, Christopher, and Karen E. Smith, eds. *European Foreign Policy: Key Documents*. New York: Routledge, 2000.

Humphreys, Peter. "EU Audiovisual Policy, Cultural Diversity and the Future of Public Service Broadcasting." In *Mediating Europe: New Media, Mass Communications and the European Public Sphere*, edited by Jackie Harrison and Bridgette Wessels, 226–266. New York: Berghahn, 2008.

Kaiser, Wolfram, and Kiran Klaus Patel. "Multiple Connections in European Cooperation: International Organizations, Policy Ideas, Practices and Transfers 1967–1992." *European Review of History* 24, no. 3 (2017): 337–357.

Krebber, Daniel. *Europeanisation of Regulatory Television Policy: The Decision-Making Process of the Television Without Frontiers Directives from 1989 and 1997*. Baden-Baden: Nomos, 2002.

Mandler, Peter. *The Fall and Rise of the Stately Home*. New Haven, CT: Yale University Press, 1997.

Notter, F. "Premier aperçu de l'Année européenne du patrimoine architectural 1975 en Suisse [First Preview of the 1975 European Year of Architectural Heritage in Switzerland]." *Patrimoine* 68, no. 1973 (1975): 20–25.

Patel, Kiran Klaus. "Introduction." In *The Cultural Politics of Europe: European Capitals of Culture and European Union since the 1980s*, edited by Kiran Klaus Patel, 1–15. London: Routledge, 2013.

Patel, Kiran Klaus. "Provincialising European Union: Co-operation and Integration in Europe in a Historical Perspective." *Contemporary European History* 22 (2013): 649–673.

Sassatelli, Monica. *Becoming Europeans: Cultural Identity and Cultural Politics*. Houndmills: Palgrave, 2009.

Schwartz, Ivo. "Fernsehen ohne Grenzen: Zur Effektivität und zum Verhältnis von EG-Richtline und Europarats-Konvention [Television without Frontiers: Efficiency and the Relationship between the EC Directive and the Council of Europe Convention]." *Europarecht* 24, no. 1 (1989): 1–12.

Shore, Cris. *Building Europe: The Cultural Politics of European Integration*. London: Routledge, 2000.

Smith, Rachael Craufurd. "The Evolution of Cultural Policy in the European Union." In *The Evolution of EU Law*, edited by Paul Craig and Gráinne de Búrca, 869–895. Oxford: Oxford University Press, 2011.

Staiger, Uta. "The European Capitals of Culture in Context: Cultural Policy and the European Integration Process." In *The Cultural Politics of Europe: European Capitals of Culture and European Union since the 1980s*, edited by Kiran Klaus Patel, 19–38. London: Routledge, 2013.

Trunk, Achim. *Europa, ein Ausweg. Politische Eliten und europäische Identität in den 1950er Jahren* [Europe, a Way Out. Political Elites and European Identity in the 1950s]. Munich: Oldenbourg, 2007.

Witte, Bruno de. "Cultural Linkages." In *The Dynamics of European Integration*, edited by William Wallace, 192–210. London: Pinter, 1990.

Witte, Bruno de and Anne Thies. "Why Choose Europe? The Place of the European Union in the Architecture of International Legal Cooperation." In *The EU's Role in Global Governance: The Legal Dimension*, edited by Bart van Vooren, Steven Blockmans and Jan Wouters, 23–38. Oxford: Oxford University Press, 2013.

Between cooperation and competitive bargaining: the Council of Europe, local and regional networking, and the shaping of the European Community's regional policies, 1970s–90s

Birte Wassenberg

ABSTRACT:
In many ways, the Council of Europe paved the way for European Community (EC) action in local and regional affairs. It was the first European organisation to establish a conference of local and regional authorities in 1957, in which local actors and associations were represented and tried to influence the shaping of European regional policies. This article analyses the links between the Council of Europe and the EC in the development of regional policies from the 1970s to the 1990s by focusing on three transmission vectors: through institutional cooperation between the two European organisations; through competitive bargaining among local and regional groups; and through intensive lobbying at EC level. It argues that the transfer of ideas was not so much achieved through cooperation between the organisations' experts or political committees but rather by means of transregional networking promoting the idea that local and regional authorities had to be associated with the elaboration and implementation of European regional policy. From 1988, these networks shifted their attention away from the Council of Europe towards the EC because of the possibility to receive direct funding from the European Commission.

Today, local and regional affairs constitute one of the major policy fields both of the Council of Europe (CoE) and the European Union (EU). For the on-going planning of its cohesion policy for the period from 2014 to 2020, the EU has reserved €351.8 billion out of a total budget of €1,082 billion to reduce economic disparities between its member-states' regions.[1] The CoE even uses the criterion of local and regional democracy as one of the major conditions for membership of the organization, which means that the monitoring of local and regional elections has become one of its main activities.[2] Furthermore, since 1994, the CoE and the EU have both set up an institution where local and regional authorities are represented and have become involved in both organizations' decision-making processes: the EU Committee of the Regions and the Congress of Local and Regional Authorities of the CoE.[3] Judging from these similarities, one might be tempted to conclude that both organizations have developed local and regional policy in parallel, without necessarily taking notice of the other's activities in this field.

This article will argue instead that there has been a transfer of ideas between the CoE and the European Community (EC) about local and regional affairs and that this process has strong roots in the 1970s. The key players in this 'interlinking' process were not so much the European organizations and their institutional bodies themselves – expert groups, parliamentary assemblies and so on – but also certain local and regional networks and within those a number of leading politicians. The transfer dynamics operated either through cooperation or competitive bargaining. This article will therefore not only take into account the institutional actors within the two organizations, but also emphasize the role of associations and groups of local and regional actors who tried to influence the development of these policies in both organizations and thus transported ideas from one to the other.[4] This approach is also reflected by the use of sources which do not only originate from the institutional archives of the CoE (Parliamentary Assembly, Committee of Ministers) and the EC (European Commission), but also from local and regional associations (mainly the Association for European Border Regions, but also the Conference of Local and Regional Authorities which only became an 'official' CoE institution in 1994).

When examining the interactions between the CoE and the EC for the development of regional policy, we must take three key factors into account. First, it was the CoE that first addressed local and regional matters from the beginning of the 1950s onwards; consequently, ideas could only be transferred from the CoE towards the EC, at least in the early stage.[5] Indeed the CoE started very early to associate local and regional actors with its activities directly. Within its Consultative Assembly, it was the French representative Jacques Chaban-Delmas, Mayor of Bordeaux and co-founder of the Conseil des communes d'Europe (CCE) as a Europe-wide organization of cities, who proposed the creation of a special Committee on Local and Regional Affairs. In September 1952, a mere three years after the CoE had been founded, this body was established.[6] The motives behind this were mainly to increase the power of local authorities within the CoE, but the Committee also reflected a general trend at the time towards European regionalization.[7] In 1957, this led to the creation of an annual Conference of Local Authorities, which brought together local political representatives from towns of the CoE's member-states to discuss matters of local concern and which later on served as a basis for the transfer of ideas to the EC.[8]

Secondly, local and regional affairs were and are still today not treated in the same way by the two European organizations. Whereas the CoE, from the outset, made an effort to associate local and regional actors to its activities and focused on political issues related to the subject, the European Community developed a more economic approach to the matter, considering regions as territorial units whose economic standards should be developed in order to reduce disparities between them.[9] The main actors for the development and implementation of the EC's regional policy ever since its establishment with the Treaties of Rome in 1957 were therefore the member-states and not local or regional authorities.[10] Thirdly, as regional policy mainly focused on questions of economic development within Western Europe, there were few links to Cold War dynamics. The international climate, and especially the periods of crisis or *détente*, therefore did not have a major impact on this policy area or on the relations between the CoE and the EC with regard to this subject.[11] This only changed after the fall of the Berlin Wall in November 1989 when regional policy became an opportunity for both European organizations to break the Cold War logic and open up to the East.

After a short summary on the relationship between the two organizations during the 1950s and 1960s, this article will analyse three types of transfer that operated between the CoE and the EC in the field of regional policy: the first deals with the institutional cooperation on local and regional matters between the two organizations launched in 1969 and which was intensive until 1980; the second with competitive bargaining between local and regional associations in order to influence regional policy in both organizations as a phenomenon characteristic for the period from 1971 to the mid-1980s; and the third illustrates how lobbying by local and regional associations shifted away from the CoE towards the EC, taking the example of the origins of the Community's Interreg programme to support cross-border cooperation (1987–90).

The failure of structured relations on local and regional matters (1952–60s)

The CoE, founded in 1949 by 10 European states, was the first European organization to consider local and regional matters. In contrast, the six member-states of the European Coal and Steel Community (ECSC) – as the EC's predecessor – did not deal with this policy issue during the early 1950s.[12] Still, the CoE's two institutional bodies – the Consultative Assembly's Committee on Local and Regional Affairs and the Conference of Local Authorities – could serve as vectors for the flow of information from the Strasbourg organization to the EC.

To a certain extent, this influenced the EC's provisions with implications for regional policy. The CoE's Committee on Local and Regional Affairs thus claimed, from its foundation in 1952, that the ECSC had not considered the local and regional impact of the European integration process.[13] A first response to this claim can be found in the preamble of the EC's Treaties of Rome that stated that the Communities should 'strengthen the unity of their economies and ensure their harmonious development by reducing the differences existing between the various regions and the backwardness of the less favoured region'.[14] The CoE's Conference of Local Authorities also influenced the shaping of the EC's emerging regional-policy tools. The Conference's delegate René Radius presented two reports respectively in 1957 and 1958 asking for the EC to provide for financial compensation to disadvantaged regions to be allocated in the form of subsidies.[15] The Six took some of these demands into account and thus the first 'regional policy tools' implemented after the adoption of the Treaties of Rome provided for loans to rural regions and ECSC loans to regions in industrial decline.[16] The EC's bigger financial resources thus became the main reason why some actors in the CoE invited it to become active in the domain of regional policy – as a factor that also explains some of the dynamics of the interaction between the two organizations in cultural policy, as Oriane Calligaro and Kiran Klaus Patel demonstrate in their contribution to this special section.

When it came to establishing institutional links with Brussels, ensuring a regular flow of information from the Strasbourg organization to the EC, the CoE failed, however. At the first Conference in January 1957, the local representatives adopted a resolution calling for the setting-up of a special 'Committee of Six' responsible for relations with the EC member-states.[17] This Committee would be composed of local delegates from the EC member-states and be in charge of relations between the two European organizations. At first, the prospects for implementing this project seemed promising. At the Paris meeting of the Consultative Assembly's Local and Regional Affairs Committee in May 1958, the Committee of Six was indeed created.[18] At the second Conference of Local Authorities in Strasbourg in

October 1958 the Italian representative Natale Santero presented a scheme for the future functioning of this Committee which was supposed to be established as a 'link institution' between the CoE and the EC.[19] The report clearly favoured the direct implication of local authorities in the activities both of the CoE and the EC, via the Committee of Six. Although an integral part of the Conference of Local Authorities, it would be able to work for both the Local Affairs Committee of the CoE's Consultative Assembly and for the EC.[20] However, the CoE's decisive decision-making body, the Committee of Ministers, did not support the idea of giving such a crucial position to a committee composed of local representatives. In 1960, it refused to follow up a resolution adopted by the Conference and a recommendation by the CoE's Consultative Assembly, both of which aimed at formalizing the mediator role of the Committee of Six between the CoE and the EC. Without official recognition by the Committee of Ministers, this institutional link between the two European organizations for local and regional affairs could not be established.[21] Even if the CoE's Committee of Ministers had accepted this institutional link, the EC would likely have refused this proposal – judging from the experience of the so-called Eden Plan of 1952, as an earlier attempt to link the two organizations more closely on a broad range of policy issues.[22]

Thus, in the 1950s and 1960s, the CoE and the EC did not create a common institutional framework to discuss regional policy matters. However, this did not mean that there was no flow of ideas between the two organizations. On the one hand, the CoE still had a representation of local authorities that could influence the activities of the Strasbourg organization and although it had no means of directly influencing the EC's emerging regional policy, a transfer of ideas could still take place informally, via the Conference of Local Authorities. On the other hand, institutionalized links between the CoE and the EC were not really necessary when associations and local and regional interest groups could lobby both organizations to try to shape local and regional policy according to their own goals.

Regular expert and political cooperation on regional matters (1969–80)'

From the end of the 1960s it became apparent that a lack of an institutional framework to coordinate regional policy between the two European organizations did not hamper the establishment of cooperation on local and regional issues. The first type of relation that developed between them on regional policy was the setting up of regular contacts between the EC's Commission and the political and expert groups in the Strasbourg organization.

In the 1970s, both organizations were able to benefit from this cooperation. On the one hand, the period from 1970 to 1983 was marked by the growing threat of competition between the CoE and the EC. At the summit of The Hague in 1969, the EC took an important decision that threatened the position of the CoE in the European architecture and encroached on its activities: the six member-states finally broke the deadlock regarding enlargement and this opened the door for the accession of the United Kingdom, Ireland and Denmark in 1973.[23] The CoE could thus no longer advocate its leading political role as the organization representing the 'greater' Europe.[24] It had to look for new possibilities for cooperation with the EC, using, for example, its experience in various policy fields in order to transfer what it considered good practice or ideas to the EC. Local and regional affairs was one of these fields. Within the EC, there was indeed a demand for learning from the CoE's experience in this area. With the growing trend towards regionalization in Europe, and the prospect of the first EC enlargement which would require an increase in regional funds, the European Commission realized that the CoE could provide valuable information to help it design its new regional policy.[25]

From 1969 on, the EC's European Commission delegated members of the Directorate General for Regional Policy (DG XVI) to participate in different working panels of the CoE.[26] This participation was not limited to the intergovernmental expert committees set up by the CoE's Committee of Ministers, but also included the sessions of its Consultative Assembly and of the Conference of Local Authorities.[27] The European Commission was particularly interested in fostering cooperation with the CoE when the latter organized a first Conference of European Ministers of Spatial Planning in September 1970 in Bonn.[28] For the preparation of this Conference, a representative of the Commission's DG XVI wrote a memorandum explaining in detail the EC's concepts of regional policy so that the CoE could pass the information on to the responsible member-state ministers of spatial planning.[29] Cooperation between the two organizations improved steadily. In 1972, the Secretariat General of the CoE tried again to institutionalize its links with the European Commission by inviting it to nominate a 'permanent representative' to its Expert Committee on Municipal and Regional Affairs.[30] The European Commission agreed to participate in this committee as an observer from 1973 onwards.[31] This interest was also linked to the consequences of EC enlargement to the UK, Ireland and Denmark, which put the question of regional funding at the heart of the agenda for future Community policies. In order to palliate regional disparities with regard to the new member-states' regions, especially in Ireland, the EC planned a new policy instrument with huge implications for regional policy in 1974, the so-called European Regional Development Fund (ERDF). For the representatives from Brussels, the advantages of an observer status in the CoE were therefore twofold: on the one hand, they could obtain information from the CoE on regional statistics and cartographical elements for the reform of the EC's regional policy.[32] On the other hand, their presence in the committee allowed them to defend the outline of their new regional policy among the member-states of the CoE. Thus, for example, referring to the ERDF, a Commission delegate stressed vis-à-vis the CoE and other stakeholders that it would deal with economic disparities between European regions.[33] Again, the EC's larger financial means impacted on the relationship between the two organizations.

After the adoption of the new regional policy and the ERDF in 1975, the European Commission continued to participate in the CoE's regional expert committee, mainly taking an interest in the Council's studies on regionalization, cross-border cooperation and economic problems in rural areas.[34] There was also high-level support for this cooperation between the CoE and the EC on regional matters, as confirmed during an intervention by Roy Jenkins, President of the European Commission, before the CoE's Committee of Ministers in November 1977. However, the unofficial request from the CoE to be able to delegate a representative to the EC committee on regional policy was not met positively by the Commission.[35] This shows that reciprocity in the exchange of information between the CoE and the EC was not guaranteed.

From the beginning of the 1980s, the European Commission started losing interest in the CoE's activities on regional matters.[36] Several policy areas of the CoE also still seemed to represent an interest for the Commission: socio-economic problems (migration and employment), management of natural resources in urban areas and general questions of local and regional affairs.[37] However, in 1981, a representative of the European Commission, participating in a meeting of regional directors responsible for regional and local affairs organized by the CoE, clearly expressed his disappointment: 'This meeting discussed little that was of interest to the European Commission.' In an internal memorandum, he was more explicit:

> I feel I should say that the meeting confirmed my impression that there is nothing of real substance happening within the Council. The discussion which could have been disposed of in several hours extended to two days, a good part of which was taken up in the argument about how the number of trips to expert group meetings paid by the Council could be reduced.[38]

Indeed, whereas the CoE continued to invite the European Commission to take part in its various meetings,[39] the latter started to withdraw. An internal memorandum of the Commission's DGRP in 1981 confirmed that a certain number of high-level civil servants participated 'more or less' in the Council's activities in 1979–80.[40] Several factors explain the European Commission's disengagement at the turn of the 1980s. First, the EC's regional policy was in place and the European Commission did not need any further information from the CoE to shape this policy. Second, the archival material suggests that the CoE's expert group was seriously struggling with growing inefficiency and lack of tangible results. In the early 1980s, the CoE was suffering an identity crisis, lacking both the financial means for important policy programmes and the legal tools to implement these policies efficiently – quite similar to developments in cultural policy, as shown in Oriane Calligaro and Kiran Klaus Patel's contribution to this special section.[41] Finally, in the 1980s, the CoE was withdrawing from the economic-policy field, concentrating more on its core issues of defending human rights, democracy and the rule of law.[42] Therefore, only the political issues dealt with by the Conference of Local Authorities (such as local autonomy and legal tools for cross-border cooperation)[43] and the national spatial planning policies in the member-states' Conferences on Spatial Planning organized by the Council remained of interest to the European Commission.

Influencing regional policy in both European organizations 1971–mid-1980s

The second type of interconnection between the CoE and the EC in local and regional matters was established through the vector of local and regional groups which competitively lobbied both organizations, with the EC however becoming more interesting for all of them in the long run.

As a matter of fact, from the beginning of the 1970s, the idea of a 'Europe of regions' was gaining importance and the number of interest groups representing regional affairs in Europe increased greatly. Thus far, the Conference of Local Authorities had been largely influenced by associations of local actors.[44] But in the early 1970s, the regional element gained importance in Western Europe. With the crisis of legitimacy of Western European States first revealed in 1973 by Jürgen Habermas, there was indeed a decline of confidence in the classic administrative functions, political institutions and leadership of the national state and thus regionalist theories became an attractive alternative. There was a wave of regionalization especially in Italy and Belgium, where new or more powerful regional governments were created. Meanwhile, first demands for regional decentralization also emerged in France. The idea of a 'Europe of regions' was also defended by one of the leading figures in the CoE's Consultative Assembly, Denis de Rougemont[45] Together, these processes revealed the growing importance of regional policies across Western Europe.[46]

The new regional actors wanted to establish themselves as a lobbying force at the European level and to act independently from the local authorities' groups. They began to organize themselves in order to defend collectively their own views on regional policy which were not necessarily the same as those of local authorities.[47] Competition soon played an important role, mainly with the already existing associations, the aforementioned Conseil des communes d'Europe and the International Union of Local Authorities (IULA).[48]

As a first step, these new regional actors established two new regional associations: the Association of European Border Regions (AEBR) and the Conference of Regional Peripheral Maritime Regions (CRPM) which, from then on, lobbied for the integration of their specific interests into the European organizations' regional policies.[49] The AEBR was founded in 1971 in Isselburg-Anholt (Germany) by 10 border regions and aimed to promote cross-border cooperation in Europe.[50] Its members were mainly cross-border groups and local or regional authorities from the first Euro-regions in Western Europe (for example on the Dutch-German and the Franco-German-Swiss borders).[51] The CRPM was constituted during a Conference in Saint-Malo in June 1973 and brought together 23 European maritime regions, under the leadership of the Comité d'études et de liaisons des intérêts Bretons. It was mainly a French initiative and aimed to raise awareness for specifically maritime problems and the need for financial support for maritime regions.[52]

The second step was to create a representation of regional interests in the CoE. For this purpose, the Conference of Local Authorities had to be restructured. Within the CoE's Consultative Assembly, several members favoured a shift towards the 'region' as a major actor for European cooperation.[53] Following the regionalist views of Denis De Rougemont, laid out in 1970 in a 'Letter to Europeans'[54] and distributed to the members of the CoE's Assembly, the German delegate Klaus-Peter Schultz presented a report in 1971 which called for the CoE to become the promoter of the integrationist model of 'a Europe of regions'.[55] In reality, this meant to reform the Conference of Local Authorities so as to integrate political representatives from European regional authorities. During its ninth session in 1972, the Conference indeed asked for the possibility to designate delegates from a 'region' or a 'group of regions'.[56] The resolution adopted by the members not only insisted on the necessity of an internal reorganization of the Conference, but also on its official mission as a promoter of local and regional interests in the EC.[57] A second resolution adopted in 1974 asked for the recognition of the Conference as the official representation of local and regional interests within the CoE.[58]

Responding to these demands, the Committee of Ministers finally accepted the revision of the Conference's original Charter,[59] which allowed for the designation of regional representatives and the change of its official name: in 1975, it became the Conference of Local and Regional Authorities in Europe (CLRAE). The lobbying by the new regional associations had been successful in two respects: first, they achieved representation by regional authorities within the Conference itself; and, second, just as the local authorities' groups, the AEBR and the CRPM were granted a consultative status to this Conference.[60]

On this basis, these regional associations started to establish even more efficient forms of lobbying. Whereas the AEBR concentrated its actions on the CoE, the CPRM favoured lobbying EC institutions, especially the European Commission. This was due to the fact that, above all, the AEBR wanted political recognition for border regions and the development of legal tools for cross-border cooperation (which could be accomplished by means of CoE conventions) whilst the CPRM's objective was to obtain economic support for maritime regions for which the EC with its larger budget was a better target.[61] The differences in legal setup and financial means thus explain why the two regional associations turned to different European organizations.

The AEBR thus tended to focus its activities on the CoE, although its first President, the Social Democrat Alfred Mozer, had worked as Cabinet Director for the European Commission until 1970.[62] Mozer knew, however, that the best opportunity to defend the interests of border regions at European level was at the CoE, where the AEBR could fight for direct representation in the Conference and where the concerns of border regions could be directly integrated into the European organization's activities.[63] Furthermore, one of the AEBR's founding fathers, the German Socialist Karl Ahrens, was a member of the CoE's Consultative Assembly and therefore sought to use this position to promote the interests of border regions.[64]

Indeed, the CoE's Consultative Assembly had already shown its support for border regions on 29 January 1969 when the French delegate, Pierre Weber, first proposed the organization of a conference of border regions and cross-border associations in Strasbourg.[65] This conference took place from 29 June to 1 July 1972 and brought together not only local and regional authorities from European border regions, but also experts from universities and representatives of the AEBR.[66] It was the first occasion for the AEBR to draw attention on the specificity of border regions. The German representative Viktor von Malchus thus highlighted not only the economic disparities between border regions, but also the legal difficulties they encountered when working together across the border.[67] Von Malchus put forward the idea that the CoE should elaborate a legal tool for cross-border cooperation, the so-called Madrid Framework Convention on Cross-Border Cooperation. This proposal was a small 'revolution', for, normally, border regions did not have the legal competence to engage in cooperation with their neighbours, as, generally, foreign policy was reserved for the nation-state. The demand was taken up again at the second conference of cross-border regions, organized in Innsbruck (Austria) in September 1975 where all of the participants agreed that a legal tool for cross-border cooperation was necessary.[68]

But it took some effort for the AEBR and other cross-border groups to convince the CoE member-states. They finally managed to inscribe the idea on the agenda of the first Conference of Ministers responsible for Local Authorities organized in Paris in November 1975, where the ministers agreed on the principle of a Framework Convention on Cross-Border Cooperation, which was then quickly drafted by the different CoE expert groups.[69] AEBR lobbying of the Consultative Assembly and the Conference on Local and Regional Authorities subsequently influenced the drafting process.[70] The Madrid Convention was adopted by the CoE on 21 May 1980.[71] For the first time, a European organization possessed a legal tool for cross-border cooperation. While it did not directly authorize local and regional authorities to conclude contracts with their neighbours across the border, it proposed a series of model conventions for member-states to use to adopt bilateral inter-governmental agreements on cross-border cooperation. Politically, this Convention was a big step towards the political recognition of the specific needs of border regions and their right to establish permanent relations with their neighbours.[72] AEBR lobbying in the CoE had therefore been successful.

The AEBR did not completely ignore the EC in this matter. During the drafting of the Convention, the AEBR president, Horst Gerlach, who was a member of the European Parliament, tried to find support for the idea of a similar legal instrument for cross-border cooperation at Community level and to associate the European Parliament with the work of the CoE.[73] His efforts were of little avail, however, thus strengthening the link between the AEBR and the CoE.

In contrast to the AEBR, since its establishment, the CRPM was looking for a strong link with the EC because it hoped to influence regional policy funding so as to obtain financial support for maritime regions.[74] At its founding meeting in Saint-Malo, the CRPM created a working group in charge of relations with EC institutions, which met for the first time in Brussels in 1973.[75] The working group aimed at contributing to the definition and implementation of different EC policies. However, the CRPM also wanted a consultative body, comparable to the Conference of Local and Regional Authorities in Strasbourg, to be set up in Brussels.[76] In this respect, the CPMR was again in competition with the already well-established local authorities' interest groups who were also keen to set up official representations in Brussels.[77] Here, we can identify a new case of competitive bargaining among local and regional groups.

The story becomes even more complex considering two additional factors. First, the idea of regional representation at EC level can also be traced back to someone who was active in both European organizations; this issue had in fact already been raised by the former Belgian President of the Consultative Assembly, Fernand Dehousse, during the late 1960s. A fervent defender of regionalism from Wallonia, Dehousse had been both a member of the CoE's Consultative Assembly and of the European Parliament in the 1950s and was invited to the Conference of Local Authorities in 1968.[78] As one of his first activities in the Conference, he gave a speech in which he called for the creation of a 'Senate of Regions' within the EC, as a sort of 'second chamber' of the European Parliament.[79] The transfer of ideas between the two European organizations here was achieved by someone who had been an official member of both assemblies and who tried to use the CoE's Conference of Local Authorities as a model and a lobbying platform for the creation of a similar representative body, but for regions, not local authorities, at EC level.[80]

Second, the competitive bargaining game among organizations also included the Conference of Local Authorities of the CoE, for the latter was still trying to achieve its original idea of creating a 'Committee of Six' responsible for relations with the EC. In 1972, it adopted a resolution inviting the Committee of Ministers of the CoE to adopt a partial agreement, by which the Conference would be authorized to organize specific plenary sessions for the delegations of the EC member-states.[81] The president of the Conference, Giancarlo Piombino, Mayor of Genoa, in particular pushed for such a new institutional link with the EC.[82] In 1974, the Conference proposed several measures to achieve this goal: first, to invite the president of the European Commission and the commissioner in charge of local and regional policy for hearings; second, to transmit officially all resolutions and opinions of the Conference to the EC; and, third, to organize exchanges of views between the president of the European Commission and a delegation from the Conference.[83] One proposal was also to arrange for regular meetings in Brussels between the Committee of Six and the representatives of the local groups (the CCE and the IULA) so as to inform each other of their respective 'bargaining' activities.

Even if the European Commission did not take up these proposals immediately, this meant direct competition for the CPMR, which only obtained consultative status with the Conference after its reform in 1975.[84] It organized, from 14 to 16 October 1975, a Conference in Galway (Ireland) where over 200 representatives of more than 60 regions were invited to express their views on the EC's regional policy and took up again Dehousse's original idea to create a 'Senate of Regions' in Brussels.[85] The CRPM considered it a success of its lobbying that the EC Commissioner on Regional Affairs, George Thomson, attended this conference to explain the Commission's implementation of its regional policy.[86]

However, the lobbying weight of the local groups was stronger. In 1976, the European Commission accepted their idea of creating a Consultative Committee in Brussels, where mainly members of the CCE and the IULA would be represented. To some extent, this Committee was in fact the creation of the 'Committee of Six' at EC level, but it did not have the same status as the Conference of Local and Regional Authorities of the CoE. The Committee functioned with no legal basis, no financial means and no secretariat.[87] In sum, it gave a clear advantage to local groups in the competitive bargaining process: it reinforced the representation of local interests in the EC, whereas regional associations did not participate in the Committee. The regional groups had lost the bargaining game.

This situation led in 1979 to joint action by the two originally opposed regional associations. Together with two other regional groups,[88] the AEBR and the CPMR formed a Liaison Bureau of European Regional Organizations in order to lobby EC institutions.[89] Local and regional interest groups had now created competing lobbying structures in order to influence EC regional policy but only the local interest groups had an officially recognized committee in Brussels.

However, the Consultative Committee in Brussels was not directly associated with the decision-making process of EC regional policy.[90] Therefore, the Conference of Local and Regional Authorities of the CoE, where the local and regional groups were both represented, still defended some common views on EC regional policy. It adopted a first opinion on the new European Regional Development Fund in 1974 in which it criticized the fact that the Community considered the region only as an economic unit, but did not take into account its political function.[91] According to the Conference, the EC's regional policy was too dependent on the member-states and omitted to take into account the opinions of the local and regional authorities themselves. At the Galway Conference organized by the CPMR in 1975, the representations of regions defended the same view.[92] They clearly considered the EC's regional policy to be 'state subsidies for the EC member-states in order to develop national strategies for their regional development'.[93]

In the end, the Conference of Local and Regional Authorities managed to influence at least some elements of the EC's regional policy. First, it adopted a resolution on 24 May 1977 insisting on the necessity for the EC to associate local and regional authorities with the drafting and implementation of regional policy.[94] This resolution was indeed taken up by the European Commission when it submitted its proposal for the future orientation of the EC's regional policy to the European Council on 3 June 1977. For one, it defined regional policy as a permanent task for the Community where 'the EC institutions, member-states, social partners and representatives of local and regional authorities should be consulted'.[95] For another, in 1979, the Conference asked the EC to increase the funding for the reconstruction of regions in industrial decline.[96] This proposal, which was also supported by the Consultative Committee in Brussels, finally encouraged the European Commission to increase its funding for regions in economic decline in 1983.[97]

In sum, the competitive bargaining of local and regional lobby groups at both organizations did not lead very far. The local groups were successful in obtaining a Consultative Committee at EC level but this Committee did not have any decision-making power.

Lobbying by regional groups was most efficient when used by one association for a specific purpose such as when the AEBR lobbied for the Madrid Convention. The best impact on EC regional policy until the mid-1980s was still achieved by the CoE's Conference of Local and Regional Authorities where common instead of competitive bargaining prevailed.

Regional lobbying shifting towards the EC: the origin of the Interreg initiative (1987–90)

After the adoption by the EC of the Single European Act in 1987, those regional groups (especially the AEBR) that thus far had given priority to the CoE as a target shifted their interest away from the Strasbourg organization towards the EC. This can be explained by the new policy orientations of the two European organizations.

From the mid-1980s, the CoE developed new priorities, which did not include regional policy as a major concern.[98] At the time, developments in the Eastern bloc came to play an important role for the Strasbourg organization starting with Mikhail Gorbachev's announcement of reform measures in the Soviet Union in 1987 on democratization and economic liberalization (Glasnost and Perestroika) and leading to the fall of the Berlin Wall on 9 November 1989 which marked the end of the division of Europe and the Cold War. For the CoE, this presented the opportunity to take on a new role as the first pan-European organization to open up to the countries of Eastern Europe, a role Gorbachev supported in a speech at the Consultative Assembly on 5 May 1989 in which he called for the creation of a 'common European home'.[99] It therefore started to foster cooperation with the Eastern bloc[100] – including the Soviet Union – and, from 1990 onwards, embarked on a spectacular enlargement process leading to the integration of all Central and Eastern European states by 1993. This meant helping the democratization process in these countries and monitoring respect for human rights and the rule of law. Promoting local and regional democracy was also part of this task but this had nothing to do with the regional policy sought by the regional groups, that is, as a means of acquiring financial support for disadvantaged (Western) European regions. In an enlarged pan-European organization, in any case, it would be the Eastern regions which would be the main beneficiaries of regional policy and not those represented in the existing lobbying groups.[101] The CoE was therefore no longer such an interesting target for the regional associations.

Whereas regional policy was not of major concern for the CoE during the period from 1987 to 1990, it became an important policy issue for the EC. The EC's prime objective was to strengthen internal relations before enlarging to the East: the accomplishment of the Single European Market by 1992 was a priority for Brussels.[102] This also required the strengthening of regional funds in order to reduce regional economic disparities which threatened to disrupt the free circulation of goods, capital, people and services in the EC.[103] With the introduction of a new Chapter V on 'social and economic cohesion' in the Single European Act, the mechanism of the Structural Funds was reformed in 1988.[104] Amongst other measures, the ERDF could financially support pilot projects and it promoted an exchange of experience and the development of relations between regional authorities within the EC.[105] This made the EC very attractive for lobbying by regional groups.

Its financial resources were the main reasons why regional groups and organizations refocused their attention away from the CoE towards the EC, where they saw a chance for local and regional authorities to receive financial support directly for their activities at local and regional levels.[106] The lobbying initiatives were facilitated by the fact that the European Commission decided on 24 June 1988 to create a Consultative Council of Local and Regional Authorities at the Directorate General for Regional Affairs (DG XVI) which was to express its opinion on the implementation of the Community's regional policy.[107] For its part, the CoE did not have any financial tools to support regional projects and did not consider this to be a priority: its action continued to concentrate on the political implication of local and regional authorities in European cooperation.[108]

The AEBR's changing priorities epitomize the shift away from the CoE to the EC. Representatives of this organization for border regions realized that the EC's new regional policy presented a formidable opportunity to receive funding for cross-border cooperation.[109] Therefore, lobbying the EC became more and more attractive for the association. In the field of cross-border cooperation, the AEBR had established itself as the leading lobbying group and competition with other associations such as the CPRM did not hamper its intervention. In 1984, the AEBR had already participated in a Conference on European Regions organized by the European Parliament where it had introduced a resolution on the promotion of cross-border cooperation and the reinforcement of the role of regions in Europe that was fully integrated into the final declaration.[110] After that, relations with the EC were mainly developed with the European Commission from 1988 on, when the new regional policy was to be implemented.

Ultimately, the AEBR's lobbying resulted in the adoption of the EC's first programme supporting cross-border cooperation, the so-called Interreg Initiative.[111] The AEBR lobbied on two fronts: as a member of DG XVI's Consultative Council[112]; and through direct dialogue with the Commission. On 14 July 1988, Karl Ahrens, the AEBR President, had a meeting with Peter Schmidhuber, the European Commissioner for Regional Policy. This channel proved the most efficient. During the meeting, they discussed regional policy issues, mainly the reorganization of the structural funds and the concepts of a new spatial policy.[113] One of the topics on the agenda was the possibility to establish regional cross-border programmes. The European Commission accepted that the AEBR prepare a draft proposal on a 'European spatial planning concept'.[114] In September 1988, the AEBR paper was presented to the European Commission as 'the basis for an efficient regional policy from which border regions could profit in the long run'.[115] The paper was then used by the European Commission to define its first Community initiative on cross-border cooperation: entire passages from it were indeed integrated into the official text adopted by the EC on the matter two years later.[116]

Thanks to the AEBR's lobbying, the EC became aware of the fact that the Single European Market on its own would not resolve all problems at European borders, for example, in the fields of spatial planning (infrastructure) and social security (legislation on cross-border workers), and that it was best to charge the border regions themselves with finding solutions for these problems through the implementation of joint cross-border projects.[117] A first step in this direction was taken in 1989, when the European Commission introduced a pilot programme in which it co-financed a small number of cross-border projects in five European 'test' cross-border regions.[118] It was not surprising that the Northern Franco-German Region Pfalz-Mittlerer Oberrhein Nord Alsace (PAMINA) was selected as one of these pilot regions: two members of PAMINA, the *Département du Bas-Rhin* and the *Communauté d'intérêt moyen Alsace-Breisgau* (CIMAB) had been active members of the AEBR for years.[119]

On this basis, the European Commission in 1990 adopted the Interreg programme as a Community Initiative Policy (CIP) which supported cross-border projects at all (internal and external) EC borders for a five-year period with a total budget of 1 billion ECU.[120] The AEBR had thus succeeded in obtaining direct financing for border regions and in ensuring that they could participate in the implementation of the European regional policy. This cross-border initiative also carried a lot of symbolic meaning: as Michel Barnier, at the time the European Commissioner for Regional Policy, emphasized looking back 10 years later, Interreg had been meant to 'promote the rapprochement of people at the borders of the European Community'.[121] The AEBR had thus also helped key EC decision-makers to substantiate their claims to realize the 'European spirit' of cross-border cooperation.

The AEBR's lobbying did not stop with Interreg. In 1990, the Association itself obtained funding from the European Commission to establish a network of European border regions. The pilot project Linkage Assistance for European Border Regions was meant to foster an exchange of experience between European border regions.[122] One of its objectives was to encourage the creation of Euro-regions at the Eastern (external) borders of the EC in order to promote cooperation between East and West European border regions. This measure was coupled with a special EC programme (Phare) to finance technical support projects for economic and political development in Eastern European states. With this new initiative, the EC provided the first funding for East–West cooperation – a policy field in which the CoE had already been invested since 1989.[123] This demonstrates clearly that the AEBR now favoured lobbying at EC level, in spite of the CoE's 'priority field' of East–West cooperation.

Conclusion

The analysis of inter-organizational relations between the CoE and the European Community in the field of regional policy reveals a very complex picture: like in other policy fields, for example cultural policy,[124] there was definitely a flow of ideas from the CoE towards the EC.

The CoE was the first European organization to consider local and regional affairs and could therefore have served as a model for the EC's regional policy. But the Strasbourg organization focused on the political engagement of local and regional actors in European cooperation – which was of no interest to the EC in the 1970s and 1980s. Within the CoE, it was the Consultative Assembly that supported the creation of a Conference of Local Authorities in 1957, where local actors were directly represented. This Conference tried to influence the shaping of the EC's regional policy, by insisting on the necessity of reducing regional disadvantages and generally taking into account regional concerns. But apart from this general goal, which was indeed mentioned by the European Regional Development Fund in 1975, the results of the Conference's efforts were meagre. As long as the EC's approach consisted of considering regions as territorial development units without taking into account their political functions, the influence of the CoE's Conference remained weak.

The flow of ideas from one European organization to the other was also affected by some additional players in the field of regional policy. Indeed, the complexity of relations between the CoE and the EC regarding local and regional issues resulted from the role of non-state actors as supplementary communication vectors. During the 1950s and the 1960s, the Conference of Local Authorities did not succeed in establishing formal links with the EC. Thus no institutionalized 'channel' was set up for the transfer of ideas. Since no official liaison committee was created between the two organizations, local and regional groups seized the opportunity to bridge this gap and engage in competitive lobbying of both the CoE and the EC. The flow of transfer thus became multi-dimensional. This article has highlighted three types of mutual relations: classical inter-organizational cooperation; competitive bargaining by transregional groups; and the lobbying focus on the EC from the end of the 1980s onwards.

Of these three types of relations, inter-organizational cooperation was a comparably weak element. The exchange of information between the two organizations on regional policy was unstable and largely depended on the willingness of the European Commission to participate in the CoE's expert groups or the Conference on Local Authorities. Until the early 1980s, the European Commission was keen to obtain statistical information on urban and regional spaces which the CoE had gathered, but there was a clear lack of reciprocity with the European Commission refusing to grant the CoE access to its expert groups. Once the EC had implemented the European Regional and Development Fund, it lost interest in the Strasbourg organization.

In contrast, competitive bargaining by local and regional groups became a very dynamic factor influencing regional policy in both organizations. This activity was not always efficient, however, as many networks with different objectives competed with each other. Their lobbying was uncoordinated and oscillated between the two organizations, depending on which one they expected to satisfy their specific demands. Thus, the Association for European Border Regions needed a legal tool for cross-border cooperation, which the CoE was more likely to provide. Therefore, the AEBR at first focused its attention on the CoE. The Conference of Peripheral Maritime Regions, on the other hand, wanted to create a representative body in Brussels where it could lobby for financial support from the EC. Various local authorities' associations also wanted representation in Brussels. These conflicting local and regional interests finally resulted in the creation of a weak consultative body which did not have the same position as the CoE's Conference of Local and Regional Authorities created in 1975. Competition between local and regional groups was therefore an obstacle to gaining a strong lobbying position in Brussels.

The most efficient influence on the EC's regional policy was achieved at the end of the 1980s when the AEBR shifted its interest away from the CoE towards the EC. Intensive lobbying by the AEBR made the European Commission reconsider its approach to regional policy which resulted in the European Commission's Interreg initiative of 1990, where local and regional actors were directly associated with the implementation of EC regional programmes. This development shows that regional groups gradually preferred the EC as the financially more powerful organization. In comparison, the CoE could not offer the same support for their activities. In this respect the regional policy field largely resembles other policy areas, including cultural policy, where the EC's intervention progressively out-competed the CoE because it had more financial means for these policies and more binding legal tools to ensure their implementation.

Notes

1. Archives of websites of the DG Regio, European Commission, Cohesion policy 2014–2020, on: http://ec.europa.eu/regional_policy/archive/what/future/index_en.cfm, 2.2.2015. See Wassenberg and Reitel, *Territorial Coo peration in Europe*, 30–42

2. Bauer, *Der Europarat nach der Zeitenwende 1989–1999,* 103, see also Wassenberg, *History of the Council of Europe,* 135.

MULTIPLE CONNECTIONS IN EUROPEAN COOPERATION

3. For the Committee of the Regions see Warleigh, *The Committee of the Regions: Institutionalizing Multi-Level Governance?*, 7; for the Congress of Local and Regional Authorities see Wassenberg, *Histoire du Conseil de l'Europe (1949–2009)*, 427.

4. Mainly the Association of European Border Regions (AEBR), the Conference on Peripheral Maritime Regions (CPMR) and the Conseil des Communes d'Europe (CCR). For the lobbying of these groups see Ramirez, 'Cross-Border Lobbying: The Association of European Border Regions (AEBR) Activities with the European Union', 283–97. For a typology of inter-organizational links between the Council of Europe, the EC and other organizations, see Patel, 'Provincialising European Union'.

5. See Guerra, *Les régions au Conseil de l'Europe*.

6. ACE, Consultative Assembly (CA), *Demand for the Inscription to the Order of the Day of the Session*, Doc. 85, 29 November 1951; *Report on the Creation of a Specialized Authority on Local and Regional Affairs*, 26 September 1952, Doc. 89; *Resolution 20*, 27 September 1952.

7. See Wirsching, *Demokratie und Globalisierung*.

8. ACE, CA, *Resolution 76 on the Convocation of a Conference of Representatives of National Associations of Local Authorities from the Member States*, 14 October 1955; ACE, Conference of Local Authorities (CLA), *Minutes of the Debates of the 1st Session*, 17 January 1957. See Meyer, *Le Conseil de l'Europe et la Région (1957–1962)*.

9. Wassenberg and Beck, *Living and Researching Cross-Border Cooperation (Volume 3)*, 300–2 (Conclusion).

10. See Marx, *EG-Regionalpolitik, Fortschritt und Stagnation im Spannungsfeld von Integrationsziel und nationalstaatlichen Interessen*, 158–60.

11. Pinto, 'Accompagner les mutations de l'Europe centrale et orientale', 53–63; Courcelle, *Le Conseil de l'Europe, enjeux et représentations*, 122.

12. See *50 Years of Local and Regional Democracy*, 7.

13. ACE, CA, *Report on International and National Bodies of Local Authorities and Studies on their Own Means to Involve these Bodies and the Local Authorities Themselves in the Diffusion of the European Idea*, Doc. 210, 23 September 1953.

14. Treaty of Rome, Preamble, 25 March 1957.

15. ACE, CLA, *Report on the Local Problems Created by the Creation of the Common Coal and Steel Market and the ESCE Activities*, 17 January 1957, 15–16; *Report on the Local Incidences of European Economic Integration*, 29–31 October 1958.

16. Clout, Blacksell, King and Pinder, *Western Europe: Geographical Perspectives*, 203–5.

17. ACE, CLA, *Resolution 1 on the Creation of a Special Committee*, 17 January 1957.

18. Meyer, *Le Conseil de l'Europe et la Région (1957–1962)*, 60.

19. ACE, CLA, *Report 'Santero'*, 29–31 October 1958, 137.

20. ACE, CLA, *Resolution 9 on the Participation of Local Authorities in the Establishment and the Activities of European Institutions*, 29–31 October 1958.

21. ACE, CA, *Resolution 20 on the Charter of the European Conference of Local Authorities*, 25 January 1960; *Recommendation 120 on the Charter of the European Conference of Local Authorities*, 28 September 1960.

22. Fischer, 'Vierzig Jahre Europarat – Vom gescheiterten Föderator zum kreativen Trainingscenter', 119–26.

23. Wassenberg, *History of the Council of Europe*, 71–2.

24. Maschke, '30 Jahre Europarat, Rückblick und Perspektiven', 161.

25. Deyon and Rémond, *Régionalismes et régions dans l'Europe des quinze*, Conseil de l'Europe, *Les institutions régionales et la régionalisation dans les États membres*.

26. Archives of the European Commission (AEC), BAC 86/1989, N° 48, 1968–1975, Notice to the Directorate General for External Relations on the participation of M. Van der Kelk in the expert group on demographic regional problems, 2 December 1968; Information notice by the European Commission on the session of the Parliamentary Assembly of the Council of Europe on spatial planning 12–16 May 1969, 23 May 1969.

MULTIPLE CONNECTIONS IN EUROPEAN COOPERATION

27. AEC, BAC 86/1989, N° 48, 1968–1975, Notice to Mr. Sigrist, Director General on External Relations on a joint meeting of the Commission and the General Secretariat of the Council, 27 October 1969.
28. For the decision of the Committee of Ministers to organize this conference, see ACE, CM, *Minutes of the Committee of Minister's Meeting*, December 1968.
29. AEC, BAC 86/1989, N° 48, 1968–1975, Notice on a meeting between the European Commission and the General Secretariat of the Council of Europe (Strasbourg-June 1971) on the contribution of the General Directorate on Regional Policy, 15 March 1971.
30. AEC, BAC 86/1989, N° 48, 1968–1975, Letter to the President of the European Commission Sicco Mansholt by the Secretary General of the Council of Europe, Lujo Toncic-Sorinj, 20 October 1972.
31. AEC, BAC 86/1989, N° 48, 1968–1975, Notice to Mr. Sigrist, Directorate General for External Relations on the Letter of the Council of Europe of 6 February 1973, 7 March 1973.
32. AEC, BAC 86/1989, N° 48, 1968–1975, Letter to Mr. Locatelli in the Council of Europe by J. Van Ginderachter, 6 November 1973.
33. AEC, BAC 86/1989, N° 48, 1968–1975, Draft intervention by Mr. Camier addressed to the Directorate of Environment and Spatial Planning of the Council of Europe, 30 September 1974.
34. AEC, BAC 86/1989, N° 49, 1975–1982, Notice by Mr. Camier on the Committee of Cooperation of the Council of 11–12 December 1975, 24 December 1975.
35. AEC, BAC 86/1989, N° 49, 1975–1982, Notice by Mr. G. De Freye, DG Regional Policy to Mr. Renicki on the participation of the Council of Europe in the activities of the Regional Policy Committee, 9 April 1979.
36. AEC, BAC 86/1989, N° 49, 1975–1982, Notice to Emile Noël, Secretary General, by Pierre Mathijsen, Directorate General for Regional Affairs, 12 June 1981.
37. AEC, BAC 86/1989, N° 49, 1975–1982, Notice to Roy Denman, Director General for External Relations, by Pierre Mathijsen, Directorate General for Regional Affairs, 2 June 1980.
38. AEC, BAC 86/1989, N° 49, 1975–1982, *Report by H. Quigly to Mr. Renicki, Wäldchen, Van Gindernachter, Lenarduzzi, Messina, Boisdequin on the Meeting of Council's Steering Committee on Regional and Municipal Matters of 20–21 May 1981*, 1 June 1981.
39. AEC, BAC 86/1989, N° 49, 1975–1982. See letters of invitation by the Council of Europe on 9 September 1980, 1 October 1980, 13 October 1980, 31 October 1980, without response by the Commission.
40. AEC, BAC 86/1989, N° 49, 1975–1982, Notice by van Ginderachter to Mr. Wäldchen on the activities of the Council of Europe followed by the services of the DG XVI, 25 May 1980.
41. Wassenberg, *Histoire du Conseil de l'Europe,* 586.
42. *Ibid.,* 310.
43. Cf. COE, Bureau of Treaties, *Madrid Convention* 1980 and *Charter of Local Self-Government* 1985.
44. Mainly the Conseil des communes d'Europe (CCE), the International Union of Local Authorities (IULA) and the Forengen Norden, cf. interview with Ulrich Bohner, high-ranking civil servant in the Council of Europe in the Department for Spatial Planning and Regional Affairs (1972–2009), Secretary General of the Conference of Local and Regional Authorities, 25 May 2014, cf. also Guerra, *Les régions au Conseil de l'Europe,* 72.
45. De Rougemont, *Vers une fédération des régions,* 1968 and *Lettre ouverte aux Européens,* 1970.
46. In 1970, 15 'ordinary' regions were formed in Italy, three regions in Belgium and, in 1972, the so-called Etablissements régionaux publics were set up in France.
47. Malchus, *Partnerschaft an europäischen Grenzen,* 15.
48. *Ibid.*
49. Interview with Jens Gabbe, Secretary General of the AEBR (1987–2006), 8 June 2014.
50. AEBR, *30 ans de travail en commun,* 17.
51. Wassenberg, 'Qu'est-ce qui motive la coopération transfrontalière dans l'espace franco-germano-suisse?', 95–117.
52. See Pierret, *La face cachée de l'Union,* 97–8.

MULTIPLE CONNECTIONS IN EUROPEAN COOPERATION

53. For example ACE, CLA, '*Problèmes de l'organisation politique des pouvoirs locaux européens et des régions européennes*', Communication by Fernand Dehousse, 31 October 1968; ACE, CLA, '*Message*' by Jacques Chaban-Delmas, French Prime Minister, 26–30 October 1970.
54. De Rougemont, *Lettre ouverte aux Européens*, 183–4.
55. See Ruge, *Die Erfindung des 'Europa der Regionen*'; ACE, CLA, *Report on the Role of Local Authorities in the Framework of the Council of Europe's Mission in the Near Future*, 25–29 September 1972, 3.
56. ACE, the Parliamentary Assembly, supports this demand: see *Recommendation 694 Concerning the 9th Session of the CLA*, 24 January 1973.
57. ACE, CLA, *Resolution 74 Concerning the Role of Local Authorities in the Framework of the Council of Europe's Mission in the Near Future and the Development of Activities of the EC in the Spheres of Competence of Local and Regional Authorities*, 25–29 September 1972.
58. ACE, CLA, *Resolution 76 Concerning the Role of the Conference of Local Authorities in Europe Today, 16–20 September 1974*, 16–20 September 1974.
59. The Charter for the institutionalization of the Conference had been adopted on 13 September 1961, ACE, CM, *Resolution 61/20*, 13 September 1961.
60. Council of Europe, *50 Years of Local and Regional Democracy*.
61. Noël, 'La Conférence des régions périphériques maritimes d'Europe. Une initiative originale pour une politique régionale européenne', 267–9.
62. Interview with Jens Gabbe; AEBR, *30 ans de travail en commun*, 6; 'Die AGEG', 26.
63. Interview with Jens Gabbe; ACE, Conference of Local and Regional Authorities of Europe (CLRAE), *Report on Cross-Border Cooperation in Europe, CPL (15) 6 Final*, 23 May 1980, 52.
64. *Ibid.*
65. ACE, CA, Proposal for a recommendation on cooperation between border regions presented by Mr. Weber, 29 January 1969.
66. ACE, CA, Ahrens, Karl, *Report on the European Confrontation of Border Regions*, Doc. 2876, 5 January 1971, 4.
67. Malchus, *Die Zusammenarbeit europäischer Grenzgebiete, Stand der Frage und jüngste Entwicklung, Basisbericht für das 1. Europäische Symposium der Grenzregionen.*
68. Malchus, *Die Zusammenarbeit europäischer Grenzgebiete, Basisbericht für das 2. Europäische Symposium der Grenzregionen.*
69. ACE, CM, *Reports Presented at the Second Meeting of the European Ministers in Charge of Local Authorities, CME/Loc (76) 28*, 1976.
70. ACE, CA, *Opinion on the Framework Convention on Cross-Border Cooperation*, Doc. 4420, 1979.
71. Series of European Treaties n° 106, entered into force on 22 December 1981.
72. Interview with Jens Gabbe.
73. Wassenberg, *La coopération transfrontalière franco-germano-suisse dans l'espace du Rhin-supérieur de 1975 à 2000. Vers une eurorégion?*, 149.
74. Noël, 'La Conférence des régions périphériques maritimes d'Europe. Une initiative originale pour une politique régionale européenne', 265.
75. Pierret, *La face cachée de l'Union*, 189.
76. Interview with Ulrich Bohner.
77. *Ibid.*
78. Guerra, *Les régions au Conseil de l'Europe*, 108.
79. ACE, CLA, '*Problèmes de l'organisation politique des pouvoirs locaux européens et des régions européennes*', Communication by Fernand Dehousse, 31 October 1968.
80. Interview with Ulrich Bohner.
81. ACE, CLA, *Resolution 74*.
82. Cf. ACE, CLA, Follow-up by the Committee of Ministers and the Consultative Assembly of the Resolutions of the 9th Session of the Conference, 16–21 September 1974; Letter by Piombini to Rudolf Kirchschläger, president of the Committee of Minsters, 14 June 1974, Doc CPL (10) 4.
83. ACE, CLA, *Opinion 18 on the Relations Between the Conference and the EC*, 16–20 September 1974.

MULTIPLE CONNECTIONS IN EUROPEAN COOPERATION

84. ACE, CM, *Resolution 4 on the Amendment of the European Charter of Local Authorities*, 19 February 1975.
85. Cf. 'Première Convention des autorités régionales de l'Europe périphérique', 9–14.
86. ACE, CLRAE, *Aide-mémoire* on the Conferences of Local and Regional Authorities of Europe by G. van der Auwera, Division XVI-A-1, 23 January 1978.
87. Guerra, *Les régions au Conseil de l'Europe*, 198; see Assembly of European Regions (AER), *Régions d'Europe*, 8.
88. Together with the Committee of Alpine Regions and the Pyrenees Community.
89. Guerra *Les régions au Conseil de l'Europe*, 209; See AER, *Régions d'Europe*, 9.
90. Interview Ulrich Bohner.
91. ACE, CLRAE, *Opinion 17 on the Regional Policy of the European Economic Community*, 16–20 September 1974, 3.
92. Guerra, *Les régions au Conseil de l'Europe*, 204.
93. *Ibid.*
94. ACE, CLRAE, *Resolution 89 on the Regional Policy of the Member States of the Council of Europe and European Institutions*, 24–26 May 1977.
95. AEC, Proposal for Future Orientation of the Regional Policy, 3 June 1977.
96. ACE, CLRAE, *Resolution 108 on the Regional Policy of the Member States of the Council of Europe and European Institutions*, 16–18 October 1979, 6.
97. Guerra, *Les régions au Conseil de l'Europe*, 207; *Déclarations adoptées lors des Conférences européennes organisées par la CPLRE (ou avec son concours) 1970–1985.*
98. Wassenberg, *History of the Council of Europe,* 130.
99. *Les voix de l'Europe : 1949–1996*, 161. See Rey, 'Europe is Our Home', 33–65.
100. Dremzewski, Andrew, 'Programmes de coopération et assistance du Conseil de l'Europe aux pays d'Europe centrale et orientale dans le domaine des droits de l'homme: 1990-Septembre 1993', 195.
101. Interview with Jens Gabbe.
102. Wassenberg, *History of the Council of Europe,* 131.
103. See interview with Jean Peyrony, former expert at the DG Regio, European Commission, 25 May 2015; Wassenberg, *La coopération transfrontalière franco-germano-suisse dans l'espace du Rhin-supérieur de 1975 à 2000,* 313.
104. AEC, EC *Decision n° 2025/88 of the Council*, OJEC L185, 14 June 1988.
105. Mestre, 'La Communauté économique européenne et le développement de la coopération transfrontalière', 63.
106. Interview with Jean Peyrony; Interview with Patrice Harster, head of the PAMINA Eurodistrict in the Upper Rhine Region and responsible for the setting-up of the first Interreg pilot-project PAMINA in 1990, 16 September 2015.
107. Engel, 'Europa der Regionen', 148.
108. Interview with Ulrich Bohner.
109. Interview with Jens Gabbe.
110. Archives of the Association for European Border Regions (AEBR), Minutes of the annual meetings 1985–1988.
111. See Beck, *Netzwerke in der transnationalen Regionalpolitik, Rahmenbedingungen, Funktionsweise, Folgen*, 110.
112. Interview with Jean Peyrony.
113. *Europe 2000. Les perspectives de développement du territoire communautaire.*
114. AEBR, Minutes of the Annual Meeting 1989.
115. AEBR, Minutes of the Annual Meetings 1985–1988.
116. Interview with Jens Gabbe: see AEBR position paper on cross-border cooperation 1988 and *Communication C(90) 1562/3 to the Member States Fixing the Orientations for Operational Programmes in the Framework of a Community Initiative on Border Regions (INTERREG)*, OJEC n° C215/4, 30 August 1990.
117. AEBR, *25 ans de travail en commun,* 22.

118. Beck, *Netzwerke in der transnationalen Regionalpolitik. Rahmenbedingungen, Funktionsweise, Folgen*, 119.
119. Interview with Patrice Harster.
120. AEC, *Communication C(90) 1562/3 to the Member States Fixing the Orientations for Operational Programmes in the Framework of a Community Initiative on Border Regions (INTERREG)*, OJEC n° C215/4, 30 August 1990.
121. Speech by Michel Barnier, European Commissioner in *Les 10 ans d'INTERREG*.
122. AEBR, pilot-project LACE, 1990, draft proposal.
123. Wassenberg, *Histoire du Conseil de l'Europe*, 397.
124. ARA, *Les 10 ans d'INTERREG*, brochure, Région Alsace, mai 2000.

Disclosure statement

No potential conflict of interest was reported by the author.

Bibliography

Archival material
Archives of the Council of Europe (ACE)
Archives of the European Commission (AEC)
Archives of the Association for European Border Regions (AEBR)
Archives of the Region Alsace (ARA)

Grey Literature
ACE, Consultative Assembly (CA), *Report on the Creation of a Specialized Authority on Local and Regional Affairs*, Doc. 85, 26 September 1952.
ACE, CA, *Resolution 20*, 27 September 1952.
ACE, CA, *Resolution 76*, 14 October 1955.
ACE, CA, *Report on International and National Bodies of Local Authorities and Studies on their Own Means to Involve these Bodies and the Local Authorities Themselves in the Diffusion of the European Idea*, Doc. 210, 23 September 1953.
ACE, CA, *Recommendation 120*, 28 September 1960.
ACE, CA, *Report on the European Confrontation of Border Regions*, Doc. 2876, 5 January 1971.
ACE, CA, *Recommendation 694*, 24 January 1973.
ACE, CA, *Opinion on the Framework-Convention on Cross-Border Cooperation*, Doc. 4420, 1979.
ACE, Committee of Ministers (CM), *Resolution 61/20*, 13 September 1961.
ACE, CM, *Resolution 4*, 19 February 1975.
ACE, CM, *Reports Presented at the Second Meeting of the European Ministers in Charge of Local Authorities*, CME/Loc (76) 28, 1976.
ACE, Conference of Local Authorities (CLA), *Report and Demand for Opinion on the Local Problems Created by the Creation of the Common Coal and Steel Market and the ESCE Activities*, 17 January 1957.

ACE, CLA, *Resolution 1,* 17 January 1957.

ACE, CLA, *Report and Demand for Opinion on the Local Incidences of European Economic Integration,* 29-31 October 1958.

ACE, CLA, *Opinion 8 on the Local Incidences of the ECSC,* 29–31 October 1958.

ACE, CLA, *Report "Santero",* 29-31 October 1958.

ACE, CLA, *Resolution 9,* 29-31 October 1958.

ACE, CLA, *Resolution 20,* 18-25 January 1960.

ACE, CLA, *Report on the Role of Local Authorities in the Framework of the Council of Europe's Mission in the Near Future,* 25-29 September 1972.

ACE, CLA, *Resolution 74,* 25-29 September 1972.

ACE, CLA, *Resolution 76,* 16-20 September 1974.

ACE, CLA, *Opinion 18 on the Relations between the Conference and the EC,* 16-20 September 1974.

ACE, Conference of Local and Regional Authorities of Europe (CLRAE), *Report on Cross-Border Cooperation in Europe, CPL (15) 6 Final,* 23 May 1980.

ACE, CLRAE, *Opinion 17 on the Regional Policy of the European Economic Community,* 16-20 September 1974.

ACE, CLRAE, *Resolution 89,* 24-26 May 1977.

ACE, CLRAE, *Resolution 108,* 16-18 October 1979.

AEBR, *30 ans de travail en commun,* brochure, Gronau, 2001, p.17.

AEC, BAC 86/1989, N° 49, 1975-1982, *Report by H. Quigly to Mr Renicki, Wäldchen, Van Gindernachter, Lenarduzzi, Messina, Boisdequin on the Meeting of the Council's Steering Committee on Regional and Municipal Matters of 20-21 May 1981,* 1 June 1981.

AEC, *EC Decision N° 2025/88 of the Council,* OJEC L185, 14 June 1988.

AEC, Europe. *Les perspectives de développement du territoire communautaire.* DG XVI, Brussels, Luxembourg: Commission européenne, 2000.

AEC, *European Commission, Communication C(90) 1562/3 to the Member States Fixing the Orientations for Operational Programmes in the Framework of a Community Initiative on Border Regions (INTERREG),* OJEC n° C215/4, 30 August 1990.

ARA, *Les 10 ans d'INTERREG,* brochure, Région Alsace, mai 2000.

Assembly of European Regions (AER), *Régions d'Europe,* Strasbourg, 10/1995.

Déclarations adoptées lors des Conférences européennes organisées par la CPLRE (ou avec son concours) 1970-1985, Strasbourg, Council of Europe, 1986, 9-14.

Malchus, Viktor. *Freiherr von, Partnerschaft an europäischen Grenzen.* Bonn: Europa-Union Verlag, 1975.

Malchus, Viktor. *Freiherr von, Die Zusammenarbeit europäischer Grenzgebiete, Stand der Frage und jüngste Entwicklung, Basisbericht für das 1 Europäische Symposium der Grenzregionen.* AS/COLL FRONT, Council of Europe, Strasbourg, 1972.

Malchus, Viktor. *Freiherr von, Die Zusammenarbeit europäischer Grenzgebiete, Basisbericht für das 2 Europäische Symposium der Grenzregionen.* AS/COLL FRONT, Council of Europe, Strasbourg, 1975.

Région Alsace, *Les 10 ans d'INTERREG* [10 years of INTERREG], Strasbourg, May 2000.

Secondary literature

Beck, Joachim. *Netzwerke in der transnationalen Regionalpolitik, Rahmenbedingungen, Funktionsweise, Folgen* [Networks in Transnational Regional Policy, Framework Conditions, Functioning, Consequences]. Baden-Baden: Nomos, 1997.

Bauer, Hans Joachim. *Der Europarat nach der Zeitenwende 1989-1999. Zur Rolle Straßburgs im gesamteuropäischen Integrationsprozess* [The Council of Europe After the Time Turning 1989-1999. The New Role of Strasbourg in the Pan-European Integration Process]. Regensburg: LIT, 2000.

Conseil de l'Europe. *Les institutions régionales et la régionalisation dans les Etats membres* [The Regional Institutions and Regionalization in the Member States]. Strasbourg: Conseil de l'Europe, 1972.

Courcelle, Thibault. *Le Conseil de l'Europe, enjeux et representations* [The Council of Europe, Challenges and Representations]. University Paris 8, 2008.

Deyon, Pierre, and René Rémond. *Régionalismes et régions dans l'Europe des quinze* [Regionalism and Regions in the Europe of the Fifteen]. Brussels: Bruylant, 1997.

"Die AGEG [The AEBR]". In *Entwicklungsregionen in der EWG. Ursache und Ausmass der wirtschaftlichen Benachteiligung* [Development Regions in the EEC. Origins and Scope of Economic Disadvantages], edited by Bundeszentrale für politische Bildung, 26–33. Bonn: Schriften der Bundeszentrale für politische Bildung, 1973.

DREMCZEWSKI, Andrew. "Programmes de coopération et d'assistance du Conseil de l'Europe aux pays d'Europe centrale et orientale dans le domaine des droits de l'homme: 1990–Septembre 1993 [Cooperation and assistance programs of the Council of Europe for Central and Eastern European States in the field of Human Rights - September 1993]". *Revue universelle des Droits de l'Homme*, 5–6: 195. September 1993.

Engel, Christian. "Europa der Regionen [Europe of the Regions]." In *Europa von A-Z* [Europe from A-Z], edited by Werner Weidenfeld and Wolfgang Wessels, 148–150. Bonn: Europa-Union, 1995.

Fischer, Per. "Vierzig Jahre Europarat – Vom gescheiterten Föderator zum kreativen Trainingscenter [Forty Years of Council of Europe – from a Failed Federator to a Creative Training Center]." *Integration* 12 (1989): 119–126.

Guerra, Valentina, *Les régions au Conseil de l'Europe, 1957-2010* [The regions in the Council of Europe, 1975–2010]. University of Strasbourg, 2012.

Les voix de l'Europe. *1949-1996. Sélection de discours prononcés devant l'Assemblée parlementaire du Conseil de l'Europe* [The voices of Europe. 1949-1996. Selected Speeches Pronounced Before the Parliamentary Assembly of the Council of Europe]. Strasbourg: Council of Europe, 1997.

Marx, Frank. *EG-Regionalpolitik, Fortschritt und Stagnation im Spannungsfeld von Integrationsziel und nationalstaatlichen Interessen* [EC Regional Policy, Progress and Stagnation Torn Between the Aim of Integration and National Policy Interests]. Aachen: Alano, Ed. Herodot, 1992.

Maschke, Otto. "30 Jahre Europarat, Rückblick und Perspektiven [30 years of Council of Europe, Review and Perspectives]." *Österreichische Zeitschrift für Außenpolitik* 19 (1979): 161–175.

Meyer, Jean-Christophe. *Le Conseil de l'Europe et la Région (1957–1962), la mise en place de la Conférence européenne des pouvoirs locaux* [The Council of Europe and the Region (1957–1962), the Setting up of the European Conference of Local Authorities]. University of Strasbourg, 1992/1993.

Mestre, Christian. "La Communauté économique européenne et le développement de la coopération transfrontalière [The European Economic Community and the Development of Cross-Border Cooperation]". *Les régions de l'espace communautaire*, 63–78. Nancy, 1992.

Noël, Gilbert, "La Conférence des régions périphériques maritimes d'Europe. Une initiative originale pour une politique régionale européenne [The Conference of Peripheral Maritime Regions of Europe. An Original Initiative for a European Regional policy]". In *Vivre et construire l'Europe à l'échelle territoriale de 1945 à nos jours* [Living and constructing Europe at a territorial level since 1945], edited by Denéchère Yves and Vincent Bénédicte, 267–269. Brussels: Peter Lang, 2010.

Patel, Kiran Klaus. "Provincialising European Union: Co-operation and Integration in Europe in a Historical Perspective." *Contemporary European History* 22 (2013): 649–673.

Pierret, Georges. *La face cachée de l'Union* [The Hidden Face of the Union]. Rennes: Apogée, 1997.

Pinto, Diana. "Accompagner les mutations de l'Europe centrale et orientale [Accompanying the Changes in Central and Eastern Europe]". In *Les enjeux de la grande Europe. Le Conseil de l'Europe et la sécurité démocratique* [The Challenges of the Large Europe. The Council of Europe and Democratic Security], edited by Council of Europe, 53–63. Strasbourg: La Nuée Bleue-Conseil de l'Europe, 1996.

Ramirez, Martin Guillermo. "Cross-Border Lobbying: The Association of European Border Regions (AEBR) Activities with the European Union". In *Living and Researching Cross-Border Cooperation (Volume 3): The European Dimension*, edited by Birte Wassenberg and Joachim Beck, 283–297. Stuttgart: Steiner-Verlag, 2011.

Rey, Marie-Pierre. "Europe is Our Home: A Study of Gorbachev's Diplomatic Concept." *Cold War History* 4 (2004): 33–65.

Rougemont, De Denis. *Lettre ouverte aux Européens* [An Open Letter to Europeans]. Paris: Albin Michel, 1970.

Ruge, Undine. *Die Erfindung des "Europa der Regionen"* [The Inventions of the "Europe of Regions"]. Frankfurt: Campus Verlag, 2003.

"The Communities' Quest for a Regional Policy". In *Western Europe: Geographical Perspectives*, edited by Clout Hugh, Blacksell Mark, King Russel and Pinder David, 203–205. London: Routledge, 1993.

Warleigh, Alex. *The Committee of the Regions: Institutionalizing Multi-Level Governance?* London: European Research Center, 1999.

Wassenberg, Birte. *La coopération transfrontalière franco-germano-suisse dans l'espace du Rhin-supérieur de 1975 à, 2000. Vers une eurorégion?* [Franco-German-Swiss Cross-Border Cooperation in the Upper Rhine Region from 1975–2000. Towards a Euroregion?] Brussels: Peter Lang, 2007.

Wassenberg, Birte. *Histoire du Conseil de l'Europe (1949–2009)* [History of the Council of Europe (1949-2009)]. Brussels: Peter Lang, 2012.

Wassenberg, Birte. *History of the Council of Europe.* Strasbourg: Council of Europe, 2013.

Wassenberg, Birte. "Qu'est-ce qui motive la coopération transfrontalière dans l'espace franco-germano-suisse ? Approche historique [What Motivates Cross-Border Cooperation in the Franco-German-Swiss Region? A Historical Approach]". In *Vivre et penser la coopération transfrontalière (Volume 1): les régions frontalières françaises* [Living and Researching Cross-Border Cooperation (Volume 1). The French Border Regions], edited by Birte Wassenberg, 95-117. Stuttgart: Steiner-Verlag, 2009.

Wassenberg, Birte, and Bernard Reitel. *Territorial Cooperation in Europe: A Historical Perspective.* Brussels: European Commission, 2015.

Wirsching, Andreas. *Demokratie und Globalisierung, Europa seit 1989* [Democracy and Globalization. Europe Since 1989]. Munich: Beck, 2015.

50 Years of Local and Regional Democracy. Strasbourg: Council of Europe, 2008.

Re-designing military security in Europe: cooperation and competition between the European community and NATO during the early 1980s

Angela Romano

ABSTRACT

In the early 1980s, the member-states of the European Community ('the Ten') extended their foreign-policy cooperation into the field of security and disarmament. They advanced a proposal for a Conference on Disarmament in Europe within the framework of the Conference on Security and Cooperation in Europe process. As disarmament was a preserve and priority concern of NATO, the move engendered both competition and cooperation between NATO and European Political Cooperation (EPC), that is, the mechanism the Ten used to elaborate common positions. This article analyses these dynamics by paying particular attention to the exchange of ideas between the two forums. It also shows the key role of some Western European governments in inspiring competition or promoting cooperation between the two organizations, and the rationales and drivers behind their actions. The article proves that Cold War concerns played a key role in this regard: the will to preserve European détente and the need to address domestic opinion critical of an escalation of the East–West confrontation motivated their initiative in the disarmament field. At the same time, concern that the Soviets might exploit divergences across the Atlantic prompted their attempts to secure NATO's cohesion and project a strong image of unity.

Introduction

At the opening session of the Conference on Confidence- and Security-Building Measures and Disarmament in Europe (CDE), French Foreign Minister Claude Cheysson declared: 'France hoped for this conference and proposed it. The ten members of the European Community have wanted it, according to the principles presented in their statement of 20 November 1979.'[1] Cheysson was speaking on behalf on the 10 member-states of the European Community (EC), of which France held the rotating presidency, to signal that in a key area of Cold War negotiations they had decided to speak with a single voice.

The CDE, which opened in Stockholm on 17 January 1984, was an integral part of the process engendered by the Helsinki Conference on Security and Cooperation in Europe (CSCE) in 1975 and developed through periodic follow-up meetings. The CDE mandate had been agreed at the second of such meetings, held in Madrid in 1980–3. It called for a conference in two phases: the first (in Stockholm) would negotiate and adopt confidence- and security-building measures (CSBMs) designed to reduce the risk of military confrontation in Europe; the second phase would address disarmament measures. The CDE mandate specified that measures should be militarily significant, politically binding, verifiable and applicable to the whole of Europe, that is, to Soviet territory up the Ural Mountains. The CDE concluded successfully on 19 September 1986. Its final document, which entered into force in January 1987, adopted such kind of measures and established, for the first time in the Cold War period, the right to conduct on-site inspections of military forces in the field.

That the governments of the EC member-states had agreed to deal with military-security issues collectively is already impressive. Even more striking is the fact that they launched an initiative in the field and strived to have it adopted. Military security is certainly a domain in which the EC can hardly claim a pioneering role. Officially, only the European Union (EU) created by the 1992 Maastricht Treaty has been provided with a Common Security and Defence Policy. The EC never had competence in these matters, and NATO enjoyed prerogatives in the field for decades. Unsurprisingly, there has been to date no historical investigation of the interactions between the EC and NATO in this domain. The dominant narrative has it that the failure to create a European Defence Community and the consequential admission of West Germany into NATO (1955) put an end to attempts at forging a Western European actor in the security/military domain; the idea would only re-emerge with the creation of the European Union in the post-Cold War era.[2] This article demonstrates that this story is incomplete at best; the CDE initiative represents an evident foray into a new domain of EC members' cooperation.

Admittedly, their action did not unfold within the supranational framework of the European Community, but within European Political Cooperation (EPC), that is, the intergovernmental mechanism for foreign-policy coordination set in motion in November 1970. Several historians have explored the question of an EC role as a security actor, and devoted particular attention to EPC, but did not venture into considering *military* security aspects.[3] This article contends that in the early 1980s the EC governments became pro-active as a group in the field of disarmament in Europe, the CDE being their signature initiative. It argues that Cold War concerns were the main driver behind their collective engagement in the matter. They were motivated by anxiety about the endurance of détente in Europe, the pursuit and promotion of which had been both at the core of their national foreign policies since the mid-1960s and the main and most successful chapter of their embryonic common foreign policy since 1970. At the same time, they were also driven by the need to counter pacifist movements and the risk of a neutralist tendency the latter could promote in domestic public opinion. In addition, it is here argued that divergence with the US administrations on how to shape relations with the Soviets and the European order constantly nourished the EC governments' determination to launch and uphold the CDE initiative. This article acknowledges that the CSCE constituted the framework where EPC's Cold War policy was born and flourished, and maintains that EC governments were thus keen to have the CDE unfold within the forum that had proven so favourable to their unitary action.

The study of intergovernmental discussions leading to the final design of the CDE proposal and its inception provides an excellent case for analysing the EPC/NATO relationship. As disarmament was a central issue in NATO security strategy, the EC governments' action engendered competition between EPC and NATO. At the same time, overlapping membership also made cooperation obvious between the two institutions; all EC member-states but Ireland belonged to the Atlantic Alliance, and none of them aimed at marginalizing NATO. This article analyses this set of interactions by paying particular attention to the inter-organizational exchange of ideas on disarmament and European security. It proves that EPC innovated in the field of disarmament, while NATO followed suit and eventually incorporated EPC ideas in its own policy. This study is also concerned with identifying the actors mainly responsible for encouraging competition and/or cooperation. Given the high-politics nature of the case under scrutiny, the choice has been to focus on governments and high-rank individuals therein. In so doing, it demonstrates that inter-organizational dynamics also played a formative role in 'high politics' fields such as military security.[4]

The focus on government representatives is also motivated by the intention to contribute a missing piece to the recent historiography of the West's security policy in the 1970s and 1980s, which has much focused on their role. Understandably, most works dealt with SALT negotiations and Euromissiles – whether to analyse bilateral discussions or NATO debates, to reveal the origins of NATO dual-track decision or to expose its domestic-politics rationales.[5] All these valuable studies invariably focus on nuclear armaments, and completely ignore the CDE proposal. Yet the conventional forces imbalance in Europe, with the Soviet Union largely in a dominant position, was part and parcel of Western European leaders' fears of a possible decoupling between the United States' and Western Europe's security. This article draws attention to this overlooked element of the European security conundrum and the related transatlantic debate.

The article, which bases its analysis on archival sources of EC institutions, NATO and some member-states, unfolds in three steps. It first summarizes the security and disarmament-negotiations situation at the end of the 1970s, and then offers two sections exploring, respectively, the dynamics of competition and cooperation between EPC and NATO on CDE-related discussions and their outcomes. Each section also highlights the action of specific governments and individuals therein in stimulating such dynamics. In the conclusion, the article offers an assessment of the patterns of interactions between EPC and NATO in which drivers and intended goals are highlighted.

Before moving to the analysis, it is necessary to clarify some features of the two organizations here under scrutiny. The North Atlantic Treaty of 4 April 1949 created a defensive alliance and equipped it with an institution – the (North Atlantic) Council – where member-states' delegates would meet promptly to consider matters concerning security and the implementation of the Treaty. By the mid-1970s the Council met in permanent session: weekly at national representatives level; twice per year at foreign-ministers level (sometimes accompanied by defence ministers); and on an ad hoc basis at heads of state and government level.[6] The Alliance's integrated military structure was created after the outbreak of the Korean War in 1950, which raised the alert about Soviet intentions.[7] The term 'NATO' has since been used to identify both the Alliance's political apparatus and the military-integrated structure. While accepting this use, this article will highlight the difference between the political and military branches whenever necessary.

EPC worked on the principles of 'maximum informality, a commitment to consult but no legal obligation under any circumstances to agree, maximum exchange of information, the attempt always to create consensus and a common view'.[8] It had been conceived and set up as a separate entity from the European Community to deal with high-politics issues without the constraints of Community rules and institutions' competence, but it was a tool of the *EC* members. Moreover, the EC Commission became increasingly involved, and in 1981 the EC foreign ministers adopted the London Report that formally recognized the EPC/EC connection.[9] EC member-states called themselves – and were called by others – 'the Nine' in the years 1972–80, then 'the Ten' after Greece joined the EC in January 1981 (and so on). So does this article on occasion.

Security and disarmament in Europe in the late 1970s

From NATO's inception to the early 1960s, Western security strategy had been conceived in terms of the traditional balance of power; the adversary being seen as expansionist, only political and military strength would hold it in check. Things changed after mutual suspicions had brought the world to the edge of nuclear war during the Cuban Missile Crisis of 1962. With the adoption of the 'Report on the Future Tasks of the Alliance' in 1967, the so-called Harmel Report, NATO committed itself to combining military defence with détente; security could also be enhanced by involving the adversary in activities aimed at relaxing tension and by avoiding misconduct in mutual relations. The Harmel Report also called for allies' studies about possible disarmament and practical arms-control measures.[10] Six months later, in June 1968, the North Atlantic Council ministerial meeting in Reykjavik issued an appeal to the Soviet Union and its Warsaw Pact allies for negotiations on Mutual and Balanced Force Reduction in Europe (MBFR).[11]

To be precise, the appeal was issued by the countries participating in the NATO Defence Programme, that is, all members but France. Although part of the North Atlantic political organization, France had left the integrated military command structure in spring 1966 and never participated in NATO's Nuclear Planning Group. The withdrawal had been the last and most dramatic step in President Charles de Gaulle's roadmap to regain France's independence in the field of defence, which was instrumental to political assertiveness, after his failed attempts to redress the balance within NATO, which he felt dominated by the Americans. By the mid-1960s France had acquired its own nuclear capability – the *Force de Frappe* – built to retain independence in the event of a major threat and as an insurance policy in case the United States would not defend Europe.[12] Subsequent governments maintained this peculiar status of France in NATO and its independent defence policy.

NATO's call for force-reduction talks fell on deaf ears, but had a revival when the Warsaw Pact proposed the convening of a conference on European security in March 1969. Western assent to the latter was conditioned to agreements on Ostpolitik treaties, Berlin and German-German relations, as well as the opening of the MBFR talks.[13] The latter were conceived to maintain the existing level of security while reducing its costs, and were of major importance for the Nixon administration's effort to handle domestic pressures for unilateral reduction of troops in Europe. Consequently, the White House bargained bilaterally with the Kremlin, and agreement to launch both negotiations in parallel was indeed reached at the Moscow summit of May 1972. The MBFR talks opened in January in Vienna between Warsaw Pact members and NATO states minus France, where President Georges Pompidou upheld de Gaulle's legacy.[14]

The other European NATO members had shown less enthusiasm for the MBFR than the Americans; in addition, they had asked for the topic of military security to be included in the CSCE agenda. Those member-states with no troops on the Cold War front in Central Europe feared that the MBFR talks could harm their security interests; consequently, they advocated a clear link between these negotiations and the CSCE, in which they would participate with full rights. Italy, Norway, Greece and Turkey had clearly expressed this view.[15] Moreover, the EC governments shared a latent yet growing mistrust of their American ally. The Italian and German governments were most worried by the possibility of the unilateral withdrawal of US troops; they thought that an established MBFR–CSCE link would give the US Congress tangible evidence of the Europeans' willingness to negotiate arms reduction and help forestall unilateral decisions. The Belgian, Dutch and Luxembourg governments were afraid that their voices would be unheard in bloc-to-bloc negotiations, where the superpowers would obviously play a leading role and marginalize small allies. The British government, traditionally very sensitive to Benelux concerns of this kind, also preferred to give more room to the CSCE, which assured a greater involvement of minor powers as well as neutral European countries, that is, Switzerland, Sweden and Austria, whose governments tended to side with the West in multilateral negotiations.[16] The neutrals had indeed expressed the intention to bring to the CSCE some proposals on military aspects of security, and asked to link MBFR and CSCE negotiations.[17]

NATO discussions about MBFR and CSCE revealed the deterioration of European governments' confidence in the US administration. At the root of their unease was a sense that the White House was increasingly considering the international scenario in the light of its relationship with the Kremlin, and that it was prepared to subordinate the interests of its allies to it. The US–Soviet agreement on the limitation of strategic arms (SALT) signed in May 1972 had accentuated the doubts on US willingness to contemplate the use of nuclear weapons in case of conflict in Europe in a situation of strategic parity with the Soviet Union. Moreover, the US withdrawal from Vietnam and the anxiety to ensure a swift solution to the conflict had exacerbated suspicions, always present in Western European capitals, that the Americans would be prepared to sacrifice their allies if they saw it fit with their national interest. In late November 1972, UK Defence Secretary Lord Carrington wrote to Prime Minister Edward Heath about 'a more specific fear that the Americans may have actually reached secret agreements with the USSR on matters like MBFR which are of legitimate concern to NATO as a whole'.[18] Most EC leaders felt this growing sense of superpower condominium over their heads and had a neat perception of diverging interests across the Atlantic on several issues; this strengthened their determination to agree on common foreign policy within EPC.[19]

Arguably, the determination of EC governments to propose confidence-building measures in Europe was born in the mid-1970s in reaction to NATO's MBFR talks, motivated by European governments' shared sense of marginalization in European security matters. The idea of negotiating these measures was not original or exclusive to EPC, though. As already mentioned, representatives of the neutral European countries had already advanced some hypotheses during bilateral discussions that preceded the CSCE.[20] All European countries thought that confidence-building measures would defuse situations such as military manoeuvres and movements of the adversary camp that, though ordinary, could engender suspicion and lead to dangerous pre-emptive action. Most EC governments favoured these measures also to discourage intimidating displays of force and increase the political cost of Soviet interventions in Eastern Europe à la Prague 1968.[21] The coordinated efforts of the delegations of the EC countries and of neutral and non-aligned states succeeded in adding a specific item on such measures to the CSCE negotiations agenda.

The MBFR talks entered an impasse quite soon after the start in January 1973, mainly because the two opposing parties proved unable to agree on the actual force levels on both sides.[22] By contrast, the confidence-building aspect of the CSCE had better fortune. The Final Act contained a series of modest measures designed to reduce the 'dangers of armed conflict and of misunderstanding or miscalculation of military activities which could give rise to apprehension'.[23] The document also encouraged voluntary notification of smaller-scale military manoeuvres, major military movements and the invitation of observers to manoeuvres. In the course of the next years, both sides observed the compulsory elements of these provisions fairly rigorously, but the Warsaw Pact proved reluctant to engage on the voluntary notifications.[24] The CSCE follow-up meeting in Belgrade (4 October 1977 – 8 March 1978) failed to agree on any development, due to renewed superpowers' tensions, and stalemate in disarmament talks did not promise any better. This grim situation triggered the CDE proposal.

Competition between EPC and NATO

From a formal point of view, the CDE proposal was French; it was tabled in the Madrid CSCE follow-up meeting on 9 December 1980 by the French delegation on behalf of its government. It then received immediate backing from the delegations of France's EC partners, and support from NATO non-EC allies, with the exception of the United States.[25] More substantially, though, the CDE proposal was a key feature of the EC governments' common CSCE policy, approved by the EPC ministerial meeting in November 1979.[26] Only after this EPC imprimatur was the proposal subjected to NATO endorsement.[27] In addition, the latter did not rule out EPC engagement on the initiative; EPC remained both a key forum for detailed discussions on the matter and the most committed actor sponsoring the disarmament conference at the Madrid CSCE follow-up meeting.

The French origin of the CDE is almost obvious. According to Veronika Heyde, the deployment of the Soviet SS-20 missiles and ensuing debate on nuclear-weapons negotiations convinced President Giscard that France could no longer ignore disarmament talks. In the spring of 1977 the president asked the experts of the *Centre d'analyse et de prevision* (the equivalent of a Planning Staff) to elaborate a proposal that would meet French security requirements.[28] The core of French experts' considerations was that French nuclear forces should not be included in disarmament negotiations, and that Soviet superiority in conventional forces was a major threat to European security. Consequently, France should only participate in disarmament negotiations involving Soviet 'European' territory and forces. [29] The French experts conceived the idea of a general conference on disarmament in Europe with an initial focus on confidence-building measures as an alternative to the MBFR talks, which the French government did not attend and saw as fatally flawed. First, MBFR focused on too small an area of Central Europe to be military significant; second, it was concerned with reductions in manpower while neglecting the most threatening element, that is, the concentration of powerful conventional weaponry in Europe; third, it tackled the problems in the wrong order by seeking to accomplish the most difficult task of reducing forces before building mutual confidence, which the French considered the essential preliminary step.[30]

Less evident are the reasons why EC partners joined in advocating a new initiative that would overlap the MBFR talks, and agreed to promote it under the aegis of EPC rather than as a new NATO-sponsored proposal. The 1957 Treaty of Rome creating the European

(Economic) Community did not deal with security and there had been no full-scale attempt since to broaden the scope of the Community's competence to include defence. However, since the early 1970s the EC governments had started to develop a joint security concept through EPC. Since the latter's inception, most governments had pointed out that security concerns would not be excluded from foreign-policy discussions and deliberations; sure enough, EPC dealt with security issues within the scope of the CSCE. The Helsinki Conference was a tremendous learning-by-doing experience that strengthened EC governments' cohesion as a group and trained them in forging a common policy. They were successful in their endeavour, and recognized by the other CSCE participants for their unitary and effective action, which also continued in the ensuing process.[31] It should not come as a surprise, therefore, that they would again use EPC to promote the CDE initiative; they could rely on the combination of training and machinery that had proved effective. Moreover, EPC was already equipped with procedures to deal with NATO. Since 1972 EC governments had developed the practice of coordinating their views in EPC prior to the meetings of the NATO Council and working committees, including those addressing military-security issues such as confidence-building measures. They usually arrived with EPC-agreed positions and often proved reluctant to modify them to accommodate non-EC NATO allies' views.[32]

A certain degree of competition with NATO was therefore present since EPC's early days. It became more evident by the end of the 1970s, when EPC put more emphasis on security aspects following the increase in East–West tensions. In the second half of the 1970s the Soviet Union had been particularly active in African conflicts (such as Angola and Mozambique), scored a bad record in compliance with CSCE human-aspects provisions, and had embarked on a new course of military build-up. More specifically, in the second half of 1976 it had started deploying a new generation of intermediate-range ballistic missiles (SS-20) that could quickly hit designated targets throughout Western Europe. In the United States, President Carter, though committed to continue strategic arms-limitation talks (SALT 2), adopted a confrontational stance towards the Soviets in the field of human rights. Carter's stance contributed to souring the relationship between the superpowers, and put disarmament talks in jeopardy. Concerns about East–West tensions engendered by superpowers' behaviour were frequently discussed within EPC and in the European Council, where the EC heads of state and government met for informal discussions of any issue they saw fit.[33] EPC did not discuss defence issues in the narrow sense, such as military strategy, defence planning and tactics, and command structures, yet it went beyond CSCE confidence-building measures and ventured frequently into NATO's preserve to discuss disarmament.[34]

It was in this context of Cold War tension that French President Valéry Giscard d'Estaing personally presented the idea of a two-phase CDE at the UN General Assembly's special session on disarmament in May 1978. Soon after, he had a memorandum circulated to all CSCE states. Western allies and neutral countries were lukewarm about the proposal, while the Soviets resolutely rejected it. In the course of the following months, French diplomacy worked through bilateral relations to promote the CDE idea. Eventually, the French agreed to explain their proposal to the NATO Council, at a special meeting convened on 9 November 1978.[35] The French representative gave a thorough presentation, and did not shy away from questions. All delegates expressed satisfaction at France's decision to take an active role in the disarmament sphere, and declared their intention to study the proposal further.[36]

While in the special meeting the emphasis had been on security, at the next NATO Council ministerial meeting in December, Foreign Minister Jean François-Poncet made explicit the détente rationale underpinning the proposal.[37]

President Giscard also briefly expressed the CDE idea at the secret Western Four-Power summit in Guadalupe on 5–6 January 1979, where leaders 'engage[d] in an important exchange of their still-evolving personal viewpoints' on nuclear-weapons negotiations, NATO strategy and European security issues.[38] British Prime Minister James Callaghan showed perplexity at a conference involving 35 states, as well as concern that a CDE would sharply diminish any hope of reaching an agreement in the MBFR talks. US President Carter questioned whether the French proposal was cosmetic or really aimed at achieving disarmament. West German Chancellor Helmut Schmidt, on the contrary, came out strongly in support of Giscard, praising the French intention to return to multilateral discussions on disarmament.[39] The CDE, however, was not a matter for the informal and frank discussions that summitry embodied at the time.[40]

The French government, unwilling to lose control on its idea and to see it turned into a bloc-to-bloc tool, delayed detailed discussions within NATO until late 1979. Nonetheless, the French delegation to NATO would continue to give the Council progress reports on the initiative and listen to Allies' comments.[41] By contrast, it immediately started consultations with EC partners in EPC.[42] All partners demanded that a link should be established between the CDE and the CSCE, while the French proposal at the time envisaged gathering the same participants but in a parallel ad hoc framework. The British underlined the need for such a link even during Anglo-French politico-military talks.[43] The idea was that the socialist bloc's well-known interest in 'military détente' and disarmament offered a leverage to put pressure on their regimes to apply Final Act provisions and adopt new engagements in the field of human contacts/rights. On the contrary, the pursuit of military détente in a forum completely detached from the CSCE process would severely weaken the latter and deprive the West of one of the few valid tools to gradually change socialist regimes. Interestingly, this concern had been first expressed in the above-mentioned NATO special meeting by several diplomats; the Canadian delegate, in particular, had wondered whether it might be worth presenting the proposal for examination at the next CSCE meeting in Madrid, but the French representative had decisively excluded this option.[44] The idea was voiced in NATO, but EPC turned it into its own and changed the French attitude. The CDE proposal entered the 'report on the strategy of the Nine before and during the CSCE meeting' prepared by the EPC's CSCE working group; the report was submitted to the Political Committee for discussion, and eventually entered the agenda of the EPC ministerial meeting of November 1979.[45] The latter fully endorsed the CDE idea and made it an official objective for the next CSCE follow-up meeting. It is noteworthy that the ministerial communiqué presented the CDE as the Nine's approach, and only at the end did it refer to taking into account 'the various considerations which inspired the proposals made by France in May 1978'. Changes had indeed occurred. In the public statement the EC foreign ministers also listed the key CDE's features on which they had agreed

> meaningful confidence-building measures in the military field. These should be verifiable, applicable to the European continent as a whole and such that, by contributing to the improvement of the security of States, they will create conditions leading later to a process of arms control and reduction within the same geographical framework.[46]

Studying the origins of the CDE proposal thus shows that its main features were *not* determined by the NATO allies in Ankara in June 1980, as argued by scholar John Freeman,[47] but were rather discussed and agreed upon by the EC governments in EPC meetings in the first instance.

Furthermore, NATO's support of the CDE proposal did not rule out EPC engagement. Although detailed discussion of possible measures, which unfolded from early 1980 onwards, took place largely in NATO committees,[48] EPC continued its work. Irish neutrality could theoretically serve as an explanation, since the republic was a member of EPC but not of NATO. Still, it does not provide an adequate justification; the Irish could have given 'external' support to a 'NATO' proposal in Madrid negotiations, just as other like-minded CSCE participating states. The EC governments' choice not to delegate to NATO was rooted in their willingness to keep control of the pursuit of such an important goal. As will be demonstrated below, the EC member-states were first of all motivated by the determination to preserve détente in Europe and secondly concerned about domestic opinion's attitude towards pacifism. In addition, they all acknowledged the existence of deep-seated differences with Washington in relation to both the conduct of East–West relations and the meaning of détente. Even the new British government led by Margaret Thatcher since May 1979, though adopting a vigorous anti-communist rhetoric and increasing the defence budget, unambiguously stated its intention to 'persevere without respite in attempts to improve relations between East and West', and considered defence and détente as 'inseparable'.[49] It also regarded the CSCE, in particular, as an 'important and useful forum for East–West dialogue'.[50]

The Soviet invasion of Afghanistan on 26 December 1979 reinforced the EC governments' belief in their approach to European relations. The invasion proved the Kremlin's striking ability to mobilize troops of more than 100,000 soldiers within a very short time for use at the border with the Asian country; it could do the same for use at the European border. Initiatives aimed at defusing tension and preserving détente, namely the CDE and the CSCE, became even more important. All EC states' representatives explicitly expressed this view at the NATO Council meeting discussing the Allies' CSCE posture after the Afghan crisis. The representatives of Italy and Denmark affirmed their governments' intention to continue and, if possible, consolidate the détente process, and hence to strengthen the viability of the CSCE as a framework for contacts and negotiations between East and West. The German added that it was not in the West's interest to add to the crisis potential in Europe. The Belgian and the French diplomats pointed out that the CSCE provided the West with useful tools to influence Soviet policy in the political security, economic and humanitarian fields. All refused to turn the Madrid meeting into a forum for polemics.[51]

The view was very different in North America. The Canadian representative to NATO questioned the wisdom 'to continue the policy of détente – of which the CSCE was the most institutionalized expression – without coming to an understanding with the East on its application', and suggested that 'it might be more appropriate to demonstrate that détente was not an irreversible process'.[52] The worst reaction came from the Americans. The Carter administration was outraged by the Soviet move and reacted harshly, including sanctions. The year 1980 was one of presidential campaign and both candidates self-fashioned themselves as hawks against the Soviets. After the election of Ronald Reagan, whose opposition to the CSCE had been explicit, the EC governments worried that, once in office in January, the new president might withdraw the US delegation from the Madrid meeting, which opened on 11 November 1980. At the following NATO Council ministerial meeting on 12 December, EC foreign ministers Hans-Dietrich Genscher (Germany), Emilio Colombo (Italy), Lord Carrington (Britain), Charles-Ferdinand Nothomb (Belgium) and Christoph van der Klaauw (Netherlands) expressed their support for the CDE proposal and the importance of attaining its mandate at the CSCE frankly. Both détente and security were at stake, because the European Soviet territory was, in the words of Genscher, 'the very area where breaks of confidence are possible'.[53] At the NATO Council meeting of 23 January 1981 convened to discuss the strategy and objectives for the second phase of the Madrid CSCE, the representatives of the EC governments reminded their colleagues that 'the Allies had undertaken to support the French proposal' for a CDE and, in the words of Dutch diplomat van Dongen, 'should do their utmost' to support it at Madrid. The Europeans meant to put pressure on the new US administration, which 'had not yet formulated its policy to regard to this proposal'.[54]

Reagan did choose continuity, and on 16 February 1981, the head of the US delegation to the CSCE, Max Kampelman, announced that his government supported *in principle* the CDE proposal. Yet the combination of a strong stance on human rights with Reagan's confrontational rhetoric towards the Soviet Union did not augur well.

Domestic concerns also nourished this urge to decouple Europe from the intensifying superpower discord. No Western European governments underestimated the necessity to maintain an adequate level of armed forces and nuclear weapons in place to dissuade Soviet aggression. Good parts of the Western European population, though, had grown weary of the arms race; they denounced superpower struggle, actively protested 'nukes' and demanded disarmament accords. In various degrees, all Western European governments had to take domestic opinion into account when devising their security and defence policy. This pressure was comparatively light in France, where the anti-nuclear sentiment was rather weak and mostly addressed at superpowers' arsenals rather than at national weapons.[55] The problem was acute for those governments that had accepted to station new US nuclear missiles on their country's territory following NATO's 'dual-track' decision of December 1979 and were facing quite vocal and large anti-nuclear movements.[56] This was certainly the case of Belgium, Italy, West Germany and the United Kingdom, whose governments did not spare diplomatic efforts to remind the Americans that the other 'track' of the NATO decision concerning disarmament negotiations should also be implemented.[57] An initiative such as the CDE came in handy.

Finally, EC governments' unitary action in the disarmament field was nourished by their continual discussions on how to forge a European Union.[58] Whether as part of such an ambitious programme for deeper integration (Belgium, West Germany and Italy) or simply as a pragmatic step on its own (Britain, Denmark and Ireland), the idea to improve EPC was shared among the governments of the EC member-states. In particular, the idea of broadening its scope to security and defence was gaining momentum. National positions varied along the spectrum, from the negative Dutch view that 'real defence issues should be reserved for NATO and excluded from political co-operation'[59] to German Foreign Minister Genscher's bold public statement that a common European foreign policy should include co-ordination on defence. Italian Foreign Minister Colombo held very similar views.[60] The Italo-German interest in pushing the integration process further was the driver of the Genscher-Colombo initiative the same year, which proposed, among other things, to extend EPC's competence to matters of defence.[61] However, the Italian government, like most other

EC partners, would do nothing that could put the commitment of the US government to European defence at risk, especially at a time of apparent transatlantic strains.[62] Likewise, the Belgian government cautioned that any broadening of the EPC's scope should avoid weakening the Atlantic Alliance.[63] The Thatcher government was more open-minded, and Lord Carrington endeavoured throughout his mandate to put EPC on a stronger footing. Although considering defence and disarmament 'primarily the business of NATO', he thought it just natural that EPC should discuss both subjects, as they were part of 'important questions of foreign policy' that EPC had been entitled to discuss since its inception.[64] He called for a pragmatic improvement of EPC mechanisms and scope so as to achieve effectiveness and assure rapid reaction, especially in case of international crises.[65] So it was; on 13 October 1981 the EC foreign ministers approved the London Report on European Political Cooperation. The scope of EPC was not expanded to defence, though; Ireland's insistence on its neutrality requirements prevented such a bold change of mandate.[66] The London Report only stated that political cooperation included political and economic aspects of security,[67] hence formalizing the existing habit. In doing so, however, it confirmed the policy-making role of EPC, with obvious implications for the consultations in NATO. The same Irish government was clearly committed to strengthening EPC's role; on a number of occasions, it recalled 'that "the Ten" and "the West" were not synonymous terms to be used interchangeably', and that 'the Ten should not be treated as a sub-group within a broader western grouping'.[68]

By 1981, the EC governments had consulted closely on aims and tactics for the Madrid CSCE, and were pressing for reaching multilateral agreement on the CDE proposal; they defended it with determination not only against the Soviets but also vis-à-vis the US administration, whose stance at Madrid hardened in response to the worsening of the Polish crisis.[69] The Thatcher government was particularly supportive of the CDE proposal, as it had grown disillusioned with the MBFR talks.[70] Lord Carrington was concerned that European public opinion might get the feeling that their governments were putting obstacles to possible discussions on disarmament.[71] Remarkably, in the early 1981 the CDE was mentioned for the first time in the UK Defence estimates, and referred to by Defence Secretary John Nott as 'an important proposal concerning security in Europe'.[72]

The Soviets had accepted the CDE proposal as a basis for discussions. By early 1981, they had agreed in principle that CDE would apply to the whole European part of the Soviet Union, but had requested that the West would extend the confidence zone accordingly. However, provisos remained unexplained. On 31 March 1981 the delegations of neutral and non-aligned states tabled a draft concluding document that, among other things, proposed the extension of the area of application of the future CDE to 'adjoining sea and air space' of the participating countries. The Western delegations were unhappy with the draft. The NATO Council ministerial meeting of 29 April agreed that NATO experts should elaborate a counterproposal for a formula on the CDE's geographical area of application.[73]

In mid-July 1981 the NATO Council agreed on such a formula. The EPC Political Committee hoped that this would suffice to clinch agreement on CDE and enable the Soviets to make progress on all outstanding issues in Madrid. However, the North Americans posed preconditions to Western approval of the CSCE final document. Both the US and the Canadian governments made their consent dependent on the approval of the proposal for an experts' meeting on human rights and of certain measures in the humanitarian field (Third Basket). The Canadians were long-time hard-liners in this field; Foreign Secretary

Mark MacGuigan had given a passionate statement on the subject at the May 1981 NATO ministerial Council in Rome, concluding that 'human rights cannot be sacrificed for the sake of the military aspects of security'.[74] EC governments had usually been more pragmatic and anyway opposed to experts meetings on these matters, as their volatile nature could not substitute for strong operational language in the CSCE final document; they were certainly not willing to jeopardize the CDE deal for the sake of such an initiative.[75] The EC governments instructed their delegations in Madrid accordingly, and their stance did not go unnoticed in NATO. In the course of his farewell speech at the end of his service to NATO in 1981, Canadian Counsellor G. J. Smith said he was 'concerned that the strengthening of the political cooperation process of the Community was leading the Ten to give less weight to what took place in the Alliance'. This was in his view 'a regrettable trend and one which he hoped would not develop far'.[76] Five days later, the US administration decided to throw in some weight. Given that the UK held the EC rotating presidency at the time, US Secretary of State Alexander Haig sent a personal letter to Lord Carrington in which he praised cohesion and teamwork on finding a formula for the CDE area, but pressed hard on giving priority to human-rights issues. He unequivocally stated that, as important as the CDE was, the US administration could not agree to it without balancing progress on human rights; accordingly, the action of the US ambassador to CSCE, Max Kampelman, who vocally demanded progress on human-rights provisions, had his 'strong personal support'.[77]

The Soviets rejected the proposed NATO formula for the CDE geographical zone, and delegations in Madrid agreed on a summer recession until late October. As NATO consultations over the recession period did not help to reach agreement on a new NATO formula, the German permanent representative to NATO, Hans-Georg Wieck, gave a working lunch in Brussels on 12 October to discuss pending divergences. EPC political directors, heads of Madrid CSCE delegations, and NATO ambassadors from the United States, France, Germany, Italy and the UK were present. The discussions focused on the two main bones of contention between the Americans and the Europeans, namely the interpretation of the phrase 'adjoining sea and air area' in the area of application for the CDE, and the balance in the CSCE final document. The US permanent representative insisted on specifying that 'adjoining sea' meant territorial waters only, whether the French proposed a 'functional approach' that would allow the inclusion of any activity at sea or in the air that was linked with activity on the land in the scope of the CDE measures of notification. As for the second pending question, Kampelman stated that the Americans would not accept a satisfying deal on the CDE if it were not accompanied by satisfactory results on human rights. In response to Kampelman arguing that there would be no balance without adequate progress on both elements, British Political Director Julian Bullard said that the American approach was paradoxical: even if the West got agreement to a CDE on Western terms, it would still insist on demanding equally important concessions from the Soviets on human rights. In his view, the logic of balance implied that satisfactory results on the CDE should pair with reasonable language on the human-rights dimension that could be acceptable to the Kremlin. When Kampelman warned that the political situation in Congress should be taken into account, the British delegate urged the Americans 'not to try to solve their domestic political problems by creating a domestic political problem for [the] Europeans'. He also affirmed that he 'hoped the Americans would not try to suggest that a human rights experts' meeting was more important than a CDE, or that if we got what we wanted on CDE, it would be held up until we got agreement on an experts' meeting on human rights'.[78]

The position of the White House on human rights had hardened in parallel with the worsening of the internal situation in Poland, where the conflict between the authorities and the Solidarity movement was starting to escalate. Given the US government's stonewalling attitude, the EPC ministerial meeting of 13 October 1981 – the very next day after the NATO working lunch – discussed the CDE issue in detail. Lord Carrington stated that 'the CDE was a prize for which the Ten should press hard. It would be some time before the TNF and SALT discussions produced any results and agreement on a CDE could be important for European public opinion.'[79] German Foreign Minister Genscher suggested that unresolved problems of the mandate should be referred to the EPC Political Committee, a proposal to which French Minster Cheysson readily agreed.[80] This clearly showed that the foreign ministers of the EC's most powerful countries considered EPC coordination very valuable and aimed at presenting a common front vis-à-vis the Americans and in NATO consultations. EPC also forged a common position on the question of 'balance' in the final Madrid document, establishing that the latter should contain a CDE on Western terms and reasonable – not maximalist – language on human-rights dimension. When the CSCE Madrid meeting reconvened on 27 October, the opening statement given on behalf of the EC Ten explicitly stated their 'positive interest' in the initiation of 'the negotiation of an arms control regime of openness concerning the disposition of major military formations throughout Europe'. The statement also conveyed their annoyance at the length of negotiations on the matter, and the intention of concluding 'our much protracted meeting' by the middle of December. Otherwise they might 'regretfully have to draw the necessary conclusions from the continued lack of agreement'.[81]

This position had been agreed within EPC only, as a specific tactic of the Ten. There was indeed a clear lack of agreement across the Atlantic on this issue, as the US government maintained that options should be kept open for the moment. When Kampelman called again on the British, the latter explained that 'the Ten were in complete agreement' that they faced a 'political need' to convince the public opinion 'not to flirt with unilateralism', and that this 'was a strong argument for getting something out of Madrid on the CDE'.[82] The Americans complained that 'public discussion of options should be avoided', and made clear that 'they hoped the European Council would go no further than reaffirming its desire to secure a substantial and balanced concluding document by Christmas'. The British government's opinion was very different. It thought that 'the Americans [we]re using the need to avoid publicity (on which we can all agree) as a pretext for preventing the Ten taking a clear view now before discussions in NATO'. The UK position was that EPC should not abandon its decision and should give 'a clear lead to delegations by the beginning of December'. The Europeans would 'of course' consult their Allies 'as soon as possible *after* the [European] Council meeting'.[83] Coming from Washington's traditionally closest ally, this says much about EC governments' keenness to speak as one and achieve their goals.

Disagreement with the White House on priorities and tactics became even stronger after the Polish crisis reached its climax with the imposition of martial law in the country on 13 December 1981. Reagan's hardened stance against the Soviet Union, which included sanctions and refusal to continue negotiations, put the CSCE – and the prospects of CDE – in jeopardy. The history of the transatlantic clashes over the Polish crisis has been adequately covered in recent archive-based literature.[84] It will suffice here to remind that even Thatcher, who enjoyed the closest personal relationship with the US President, was furious at his unilateral action and outraged that sanctions would intentionally hit Western European allies' firms. In early November 1982 Reagan yielded and eventually agreed to resume discussions at Madrid; however, he hardened his requests on human-rights provisions. In this deeply exacerbated climate, the governments of the EC member-states fought even harder to reach an agreement on the CDE proposal. The German government was particularly vocal on this point. In autumn 1982, Genscher authored an article in which he specifically praised the CDE's potential to make the military activities in Europe more transparent and help to dispel the fear of a surprise attack and the danger of unintentional escalation.[85] During a visit to Washington in April 1983, Chancellor Helmut Kohl stated that Western European governments attached vital importance to reaching agreement on the CDE.[86]

The EC member-states eventually achieved their goal at Madrid. The difficult relationship with the Reagan administration during the last months had put a strain on transatlantic relations, but had strengthened Western European cohesion. EPC had proved able to act as a competitor to NATO, despite the latter's heavyweight credentials on security issues. As a matter of fact, the EC governments did not just promote and defend the CDE proposal, but also closely concerted common tactics and drafts for the CDE preparatory meeting in Helsinki, which took place from 25 October to 11 November 1983.[87] The assessment of their performance at this preparatory phase praised EPC's work and emphasized the positive and autonomous role that the Ten collectively were able to play within CSCE-related multilateral forums.[88]

Cooperation as the complementary dimension of EPC–NATO interaction

Competition between EPC and NATO never ruled out cooperation on matters related to the CDE. This cooperative stance started with the NATO Council final communiqué of December 1979 endorsing the French idea as 'a basis upon which to continue developing their approach in this field to bring about such a conference' at the forthcoming Madrid CSCE meeting.[89] Arguably, cooperation between EPC and NATO could also work well without the participation of the United States. The US administration had kept a reserved position, which the closest allies attributed to both latent scepticism about the CDE and concern that the latter might undermine MBFR negotiations; then the Soviet invasion of Afghanistan strengthened US reserves, which affected the whole CSCE exercise. Soviet and American postures helped to rally the other NATO allies' support of the French proposal. The Portuguese representative said that the events in Afghanistan 'must not cause the basic CSCE objectives, and particularly the quest for détente, to be abandoned'. The Turkish diplomat was even more vocal: the Ankara authorities regarded 'the quest for détente as the essential precondition for security and stability in the world'; maintained that the Madrid meeting would serve a useful purpose; and called the Allies to 'resist the temptation to use Madrid as a means of getting even with the Soviet Union'. He emphasized that his authorities attached the greatest importance to the military aspects of security discussed at Madrid and to the French proposal for a CDE; so did the Norwegian representative.[90]

The coordination between NATO and EPC had been a delicate affair since the inception of the latter. The CSCE had mostly been an EPC affair; the cohesion of the EC governments had provided the foundations for the Western positions in the Helsinki CSCE and then at the review meeting in Belgrade in 1977–8.[91] Non-EC NATO member-states had generally accepted this situation, but had shown considerable sensitivity over matters in which the Alliance had a clear interest and which were also the subject of concurrent consultation in

EPC, such as Afghanistan and preparations for the Madrid CSCE. As already mentioned, most EC governments, while keen to use EPC to elaborate and then assert unitary positions, were also careful to avoid damage to the Alliance. They thus resolved to take the other NATO allies' sensitivities into account. This proved useful for strengthening the CDE proposal, for instance its provisions for the passage from CDE Phase 1 on CSBMs to Phase 2 on disarmament. In mid-1980 the French still insisted that this should be automatic; several allies, though, were concerned that the Soviet would have no need to agree on substantial results on CSBMs, as they would get to the disarmament phase anyway, which interested them most. The Norwegians put forward the idea that CDE Phase 1 results should be evaluated at the next CSCE follow-up conference after Madrid, and only in light of that assessment should a final decision be taken on whether to call a CDE Phase 2.[92] Espoused by other delegations in the following months, this idea became part of the CDE proposal – and eventually of the CDE mandate agreed at Madrid.

The pattern of consultation at the Madrid CSCE meeting changed as well in favour of more punctual NATO coordination. The main reason, though, was that military and security questions, where NATO expertise was necessary, had a larger place in the negotiations. Since the start of the Madrid CSCE in autumn 1980, the basic unit of coordination on site was the 'Group of 16' (NATO plus Spain, which was close to becoming a member), which did not include the Irish. However, continuing the practice established at earlier meetings, the group of the Ten met before the scheduled meetings of the NATO caucus. Consequently, the delegations that belonged to both groups spent about four hours a day on Western coordination activities.[93]

Coordination at Madrid allowed, for example, for solid backing to the French proposal both in the security-basket negotiations and in the plenary sessions at a time when five proposals on a disarmament conference or military détente had been tabled, respectively from Poland, France, Yugoslavia, Romania and Sweden. The Polish proposal was the least attractive to Western governments, not only because of its imprecision but because it did not appear to require the prospective conference to take place within the CSCE. It evidently was intended to decouple the military aspects of security, which interested the socialist bloc the most, from the humanitarian and other aspects of the CSCE that were so troublesome to the socialist regimes. NATO members thought that the West should confront Eastern propaganda proposals on 'military détente' with a concrete and ambitious long-term programme for security discussions in Europe.[94] Their solidarity in backing the French proposal had not been undermined by the 'almost total silence' of the US delegates – in 1980 the Carter administration was not in a position to commit its successor's (Reagan's) to supporting the CDE. The Norwegian delegation had been very effective in attacking the Swedish proposal; the Norwegian representative criticized it for failing to grasp the nettle of the geographical parameter (Soviet territory up to the Urals), for bringing nuclear weapons into the picture, which would make things much more complicated, and for not linking Phase 2 of a CDE to approval of Phase 1's result by the CSCE follow-up meeting.[95] In substance, the Norwegian diplomats had firmly defended the key parameters of the French CDE proposal.

Caucus meetings of delegations in Madrid were thus a key vector enhancing cooperation between EPC and NATO. Cooperation was also facilitated by structural similarities of the two organizations: the machinery for political consultation was very similar, with the array of working groups feeding into a political committee which then reported to the NATO Council meeting at the level of permanent delegates ('political directors' in EPC), ministers, or, occasionally, heads of government. EPC used to meet before and after NATO meetings; this way, EC members' NATO delegations were fully informed of EPC discussions, positions and agreed proposals and equipped to advance them; likewise, detail of NATO discussions fed back into EPC.

The most important factor behind EPC–NATO cooperation, however, was the continuous work of bridge building and persuasion carried out by some European governments towards the US administration. Not only national sources, but also verbatim and summary records of NATO meetings held in NATO Archives give sound evidence of the fact that the US stance on East–West relations and human rights was the main source of tensions within the Alliance; the US attitude clearly emerges as the EC governments' point of concern and annoyance in EPC discussions. National archival sources show that several Western European representatives strove to reconcile divergences between the US and European governments. The main rationale behind these efforts was that a deep split between the United States and Western Europe would change the Soviet perception of the Atlantic Alliance in a way that could only damage Western Europe's security.

The first to seek cooperation at the transatlantic level on the CDE proposal was the French president. Since the Guadalupe summit, Giscard had showed keen interest in increased coordination between France and NATO, and the US administration was treating the French 'with complaisance'. This friendly attitude went so far that by early 1981 officials in the British Foreign Office had 'the uncomfortable feeling that there is more communication between the Americans and the French about these [defence] problems than between us and the Americans'.[96] The strength of the allies' backing for the CDE proposal in Madrid owed much to the French recognition that they needed the support of both European and Alliance partners if they wanted the CDE proposal to take off.

Indeed, the French idea only became a solid proposal after it had benefited from NATO expertise. In the preparatory phase for the Madrid meeting, the NATO working group quickly became preoccupied with technical considerations of individual measures linked to the CDE; it decided that the UK government should put forward a clear set of objectives which would make it possible to construct a coherent set of CSBMs. The British paper, circulated within NATO in March 1980, defined the goals as reducing the risk of surprise attacks, enhancing warning time in periods of tension, and preserving at an adequate level the Alliance's freedom to react to threatening events. The emphasis was deliberately on the military objectives of the CSBMs, as the UK experts agreed with the French view that measures emerging from a CDE should be militarily significant. The German, Danish and Norwegian delegates tended to put equal emphasis on the political objectives of increasing openness and mutual confidence. After intensive debate the working group submitted a report to the NATO Council in July 1980. The agreed set of objectives involved compromises on all sides, but the French probably gave in most. This reflected the fact that the original French package showed a considerable ignorance of both allied military practice and the measures put forward by the West in MBFR covering similar activities. The NATO expertise filled this void and made the CDE proposal stronger by conceiving a package of CSBMs that was clearer, simpler and with more military 'bite' than the one originally conceived by the French.[97]

The French also played an important role in October 1981, when, less than a fortnight before the CSCE would reconvene from summer recession, NATO still could not agree on a new formula on CDE area of application pertaining 'adjoining sea'. The Director of

Political Affairs at the French Foreign Ministry – Jacques Andréani – sent a message calling for urgent consultations to the opposite numbers in US, British and German governments, soliciting a common effort 'to reach a common position which could then be presented, with the customary safeguards, to our other partners in the Alliance'. The accompanying text summarized existing divergences and exposed possible options, and was 'intended to expedite progress towards such a solution'.[98] This cooperative attitude is particularly important given the change at the helm of French politics: Socialist leader François Mitterrand had been elected president of the Republic in May 1981, and the new government counted two communist ministers.

Most of the work aimed at facilitating reconciliation with the US administration was done jointly by the French, British and West German governments, in particular by their foreign ministers. Together, they tried either to bring the US administration to agree on European positions or at least to prevent it from being in the way of European goals. This was mainly the case throughout 1981, during the months of arm-twisting on the questions of defining the CDE geographical zone of application, interpreting the 'adjoining sea' phrasing, and deciding the appropriate tactics at the CSCE negotiations.[99] When agreement could not be reached due to the American unwillingness to yield on the question of territorial waters, the three Western European governments coordinated their position. They proposed that all NATO countries' delegations should adopt a 'self-denying ordinance' on not defining the meaning of 'adjoining sea' at the Madrid negotiations, with the aim of projecting Alliance cohesion vis-à-vis the Soviets.[100] It also occurred that all the NATO members' representatives 'ganged up' – both in NATO and at the CSCE – to put pressure on the Americans, whose unwillingness to abandon their interpretation of the 'adjoining sea' clause eventually annoyed everyone in the Western camp.[101] The French 'functional approach' of including sea forces linked with operations on the land proved flexible, convincing and safer for NATO security interests, and very likely to meet the acceptance of the other CSCE participants.

The British were much involved in facilitating NATO cohesion and building bridges across the Atlantic, a role they had historically played. Fundamental in this case was their sincere appreciation of the CDE proposal. The FCO's Defence Department considered it 'likely to make a positive contribution to security in Europe, as well as providing valuable political counter to the East's propaganda proposals on military détente'.[102] The British government firmly maintained that any European disarmament conference should adopt the essential features of the French proposal. Yet, in order to give the CDE chances of success, it was 'important to have US on board', and British representatives promoted these ideas in the many bilateral contacts they had with the Americans on CDE-related issues.[103]

Likewise, the German government considered that security questions would represent the central issue in the CSCE process and saw the continued participation of Canada and the United States as an essential element; 'in the field of arms control and disarmament the Soviets should be given no opportunity to create a split between the European and the North American Allies'.[104] The German government also proposed concrete measures to foster closer cooperation across the Atlantic. Already in 1980 Genscher had suggested to convene informal meetings of the NATO foreign ministers to discuss high politics issues without a set agenda and without the usual array of civil servants. Such meetings were eventually agreed upon, and NATO foreign ministers assembled for the first informal gathering at the beginning of October 1982 in Montreal.[105] Even before that, the Germans had convened in Bonn a NATO Summit on 9–10 June 1982 to lay the groundwork for an overall

Alliance strategy for the 1980s. Within the latter's scope, the Document on Arms Control and Disarmament affirmed that Western proposals offered the possibility of substantial reductions in conventional forces in Europe, as well as of confidence-building measures covering the whole of Europe.[106] Accordingly, MBFR and CDE were coupled in NATO's overall strategy, signalling that the EPC initiative had become part of the Alliance's set of policies in the field.

Cooperation on the CDE became established by the end of 1983, in view of the actual CDE negotiations due to open in January 1984. NATO foreign ministers reviewed the various proposals that had been developed so far in the field of CSBMs and on certain aspects of security and disarmament. The Final Communiqué of the North Atlantic Council of December 1983 recognized the CDE as 'an important part of the CSCE process' and providing 'new possibilities for increasing security throughout Europe'. It announced that the Allies would table 'a comprehensive package of concrete measures', were 'resolved to negotiate actively', and that '[a]s a sign of their determination' [m]inisters would themselves attend the conference.[107]

Seven days into the CDE in Stockholm, NATO countries' delegates jointly tabled a package of six confidence- and security-building measures that eventually came to define the substance of the negotiations. These provisions built significantly upon the Helsinki confidence-building measures: they lowered the notification threshold from 25,000 to 6000 soldiers involved in a manoeuvre; lengthened the period of notice required from 21 to 45 days; provided for mandatory invitation of observers; and prescribed verification by on-site inspection.[108] The NATO package was designed to provide greater transparency in military activities in Europe, reduce the chances of miscalculation, and hence build confidence and enhance stability.

At the CDE, NATO was the natural forum for coordination, since military expertise and the advice of military authorities and experts was paramount. The nature of the CDE negotiations meant that EPC played a less important role than at other CSCE meetings. EC governments continued to discuss CDE-related questions in EPC, primarily in the broader political context of East–West relations and with regard to the links between the CDE and the other elements of the CSCE process. At the same time, they valued cooperation within NATO as an essential asset to achieve results in the CDE negotiations.

Conclusions

The analysis of the debates about the CDE initiative has shed new light on the relations between EPC and NATO in the late 1970s and early 1980s in the field of East–West relations, particularly on its military-security aspects. It has demonstrated that the CDE proposal and its main features had clear origins in the EPC framework, that NATO followed suit to endorse the proposal and provided the expertise necessary to flesh it out and integrate it with NATO's overall military strategy. It has also showed that NATO endorsement did not rule out EPC engagement. Quite the contrary, EPC remained the most committed actor sponsoring the CDE proposal at the Madrid CSCE meeting.

Overall, this article has evidenced clear patterns of competition and cooperation between EPC and NATO. Present since EPC's inception in 1970, both forms of interaction became more substantial and visible a decade later. A certain degree of competition characterized the relationship between NATO and EPC since the latter's early days, as both organizations engaged in preparing common positions and proposals for the Helsinki CSCE. Moreover, the heads of state and government of the EC member-states had initiated EPC to try to speak with a single voice in the realm of foreign policy, and never excluded that EPC could discuss security matters – though strictly military security and defence were carefully avoided.

The competitive relationship between EPC and NATO intensified in the late 1970s and early 1980s, when, following a rise in Cold War tensions, EPC started to discuss the military-security aspects of East–West relations more regularly and thoroughly. Competition deepened when EPC took the initiative in defining a concrete approach to disarmament policies for Europe, namely the CDE idea. In so doing, the governments of the EC member-states consciously pushed EPC to venture into NATO's domain. They were motivated by the willingness to preserve détente in Europe, which they conceived as a process aimed at gradually overcoming the Cold War order, from the superpowers' renewed confrontation; the concern with public opinion's proclivity to neutralism; and the willingness to use the strength of the group (the EC-Ten) to avoid being marginalized as individual medium and small powers. Moreover, the EC governments' resolve was continually nourished by growing mistrust towards the US administrations, annoyance at the latter's increasing unilateralism in East–West matters, and awareness of divergent interests across the Atlantic. The main trigger for competition between EPC and NATO thus lay in the complicated relationship between the governments of the EC member-states and the United States administrations when security, cooperation and détente in Europe were at stake. It is possible to affirm that all EC governments were responsible for competition dynamics, as they all shared the above-mentioned rationales. It is noteworthy, though, that the Thatcher government was very much part of this cohort, qualifying the commonly projected image of harmonious views between the British prime minister and US President Reagan.

EPC's competition with NATO is evident not only in EPC taking the initiative in the field of disarmament in Europe, but also in the fact that it led the way at the Madrid CSCE. In particular, tactics and priorities agreed within EPC were rarely altered after NATO consultations, and sometimes applied straight to CSCE negotiations without prior coordination with the other NATO allies.

Cooperation was also present in principle since the beginning, given NATO's competence, which no Western European governments questioned, and the dual membership of all EC member-states but Ireland in EPC and NATO. However, cooperation really took off after EPC had elaborated a clear draft mandate for the CDE and CSCE negotiations had started. At the Madrid CSCE meeting the NATO caucus was much more active than the EPC group; this was partly because EC governments took into account the resentment of the other NATO members at being presented with detailed positions already agreed among the Ten, and primarily because NATO expertise was necessary in negotiations on military and security questions. However, a fundamental driver behind EPC's effort at promoting cooperation within NATO, which all governments shared, was the need to preserve Atlantic solidarity and project Western cohesion at times of strained transatlantic relations and high East–West tensions. A weakened NATO would serve neither Western European security nor détente, which were top priorities of EC governments' foreign policy. Some governments stand out for their efforts to build bridges within NATO and towards the US administration in particular: the British, the German and, most remarkably, the French. Not only did they act via bilateral channels, they also coordinated their action in secret tripartite consultations.

Cooperation within NATO was paramount in drafting military measures proposals, and in actual CDE negotiations later on.

Finally, a stronger EPC also had a positive effect on NATO's cohesion and own consultations mechanisms, as NATO came to emulate EPC structures and practices. Moreover, NATO ultimately embraced EPC's disarmament initiative as an Alliance flagship policy; proposed in July 1987 at the Vienna follow-up meeting, this became eventually the Treaty on Conventional Forces in Europe (CFE), signed in November 1990.

Finally, the CDE case shows that the Cold War continued to push EC governments towards broader and more effective foreign-policy coordination in EPC. It thus confirms recent Cold War historiography's argument that the EC member-states collectively (whether as supranational EC or by means of EPC) played a key role in shaping East–West relations since the early 1970s. This article also adds to recent European integration historiography that argues in favour of considering the 1970s and early 1980s as a constructive period of the integration process: it contributes to showing that non-supranational forms of close cooperation flourished between EC governments, and enhanced their international visibility as a close-knit group ('the Ten'). Ultimately, this nourished third countries' perception of an EC's international role, as the subtleties of EPC/EC relationship were neither evident nor explained to them. As a matter of fact, Cheysson's speech at the CDE opening session referred to 'the ten members of the European Community', not to EPC.

Notes

1. Paris COREU (suite), 11 janvier 1984, 5020, AMAE (translated from French by the author).
2. For an overview: Deighton, 'Foreign and Security Policy after the End of the Cold War', 255–67. A just-published work briefly considering 1973–4's (failed) attempts to include defence in the EC's international activity confirms the same argument: Ferrari, *Sometimes Speaking with a Single Voice*, 66–70.
3. Deighton and Bossuat, *The EC/EU: a World Security Actor?*; Bossuat, 'Origins and Development'; Möckli, *European Foreign Policy*. Specifically on the role of EC/EPC in the CSCE: Romano, *From Détente in Europe to European Détente*; on EPC and Middle East: Möckli, 'The EC-Nine and Transatlantic Conflict'; Allen and Hauri, 'The Euro-Arab Dialogue, the Venice Declaration'.
4. On such inter-organizational links: Patel, 'Provincialising European Union'.
5. Nuti et al., *The Euromissile Crisis and the End of the Cold War*; Nuti, 'The Origins of the 1979 Dual Track Decision – a Survey'; Dujardin, 'From Helsinki to the Missiles Question'; Spohr, 'Conflict and Cooperation in Intra-Alliance Nuclear Politics'; Spohr, 'Helmut Schmidt and the Shaping of Western Security in the Late 1970s'.
6. Park, 'NATO Summits', 90.
7. In 1952 Greece and Turkey became members.
8. Wallace, 'European Political Co-Operation', 9.
9. The Single European Act of 1986 gave a treaty base to EPC.
10. '*Report on Future Tasks of the Alliance*' annexed to Final Communiqué, Brussels, 13th–14th December 1967, par. 13, NATO.
11. '*Mutual And Balanced Force Reductions. Declaration adopted by Foreign Ministers and Representatives of Countries participating in the NATO Defence Program*', Reykjavik, 24th–25th June 1968.
12. 'Aide-mémoire from the French Government to the other 14 NATO countries', 11 March 1966. French forces' reintegration into NATO's military command took place in 2009; it did not entail integrating the *Force de Frappe*.

MULTIPLE CONNECTIONS IN EUROPEAN COOPERATION

13. *'Declaration of the North Atlantic Council on European Security'*, Brussels, 4th–5th December 1969, par. 14. Accessed at http://www.nato.int/docu/comm/49-95/c691204b.htm

14. CC24(1970), 27 May 1970, CAB 128/45, TNA.

15. Minute from Tickell, FCO, 23 May 1972, Doc. no. 9, DBPO.

16. Brief by FCO, 2 April 1971, CAB 133/416, TNA; Note, MAE – Sous-Direction Europe Orientale, 1 juillet 1972, 2924, AMAE. See also Bluth, 'Détente and Conventional Arms Control'.

17. Letter UK Embassy Stockholm to Tickell (WOD), 26 May 1972, FCO 28/1690, TNA.

18. Letter Ministry of Defence to PM Heath, 29 November 1972, PREM 15/1279, TNA.

19. For detail see Romano, 'Western Europe's Self-Assertion Towards the Superpowers'; and Romano, 'The Main Task of the European Political Cooperation'. Candidate states were associated to EPC beforehand: the UK since February 1972, Ireland and Denmark in May of the same year. They joined the EC on 1 January 1973.

20. Fisher, *Neutral Power in the CSCE.*

21. For a detailed analysis, see Ghebali, *Confidence-building Measures Within the CSCE Process.*

22. Dean, 'Military Security in Europe', 30.

23. *Final Act, 'Document on Confidence-Building Measures and Certain Aspects of Security and Disarmament',* 10.

24. Note by the Secretary-General, 'Confidence-Building Measures: Past and Present', 22 June 1979, C-M(79)46, NATO Arch.

25. Rose (UKDEL NATO) to Lord Carrington (FM), 22 January 1981, FCO 28/4671, TNA.

26. CSCE (80) 2/CP/, 14 mars 1980, 4211 bis, Communautés Européennes 1976–80, AMAE.

27. Final communiqué, North Atlantic Council, Brussels 13th–14th December 1979, par. 8; and Final Communiqué, North Atlantic Council, Ankara 25th–26th June 1980, par. 8.

28. Heyde, 'Multilaterale Konferenzdiplomatie unter nationaler Flagge', 39.

29. Heyde, 'Nicht nur Entspannung und Menschenrechte', 91–2.

30. Dispatch, Rose (UKDEL NATO) to Gillmore (Defence Dept), 23 January 1981, FCO 28/4671, TNA.

31. See Romano, 'The European Community and the Belgrade CSCE'.

32. Romano, 'A Single European Voice Can Speak Louder'.

33. Romano, 'G-7s, European Councils and East-West Economic Relations'; Mourlon-Druol, 'More than a Prestigious Spokesperson'.

34. Carrington (FM) to Deakins, MP, December 1980, FCO 98/959, TNA.

35. 'Summary record of a meeting of the Council held at the NATO HQ, Brussels, on Wednesday 27th September 1978', C-R(78)32, NATO Arch.

36. 'Summary record of a meeting of the Council held at the NATO HQ, Brussels, on 9th November 1978', C-R(78)39, NATO Arch.

37. 'Summary record of a meeting of the Council in Ministerial Session held at NATO HQ, Brussels, on Friday, 7th December 1978', C-R(78)47 – PART 1, NATO Arch.

38. Spohr, 'Helmut Schmidt and the Shaping of Western Security in the Late 1970s', 174. This article does not even mention the CDE.

39. Conclusions of Cabinet meeting, 11 January 1979, CAB/128/65/1, TNA. CDE was merely mentioned in 'The Guadeloupe Summit', *HL Deb 16 January 1979, House of Lords.*

40. See Mourlon-Druol and Romero, *International Summitry and Global Governance*; and Spohr and Reynolds, *Transcending the Cold War.*

41. 'Summary Record of a Restricted Meeting of the Council in Ministerial Session on Thursday 7th December 1978', PR(78)56-BIL; 'Summary Record of a meeting of the Council held at the NATO HQ, Brussels on Tuesday, 8th May 1972', C-R(79)18; 'XXVIIIth Semi-Annual Meeting of the Political Committee with Disarmament Experts', 15 November 1979, PO/79/117, NATO Arch. Also: Dispatch Rose (UKDEL NATO) to Gillmore (Defence Dept), 23 January 1981, FCO 28/4671, TNA.

42. Brief, European Integration Dept (External), 26 February 1979, FCO 98/637, TNA; Paris COREU to All COREU, 21 April 1979, FCO 98/637, TNA.

MULTIPLE CONNECTIONS IN EUROPEAN COOPERATION

43. Dispatch, Rose (UKDEL NATO) to Gillmore (Defence Dept), 23 January 1981, FCO 28/4671, TNA.
44. 'Summary record of a meeting of the Council held at the NATO HQ, Brussels, on 9th November 1978', C-R(78)39, NATO Arch.
45. Dublin COREU to All COREU, 5 September 1979, FCO 98/637, TNA.
46. European Political Cooperation statements of the Foreign Ministers and other documents 1979, AEI, 80–1.
47. Freeman, *Security and the CSCE Process,* 85–7.
48. Jackson (POCO) to Cooper (ECD external), 10 June 1981, FCO 98/1175.
49. *HC Deb 18 May 1979 vol 967 cc555–657,* 2.
50. FCO Secretary of State to all posts, 7 December 1979, FCO 28/3683, TNA.
51. 'Summary Record of a meeting of the Council held at NATO HQ Brussels on Wednesday 28th May 1980', C-R(80)21, NATO Arch.
52. Ibid.
53. 'Verbatim Record of the Meeting of the North Atlantic Council in Ministerial session held on Friday 12th Dec 1980 at NATO HQ Brussels', C-VR(80)48 Part 2, NATO Arch.
54. 'Summary Record of a meeting of the Council held at NATO HQ, Brussels on Friday 23th January 1981', C-R(81)3, NATO Arch.
55. Cooper (POCO Unit, FCO) to FitzHerbert (ECD external), 26 October 1981, FCO 98/1175, TNA.
56. For detailed analysis see: Dujardin, 'From Helsinki to the Missiles Question'; Dijk, '"A Mass Psychosis"'; Guasconi, 'Public Opinion and the Euromissile Crisis'; Nehring, 'The Last Battle of the Cold War'; Rother, 'Family Row'.
57. Gala, 'From INF to SDI', 116–118; Geiger, 'Die Regierung Schmidt-Genscher und der NATO-Doppelbeschluss'.
58. By 1976 three reports had been circulated for discussions: Tindemans, *'European Union. Report',* AEI; European Commission, *'Report on European Union',* AEI; EP, *'Reports on European Union',* AEI.
59. Budd (UK Embassy The Hague) to Cooper (POCO Unit, FCO), 13 February 1981, FCO 98/1175, TNA.
60. EC, PE 71.832/fin, 'Report on European political cooperation and the role of the European Parliament', 30 June 1981, HAEU.
61. On the Genscher-Colombo initiative see Loth, *Building Europe,* 264–5.
62. Tomkys (UK Embassy Rome) to Scott (UKDEL NATO), 24 August 1981, FCO 98/1175, TNA.
63. Richards to FitzHerbert (ECD external), 21 December 1981, FCO 98/1175, TNA.
64. Carrington (FM) to Deakins, MP, December 1980, FCO 98/959, TNA.
65. Note, Secretary of State for Foreign and Commonwealth Affairs, 17 September 1981, CAB/129/213/21; Letter, Carrington (FM) to Prime Minister, 4 June 1981, FCO 98/1175, TNA.
66. Staples (UK Embassy Dublin) to Newington (Irish Dept., FCO), 20 June 1980, FCO 98/969, TNA.
67. Note, Secretary of State for Foreign and Commonwealth Affairs, 17 September 1981, CAB/129/213/21, TNA.
68. La Haye COREU to all COREU, 12 May 1981, FCO 98/1179, TNA.
69. *Report on European Union from the Ministers of Foreign Affairs to the European Council,* 1981; idem, 1982; idem, 1983.
70. Ambassade de France, Aout 1981, COM/1/3 1981, 5857, AMAE.
71. Tel. 20281 de Dufourcq (Londres), 29 mai 1981, COM/1/3 1981, 5857, AMAE.
72. Note, Secretary of State for Defence, 16 March 1981, CAB/129/211/11, TNA.
73. Brief No. 8, POCO Unit FCO, 20 May 1981, FCO 98/1179, TNA.
74. 'Verbatim Record of the Meeting of the North Atlantic Council in Ministerial session held on Monday 4th May 1981, Rome', C-VR(81)18, NATO Arch.
75. Brief, POCO Unit FCO, 16 July 1981, FCO 46/2671, TNA.
76. Alston (UKDEL NATO) to Johnson (EESD, FCO, 15 July 1981, FCO 98/1172, TNA.
77. Louis (USA Embassy London) to Carrington (FM), 20 July 1981, FCO 46/2671, TNA.

78. Note for the record, Rose (UKDEL NATO), 12 October 1981, FCO 28/4671, TNA.
79. Tel. from Carrington (FM), 14 October 1981, FCO 98/1179, TNA.
80. Ibid.
81. 'CSCE, Opening Statement on behalf of the Ten (Madrid, 27 October 1981)', in *European Political Cooperation in the 1980s*, ed. Pijpers, Regelsberger, and Wessel, 347–8.
82. Carrington (FM) to Washington and all EC posts, 15 October 1981, FCO 28/4671, TNA.
83. Hughes (CSCE Unit) to Broomfield (EESD), 25 November 1981, FCO 98/1179, TNA.
84. Romano, 'More Cohesive, Still Divergent', 48–52; Brier, 'Poland's Solidarity as a Contested Symbol', 83–104.
85. Genscher, 'Toward an Overall Western Strategy'.
86. Selvage, 'The Politics of the Lesser Evil', 46.
87. Tel. COREU Athènes, 5 décembre 1983, 5020, Communautés Européennes, AMAE.
88. Tel. COREU Athènes, 29 novembre 1983, 5021, Communautés Européennes, AMAE.
89. Final Communiqué of the North Atlantic Council met in Ministerial Session in Brussels, 13th and 14th December 1979, par. 8.
90. 'Summary Record of a meeting of the Council held at NATO HQ Brussels on Wednesday 28th May 1980', C-R(80)21, NATO Arch.
91. Jackson (POCO) to Cooper (ECD external), 10 June 1981, FCO 98/1175, TNA.
92. 'Summary Record of a meeting of the Council held at NATO HQ, Brussels on Thursday 7th July 1980', C-R(80)27, NATO Arch.
93. Jackson (POCO) to Cooper (ECD external), 10 June 1981, FCO 98/1175, TNA.
94. Dispatch, Rose (UKDEL NATO) to Gillmore (Defence Dept), 23 January 1981, FCO 28/4671, TNA.
95. Hulse (UKDEL CSCE Madrid) to Pearce (Defence Dept), 9 February 1981, FCO 28/4671, TNA.
96. Gladstone (WED) to Gillmore (Defence Dept), 31 March 1981, FCO 98/1175, TNA.
97. Dispatch, Rose (UKDEL NATO) to Gillmore (Defence Dept), 23 January 1981, FCO 28/4671, TNA.
98. Message from Andreani, 20 October 1981, FCO 28/4671, TNA.
99. Carrington (FM) to FCO, 9 April 1981, FCO 98/1179; Carrington (FM) to Bonn and Paris, 5 July 1981, FCO 46/2671; Carrington (FM) to immediate Bonn, 20 October 1981, FCO 28/4671, TNA.
100. Carrington (FM) to immediate Paris and Bonn, 26 October 1981, FCO 28/4671, TNA.
101. Hulse (UKDEL Madrid CSCE) to Pearce (Defence Dept.), 7 July 1981, FCO 46/2671, TNA.
102. Gillmore (Defence Dept) to Rose (UKDEL NATO), 13 February 1981, FCO 28/4671, TNA.
103. FCO, Brief, 12 July 1981, FCO 46/2671, TNA.
104. 'Summary Record of a meeting of the Council held at NATO HQ, Brussels on Thursday 7th July 1980', C-R(80)27, NATO Arch.
105. Genscher, 'Toward an Overall Western Strategy', 64.
106. NATO, 'Document on Arms Control and Disarmament', 10 June 1982.
107. Final Communiqué of the North Atlantic Council met in Ministerial Session at Brussels on 8th and 9th December 1983, para. 13.
108. See Freeman, *Security and the CSCE Process*, 90–105.

Acknowledgements

I wish to thank Kiran K. Patel and Wolfram Kaiser for inviting me to contribute an article in this special issue and for their comments on earlier drafts. I am grateful to the anonymous reviewers for their thought-provoking remarks, which helped me strengthen the article in terms of its contribution to historiography. Finally, my heartfelt thanks go to Nicholas Nguyen, Johannes Geurts, and Nicholas Roche at NATO Archives for their assistance and for welcoming me so nicely at very short notice.

Disclosure statement

No potential conflict of interest was reported by the author.

ORCID

Angela Romano ⓘ http://orcid.org/0000-0003-4742-7602

Bibliography

Archival Material
Archive of European Integration, University of Pittsburgh (AEI)
Archives du Ministère des Affaires Étrangères, Paris (AMAE)
Historical Archives of the European Union, Florence (HAEU)
NATO Archives, Brussels (NATO Arch)
The National Archives of the UK, London (TNA)

Online Archival Sources
Report on Future Tasks of the Alliance (annexed to Final Communiqué), Brussels, 13th–14th December 1967. http://www.nato.int/cps/en/natolive/official_texts_26700.htm
Mutual And Balanced Force Reductions. Declaration adopted by Foreign Ministers and Representatives of Countries participating in the NATO Defence Program', Reykjavik, 24th–25th June 1968. http://www.nato.int/docu/comm/49-95/c680624b.htm
Declaration of the North Atlantic Council on European Security, Brussels, 4th–5th December 1969. http://www.nato.int/docu/comm/49-95/c691204b.htm
Aide-mémoire from the French Government to the other 14 NATO countries, 11 March 1966. http://www.cvce.eu/obj/aide_memoire_from_the_french_government_11_march_1966-en-690b3dd8-ee03-4737-85a4-d5b839b2e0dc.html
North Atlantic Council Communiqué, Brussels, December 9–10, 1971. http://www.nato.int/cps/en/natohq/official_texts_26812.htm?selectedLocale=en
Final Communiqué of North Atlantic Council Ministerial Session at Brussels on 13th and 14th December 1979. http://www.nato.int/docu/comm/49-95/c791213a.htm
Final Communiqué of North Atlantic Council Ministerial Session at Ankara on the 25th and 26th June 1980. http://www.nato.int/docu/comm/49-95/c800625a.htm
NATO, 'Document on Arms Control and Disarmament', 10 June 1982. http://www.nato.int/cps/en/natohq/official_texts_23156.htm?selectedLocale=en

MULTIPLE CONNECTIONS IN EUROPEAN COOPERATION

Final Communiqué of the North Atlantic Council met in Ministerial Session at Brussels on 8th and 9th December l983. http://www.nato.int/cps/en/natohq/official_texts_23215.htm?selectedLocale=en

Final Recommendations of the Helsinki Consultations, Helsinki 1973. http://www.osce.org/mc/40213

Final Act. www.osce.org/node/39501

HC Deb 18 May 1979 vol 967 cc555-657, Hansard, UK Parliament. http://hansard.millbanksystems.com/commons/1979/may/18/foreign-affairs

HL Deb 16 January 1979 vol 397 cc865-76. Hansard, UK Parliament. http://hansard.millbanksystems.com/lords/1979/jan/16/the-guadeloupe-summit

Tindemans, *'European Union. Report by Mr. Leo Tindemans, Prime Minister of Belgium, to the European Council', Bulletin of the European Communities, Supplement 1/76,* AEI, http://aei.pitt.edu/id/eprint/942

European Commission, *'Report on European Union. COM (75) 400 final, 25 June 1975', Bulletin of the European Communities, Supplement 5/75,* AEI. http://aei.pitt.edu/id/eprint/1761

Reports on European Union. European Parliament. Court of Justice. Economic and Social Committee', Bulletin of the European Communities, Supplement 9/75, AEI. http://aei.pitt.edu/id/eprint/5590

Grey Literature

Report on European Union from the Ministers of Foreign Affairs to the European Council. Bulletin of the European Communities, Supplement 4/80, Luxembourg: Office for Official Publications of the European Communities, 1981.

Report on European Union from the Ministers of Foreign Affairs to the European Council. Bulletin of the European Communities, Supplement 3/81, Luxembourg: Office for Official Publications of the European Communities, 1982.

Report on European Union from the Ministers of Foreign Affairs to the European Council. Bulletin of the European Communities, Supplement 7/1982, Luxembourg: Office for Official Publications of the European Communities, 1983.

Documents on British Policy Overseas, Series III, Volume II, eds. Gill Bennett and Keith A. Hamilton. London. The Stationery Office, 1997.

Secondary Literature

Allen, David, and Andrin Hauri. "The Euro-Arab Dialogue, the Venice Declaration, and Beyond: The Limits of a Distinct EC Policy, 1974–89." In *European-American Relations and the Middle East: From Suez to Iraq,* edited by Daniel Möckli and Victor Mauer, 93–107. London: Routledge, 2010.

Bilandzic, Vladimir, Dittmar Dahlmann, and Milan Kosanovic, eds. *From Helsinki to Belgrade. The First CSCE Follow-up Meeting and the Crisis of Détente.* Göttingen: Vandenhoeck & Ruprecht, 2012.

Bluth, Christoph. "Détente and Conventional Arms Control: West German Policy Priorities and the Origins of MBFR." *German Politics* 8 (1999): 181–206.

Bossuat, Gérard. "Origins and Development of the External Personality of the European Community." In *Experiencing Europe. 50 Years of European Construction 1957–2007,* edited by Wilfried Loth, 217–254. Baden-Baden: Nomos, 2009.

Brier, Robert. "Poland's Solidarity as a Contested Symbol of the Cold War: Transatlantic Debates after the Polish Crisis." In *European integration and the Atlantic Community in the 1980s,* edited by Kiran K. Patel and Ken Weisbrode, 83–104. Cambridge: Cambridge University Press, 2013.

Dean, Jonathan. "Military Security in Europe." *Foreign Affairs* 66 (Fall, 1987): 22–40.

Deighton, Anne. "Foreign and Security Policy after the End of the Cold War." In *Experiencing Europe. 50 Years of European Construction 1957–2007,* edited by Wilfried Loth, 255–267. Baden-Baden: Nomos, 2009.

Deighton, Anne, and Gérard Bossuat, eds. *The EC/EU: A World Security Actor?* Paris: Soleb, 2007.

Dijk, Ruud van. "'A Mass Psychosis': The Netherlands and NATO's Dual-Track Decision, 1978-1979." *Cold War History* 12 (2012): 381–405.

Dujardin, Vincent. "From Helsinki to the Missiles Question: A Minor Role for Small Countries? The case of Belgium (1973–1985)." In *The Crisis of Détente in Europe: From Helsinki to Gorbachev 1975-1985,* edited by Leopoldo Nuti, 72–85. Abingdon and New York: Routledge, 2008.

MULTIPLE CONNECTIONS IN EUROPEAN COOPERATION

Ferrari, Lorenzo. *Sometimes Speaking with a Single Voice: The European Community as an International Actor, 1969–1979.* Brussels: Peter Lang, 2016.

Fisher, Thomas. *Neutral Power in the CSCE: The N+N States and the Making of the Helsinki Accords 1975.* Baden-Baden: Nomos, 2009.

Freeman, John. *Security and the CSCE Process: The Stockholm Conference and Beyond.* London: Macmillan, 1991.

Gala, Marilena. "From INF to SDI: How Helsinki Reshaped the Transatlantic Dimension of European security." In *The Crisis of Détente in Europe: From Helsinki to Gorbachev 1975–1985*, edited by Leopoldo Nuti, 111–123. Abingdon and New York: Routledge, 2008.

Geiger, Tim. "Die Regierung Schmidt-Genscher und der NATO-Doppelbeschluss [The Schmidt-Genscher government and the NATO double decision]." In *Zweiter Kalter Krieg und Friedensbewegung. Der NATO-Doppelbeschluss in deutsch-deutscher und internationaler Perspektive* [Second Cold War and Peace Movement: The NATO double decision in German-German and international perspective], edited by Philipp Gassert, Tim Geiger, and Hermann Wentker, 95–120. Munich: Oldenbourg, 2011.

Genscher, Hans-Dietrich. "Toward an Overall Western Strategy for Peace, Freedom and Progress." *Foreign Affairs* 61 (Fall 1982): 42–66.

Ghebali, Victor-Yves. *Confidence-building Measures Within the CSCE Process: Paragraph-by-paragraph Analysis of the Helsinki and Stockholm Régimes.* New York: UNIDIR Research Paper, 1989.

Guasconi, Eleonora. "Public Opinion and the Euromissile Crisis." In *The Euromissile Crisis and the End of the Cold War*, edited by Leopoldo Nuti, Frédéric Bozo, Marie-Pierre Rey, and Bernd Rother, 271–290. Washington, D.C.: Woodrow Wilson Center Press, 2015.

Heyde, Veronika. "Multilaterale Konferenzdiplomatie unter nationaler Flagge. Die KSZE-Politik von Präsident Giscard d'Estaing 1974 1978 [Multilateral Conference Diplomacy under National Flag. The CSCE Policy of President Giscard d'Estaing, 1974 1978]." In *Der KSZE-Prozess Vom Kalten Krieg zu einem neuen Europa 1975 bis 1990* [The CSCE Process from the Cold War to a New Europe, 1975 to 1990], edited by Helmut Altrichter and Hermann Wentker, 29–40. Munich: Oldenbourg, 2011.

Heyde, Veronika. "Nicht nur Entspannung und Menschenrechte Die Entdeckung von Abrüstung und Rüstungskontrolle durch die französische KSZE-Politik [Not Just Relaxation and Human Rights: The Discovery of Disarmament and Armament Control by the French CSCE Policy]." In *Die KSZE im Ost-West-Konflikt Internationale Politik und gesellschaftliche Transformation 1975-1990* [The CSCE in the East-West Conflict: International Politics and Social Transformation 1975-1990], edited by Matthias Peter, Hermann Wentker, 83–98. Munich: Oldenbourg, 2012.

Loth, Wilfried. *Building Europe: A History of European Unification.* Berlin: de Gruyter, 2015.

Möckli, Daniel. *European Foreign Policy During the Cold War: Heath, Brandt, Pompidou and the Dream of Political Unity.* London: LB. Tauris, 2008.

Möckli, Daniel. "The EC-Nine and Transatlantic Conflict During the October War and the Oil Crisis, 1973–4." In *European-American Relations and the Middle East: From Suez to Iraq*, edited by Daniel Möckli and Victor Mauer, 77–92. London: Routledge, 2010.

Mourlon-Druol, Emmanuel. "More than a Prestigious Spokesperson: the Role of Summits/the European Council in European Political Cooperation (EPC), 1969–1981." In *The Commanding Heights of the European Union. The European Council: institution, actors, resources*, edited by François Foret and Yann-Sven Rittelmeyer, 43–52. London: Routledge, 2013.

Mourlon-Druol, Emmanuel, and Federico Romero, eds. *International Summitry and Global Governance. The Rise of the G-7 and the European Council, 1974–1991.* London and New York: Routledge, 2014.

Nehring, Holger. "The Last Battle of the Cold War: Peace Movements and German Politics in the 1980s." In *The Euromissile Crisis and the End of the Cold War*, edited by Leopoldo Nuti, Frédéric Bozo, Marie-Pierre Rey, and Bernd Rother, 309–330. Washington, D.C.: Woodrow Wilson Center Press, 2015.

Nuti, Leopoldo. "The Origins of the Dual Track Decision – a Survey." In *The Crisis of Détente in Europe: From Helsinki to Gorbachev 1975-1985*, edited by Leopoldo Nuti, 57–71. Abingdon and New York: Routledge, (1979) 2008.

MULTIPLE CONNECTIONS IN EUROPEAN COOPERATION

Park, Bill. "NATO Summits." In *Diplomacy at the Highest Level: The Evolution of International Summitry*, edited by David H. Dunn, 88–105. Basingstoke and London: Macmillan, 1996.

Patel, Kiran Klaus. "Provincialising European Union: Co-operation and Integration in Europe in a Historical Perspective." *Contemporary European History* 22 (2013): 649–673.

Pijpers, Alfred, Elfriede Regelsberger, and Wolfgang Wessels, eds. *European Political Cooperation in the 1980s*. Dordrecht: Martinus Nijhoff, 1988.

Romano, Angela. "Western Europe's Self-Assertion Towards the Superpowers: the CSCE Chance and its Aftermaths." In *The EC/EU: a World Security Actor?*, edited by Anne Deighton and Gérard Bossuat, 152–169. Paris: Soleb, 2007.

Romano, Angela. *From Détente in Europe to European Détente. How the West Shaped the Helsinki CSCE*. Brussels: Peter Lang, 2009.

Romano, Angela. "A Single European Voice Can Speak Louder to the World: Rationales, Ways and Means of EPC in the CSCE experience." In *The Road to a United Europe. Interpretations of the Process of European Integration*, edited by Morten Rasmussen and Ann-Kristina Knudsen, 257–270. Bruxelles: Peter Lang, 2009.

Romano, Angela. "The Main Task of the European Political Cooperation: Fostering Détente in Europe." In *Perforating the Iron Curtain: European Détente, Transatlantic Relations, and the Cold War, 1965–1985*, edited by Poul Villaume and Odd Arne Westad, 123–141. Copenhagen: Museum Tusculanum, 2010.

Romano, Angela. "The European Community and the Belgrade CSCE." In *From Helsinki to Belgrade. The First CSCE Follow-up Meeting and the Crisis of Détente*, edited by Vladimir Bilandzic, Ditter Dahlmann, and Milan Kosanovic, 205–224. Göttingen: Vandenhoeck & Ruprecht, 2012.

Romano, Angela. "More Cohesive, Still Divergent: Western Europe, the US, and the Madrid CSCE Follow-Up Meeting." In *European integration and the Atlantic Community in the 1980s*, edited by Kiran K. Patel and Ken Weisbrode, 39–58. Cambridge: Cambridge University Press, 2013.

Romano, Angela. "G-7s, European Councils and East-West Economic Relations, 1975–1982." In *International Summitry and Global Governance. The Rise of the G-7 and the European Council, 1974–1991*, edited by Emmanuel Mourlon-Druol and Federico Romero, 198–222. London and New York: Routledge, 2014.

Rother, Bernd. "Family Row: The Dual-Track Decision and Its Consequences for European Social Democratic Cooperation." In *The Euromissile Crisis and the End of the Cold War*, edited by Leopoldo Nuti, Frédéric Bozo, Marie-Pierre Rey, and Bernd Rother, 331–347. Washington, D.C.: Woodrow Wilson Center Press, 2015.

Selvage, Douglas. "The Politics of the Lesser Evil: the West, the Polish Crisis, and the CSCE Review Conference in Madrid, 1981–83." In *The Crisis of Détente in Europe: From Helsinki to Gorbachev 1975–1985*, edited by Leopoldo Nuti, 41–54. London: Routledge, 2009.

Spohr, Kristina. "Conflict and Cooperation in Intra-Alliance Nuclear Politics: Western Europe, the United States, and the Genesis of NATO's Dual-Track Decision, 1977–1979." *Journal of Cold War Studies* 13, no. 2 (2011): 39–89.

Spohr, Kristina. "Helmut Schmidt and the Shaping of Western Security in the Late 1970s: the Guadeloupe Summit of 1979." *The International History Review* 37, no. 1 (2015): 167–192.

Spohr, Kristina, and David Reynolds, eds. *Transcending the Cold War: Summits, Statecraft, and the Dissolution of Bipolarity in Europe, 1970–1990*. Oxford: OUP, 2016.

Wallace, William. "European Political Co-Operation: A New Form of Diplomacy?" *Irish Studies in International Affairs* 1 (1984): 3–14.

De-centring the European union: policy diffusion among European regional organizations – a comment

Thomas Risse

ABSTRACT

This article comments on the special issue from a political science perspective. It starts with an attempt at interpreting the contributions from a diffusion perspective. The articles show a sophisticated understanding of diffusion as "interdependent decision-making", that is multi- rather than uni-directional, focuses on diffusion as a process (not an outcome), and takes a decidedly agency-centered view. The article then highlights some of the empirical findings in this special issue. This concerns, among others, the crucial role of the Council of Europe (CoE) as a laboratory for generating new policy ideas and an agenda-setter, as well as the equally important function of the various parliamentary assemblies as mechanisms by which policy ideas diffuse. At the same time, there is also a power story in this special issue. The EC ultimately dominates the processes in most policy areas. The article concludes with remarks on the fruitfulness of an interdisciplinary dialogue between historians and social scientists as documented by this special issue.

As the editors of this special issue aptly describe in their introductory article (Kaiser and Patel, this special issue), the standard political-science account of the origins of the European Communities (EC)/ European Union (EU) is usually described as follows: In the beginning, there was economic interdependence among (mostly economic) actors in Europe leading to a functional demand for cooperation and integration. While (liberal) intergovernmentalism[1] emphasizes intergovernmental bargaining to explain European integration, neofunctionalism[2] highlights functional spill-over processes from one policy area to another as driving integration and focuses on the pivotal role of supranational actors such as the European Commission. These standard approaches have in common that they conceive of European integration as 'independent decision-making', that is, a process whereby the EC/EU and its member-states decide over integration steps virtually without any external influence and on their own. Accordingly, Jean Monnet and other founding fathers of European integration apparently never talked to or learnt from other experiences outside the EC.[3] It follows, of course, that scholars in this research tradition regard the EC experience as completely unique, as 'sui generis', as a result of which it would be futile to compare it to other regional or international organizations (ROs or IOs).

Recent scholarship on the EC/EU has started to change this rather parochial view on the European integration experience. Among historians, the editors of this special issue have been at the forefront of 'provincializing' or 'de-centring' Europe and the EC/EU.[4] In a similar vein, political scientists have started to put the EC/EU experience in a comparative perspective and have moved toward the study of comparative regionalism.[5]

The special issue speaks to this recent literature. It 'de-centres' the EC/EU not by comparing it to other regional or international organizations, but by demonstrating systematically how much the EC has actually learnt and taken on from other ROs in Europe – across most policy areas. The focus of the articles is on the scope of European integration, that is, the extension of cooperation into ever more issue areas – from human rights to culture, environment, security/disarmament and regional policies. It is not so much on the level of cooperation (intergovernmental or supranational) or on specific institutional designs.[6]

There is no way that I can do justice to the wealth of historical material documented and meticulously analyzed in this special issue. Instead, I comment on the various findings from a political-science perspective. My remarks start with an attempt at interpreting the contributions in this special issue from a diffusion approach. I argue that the articles show a sophisticated understanding of diffusion as 'interdependent decision-making', that is, multi- rather than uni-directional, focuses on diffusion as a process (not an outcome), and takes a decidedly agency-centred view. I then highlight some of the empirical findings in this special issue, as I see them. This concerns, among others, the crucial role of the Council of Europe (CoE) as a laboratory for generating new policy ideas and an agenda-setter, as well as the equally important function of the various parliamentary assemblies as mechanisms by which policy ideas diffuse. At the same time, there is also a power story in this special issue. As the editors point out in their introduction (Kaiser and Patel, this special issue), the EC ultimately dominates the processes in most policy areas – except with regard to national security, where it is the North Atlantic Treaty Organisation (NATO) that takes over (Romano, this special issue). I conclude with remarks on the fruitfulness of an interdisciplinary dialogue between historians and social scientists as documented by this special issue.

Diffusion as a multi-faceted and actor-centred process

In my view, this special issue is all about diffusion, or – as historians tend to call it – policy transfers.[7] It describes in detail where policy ideas originate from and how they spread across regional as well as international organizations. While most approaches to European integration assume 'independent decision-making', the contributions emphasize 'interdependent decision-making' or diffusion as 'any process where prior adoption of a trait or practice in a population alters the probability of adoption for remaining nonadopters'.[8] When the EC takes on the 'polluter pays principle' (PPP), it has not invented it, but it selectively adapts a policy idea which originated among environmental economists and then spread via the Organisation for Economic Co-operation and Development (OECD) and the CoE before it ultimately reaches the European Communities (Meyer, this special issue). The authors in the special issue go beyond earlier work in (mostly sociological) diffusion research that claimed policy convergence and unidirectionality from one source to various recipients (Kaiser and Patel, this special issue).[9]

The articles also demonstrate that diffusion and policy transfers are processes, not outcomes. With regard to the environment, the CoE, the OECD and finally the EC all adopted the polluter pays principle, but in different ways and rather selectively (Meyer, this special issue). (Sub-) regional policies were first 'invented' once again by the Council of Europe, but then the EC entered the picture, adopted the policy idea and changed it according to its own purposes (and the lobbying of regional networks; see Wassenberg, this special issue). In the conventional disarmament case, the EC's European Political Cooperation (EPC) devised the Conference on Disarmament in Europe (CDE), but then NATO took over and changed the content of the policy initiative (Romano, this special issue). In other words, policy convergence only constitutes a diffusion outcome in these cases insofar as the general policy idea is taken up by various ROs. With regard to the details and to institutional design features for the policy area, we observe divergence and selective adaptation to make the policies 'fit for purpose' for the various organizations. Here the articles confirm what has become the state of the art in comparative regionalism, namely that selective adaptation of policies and institutional designs is the most common outcome of trans- and inter-regional diffusion processes.[10]

If we conceive of diffusion as a process, as the special issue does, then research almost automatically focuses on the mechanisms and precise pathways by which policy ideas spread from one RO to another. Here, the articles provide enormously rich materials on the various transnational networks in Europe and beyond, through which policy ideas percolate. Moreover, the special issue demonstrates that human agency matters (see also the introduction by Kaiser and Patel, this special issue). At least implicitly, the authors argue against an overly structural view of diffusion, which has dominated the social sciences for a long time.[11] Human actors are no dummies who download some policy 'software' from a regional organization and then integrate it into their own institution. Rather, diffusion involves human choices and conscious efforts of translating ideas from one organizational context to another.[12]

The articles in this special issue document the great variety of inter-organizational and transnational networks permeating the various regional organizations in Europe and serving as transmission belts through which policy ideas travel. Hence the title: 'Multiple Connections!' Several findings stand out in this regard. First, the articles show the significance of what is called inter-regionalism, that is, interactions between various regional organizations. While most scholarly work focuses on connections between ROs in different parts of the world,[13] this special issue emphasizes inter-regionalism *within* one region. Inter-regionalism in Europe showcases some interesting features, which are usually discussed under the heading of 'overlapping regionalism'.[14] To begin with, most ROs in Europe have overlapping memberships. All EC/EU members are also members of the CoE and of the Commission on Security and Cooperation in Europe CSCE (now Organization for Security and Co-operation in Europe, OSCE), most of them are in NATO and in the OECD. This should not be problematic as long as the various ROs are functionally differentiated with regard to the tasks they cover. All NATO members are also members of the CSCE/OSCE, but there is little overlap in mandates. Things are quite different with regard to NATO, on the one hand, and the Common/European Security and Defense Policy (CSDP/ESDP), the successor of the European Political Cooperation (EPC), on the other, the more ESDP takes on traditional military-security policies and the more NATO ventures into peace-keeping and enforcement.[15]

The articles in the special issue document an interesting phenomenon, once we introduce a temporal dimension to the question of overlapping regionalism. With regard to human rights (Soriano, this special issue), cultural policies (Patel and Calligaro, this special issue), the environment (Meyer, this special issue) and regional policies (Wassenberg, this special issue), there have been considerable overlaps with regard to mandates in the early phases when policy ideas spread across various ROs. Later, however, things sort themselves out and one particular RO starts dominating the policy field with regard to regulations and policy outputs. In most cases (environment as well as regional and cultural policies, see articles by Meyer, Wassermann, and Patel and Calligaro, this special issue), the EC gained hegemony over the policy area by the 1990s (see later in this article). In the case of human rights (Soriano, this special issue), the CoE remained in charge of the European human-rights regime, but the EC adopted its practices and inserted it into its membership conditionality. In sum, overlapping mandates and policies appear to characterize the early phases when new policy ideas come onto the stage, while particular ROs control the issue area later on. Whether this is a particular European experience or whether it is comparable to the Sub-Saharan African 'spaghetti bowl' of ROs or the Latin American 'alphabet soup', should be subject for future research.[16]

Second, inter-regionalism and overlapping memberships in European ROs also provide fertile ground for the variety of transnational and transgovernmental networks[17] documented in the articles serving as 'agents of diffusion' for the various policy ideas. In some cases (see Patel and Calligaro for cultural policies, this special issue; Soriano for human rights policies, this special issue), particular individuals themselves link the various ROs via their activities in either of them. In particular, the special issue highlights three types of networks, which have also been found crucial in the diffusion of regionalism and regional governance in other parts of the world:

- Expert networks or 'epistemic communities', which are bound together by collective consensual knowledge in a particular policy field (for example, Meyer, this special issue; also Patel and Calligaro, this special issue)[18];
- Transnational advocacy networks (TAN) and social movements promoting policy ideas and international norms (for example, Soriano, this special issue; also networks of sub-regional actors acting as TAN, see Wassenberg, this special issue)[19];
- Networks among parliamentarians both in national parliaments and in regional parliamentary assemblies including the European Parliament (for example, Soriano, this special issue; Patel and Calligaro, this special issue)[20];
- Last but not least, transgovernmental networks among bureaucrats within the various ROs, but also in member-states' governments (see, for example, Patel and Calligaro, this special issue; Meyer, this special issue; Romano, this special issue).[21]

To conclude this section, the articles in this special issue offer excellent historical evidence on the mechanics of policy-diffusion processes in Europe during crucial periods of the Cold War and beyond. The authors document in detail the crucial role of agents and their transnational as well transgovernmental networks in spreading policy ideas with regard to various and rather disparate issue areas.

I would like to add a note of methodological caution, however. First, Europe with its extreme density of regional and international organizations and their overlapping memberships is probably a 'most likely case' for policy diffusion. In other words, it would be surprising if the various ROs were closed containers and *not* open to a variety of external influences – and this includes the EC/EU. Diffusion research has shown time and again that geographic contiguity matters.[22] This limits the generalizability of the findings in this special issue.

Second, the articles focus on mostly successful cases of policy diffusion, which restricts their generalizability. Future research should compare such instances of dense network interactions with cases in which policy ideas did *not* spread even though various actors tried their best to convince others of their suitability. This special issue is very good at specifying the causal mechanisms and the actor networks through which ideas are distributed. It is less well suited to determine the scope conditions under which these networks are successful. Future historical research might also look at those ideas which, e.g., the EC did *not* take up in the end or which it rejected for good.

The EC/EU de-centred – but the empire strikes back

Let me now comment on the special issue's empirical findings about Europe and the spread of policy ideas through the various regional organizations. To begin with, the articles and the editors (see introduction by Kaiser and Patel, this special issue) do an excellent job at 'de-centring' the dominant role of the EC. With one exception, the disarmament case (Romano, this special issue), none of the policy ideas examined by the various articles originated inside the EC. This focus challenges the – mostly political-science – literature on ROs in Europe, which is dominated by an EC/EU focus – with the CoE and other ROs rarely mentioned.[23] Therefore, this special issue sets the empirical record straight by demonstrating how crucial ROs other than the EC/EU have been for the diffusion of policy ideas in post-Second World War history. This account challenges empirically the dominant narratives of European (rather, EU!) integration according to which the EC/EU's extension of the policy scope over time followed mostly a functional logic to solve cooperation problems among the member-states (but see later in this article).

In a way, the CoE is the unsung hero of this special issue. In three of the cases examined (human rights, cultural as well as regional policies; see articles by Soriano, Patel and Calligaro, and Wassenberg, this special issue), the policy ideas were first explored in the framework of the Council of Europe. This does not come as much of a surprise in the human-rights area (see Soriano, this special issue), since this is the core policy domain of the CoE in charge of the European Convention on Human Rights, the most advanced regional human-rights regime on the globe. But it is astonishing that the CoE took on cultural policies and (sub-) regional policies long before the EC did. It even became active in the environmental policy area and incorporated the polluter-pays-principle before the EC became a champion in this area (Meyer, this special issue). In this latter case and again surprisingly, even NATO as a military alliance became active and spread American ideas across the Atlantic, as Meyer shows in his article. The CoE, but also the OECD, other ROs in Europe and global IOs such as the UN served a crucial role as generators of new policy ideas and agenda-setters. The articles in this special-issue document how these ROs – despite their mostly intergovernmental rather than supranational character and their lesser degree of institutionalization as compared to the EC – became laboratories for the development of new policy ideas.

With regard to human rights, environmental, (sub-) regional and cultural policies, the EC remained largely at the receiving end of the policy diffusion. The one exception is the case of the Conference on Disarmament in Europe (CDE), which originated in the framework of the EPC, the emerging foreign-policy coordination body of the EC (Romano, this special issue).[24] In this particular case, the EPC became a sort of European caucus for the EC members of NATO – without the involvement of the United States as NATO's powerful leader.[25] The case might, therefore, be rather special.

In all other cases documented in this special issue, the EC eventually took up the policy ideas, which were diffused through the various networks discussed above. In the case of the CoE and the EC, the networks of parliamentarians deserve special attention. Note that in the cases of human rights and cultural policies (articles by Soriano and Patel and Calligaro, this special issue), the European Parliament (EP) was not yet directly elected and did not have strong parliamentary competences. Yet, both national MPs and MEPs were crucial in many cases, linking the CoE with the EC in the diffusion of ideas.

So far, so good! The special issue successfully de-centres the EC with regard to the agenda-setting phase of new policy ideas. Yet, 'the empire strikes back!' In three of the five case studies analyzed (environmental, cultural and (sub-) regional policies, see articles by Meyer, Patel and Calligaro, and Wassenberg, this special issue), the EC eventually takes on the policies, adjusts them to its own institutional circumstances – and then dominates the policy area in Europe. With regard to human rights (Soriano, this special issue), the CoE remains the dominant player, but the EC aligns its (accession) policies with the European Convention on Human Rights.

The editors argue in their introductory essay (Kaiser and Patel, this special issue) that three factors explain why the EC ultimately controlled the various policy areas thereby crowding out the other ROs: the EC's focus on market integration, its legal integration and its financial resources (see also Patel and Calligaro on cultural policies, this special issue). In other words, this is about power! The huge asymmetry between the EC and the other ROs in Europe comes into play in the diffusion of ideas, not in the agenda-setting phase, but in later stages of the policy cycle.[26] Financial resources and legal integration – as the ability to enforce supranational legislation through the European Court of Justice (ECJ) and the national legal system – are about power capacities. No wonder that human rights are the one domain where the CoE stood its ground: the European Court of Human Rights (ECHR) commands similar legal enforcement powers in its policy domain as the ECJ.

With regard to market integration, the editors point out (Kaiser and Patel, this special issue), that it created functional connections to the other policy domains allowing the EC/EU to use them as instruments for its never-ending task expansion. This is, of course, a functional argument consistent with mainstream theories of European integration, whether neofunctionalism or (liberal) intergovernmentalism. If this argument were correct, the successful spread of policy ideas into the EC's remit would ultimately depend on their functionality for market integration thereby introducing a scope condition for the successful implementation of policy ideas in the EC/EU. An alternative view would argue that this is all about social constructions and framing.[27] Actors who want the EC/EU to take on new policies have to make functional arguments related to market integration in order to expand the scope of EC policies successfully. The editors' argument (Kaiser and Patel, this special issue) is consistent with both views, but the latter interpretation is more in line with an actor-centred approach that is also open for historical contingencies. Otherwise, one would have introduced functional approaches in a diffusion process through the back door.

This is not to argue that functional stories got it all wrong. Indeed, the diffusion of regionalism shows that new policy ideas are rarely taken up if they do not talk at all to a real policy problem at hand. Regarding environmental policies, for example, it is hard to imagine that environmental issues would have entered the agenda of ROs and IOs in the late 1960s without the widespread awareness of air pollution, acid rain and the like – and the social mobilization surrounding these issues (see Meyer, this special issue). With regard to cultural policies (Patel and Calligaro, this special issue), the various debates about Europe's cultural heritage are about identity politics and the efforts by political elites to construct a European identity underpinning European integration.[28] In other words, one should not throw the baby out with the bathwater when it comes to functional accounts, but one has to realize that this is not all about economics.[29]

Be this as it may, the special issue shows that the diffusion of policy ideas cannot (and should not) ignore power, be it material resources, institutional power (legal enforcement capacity) or structural power (market integration).[30] At the end of the day, the EC is able to crowd out other regional organizations from the various policy domains in three of the five issue areas examined in this special issue because of its superior material, institutional and structural capabilities. The CDE only serves to prove the point (Romano, this special issue). While the EPC invents the idea of a disarmament conference in Europe in the framework of the CSCE, NATO ultimately takes up the CDE proposal and implements it. Military security, however, is one issue area in which NATO is more powerful than the EC or the EPC at the time. It has more institutional resources, but it also has one member, the United States, without which disarmament in Europe during the Cold War cannot take place. In other words, the article about military security – or 'high politics' – confirms the argument that power matters in diffusion processes. Policy ideas might spread through processes of deliberation and persuasion, but they have ultimately to be taken up by powerful actors in order to stick and get implemented.

Conclusions

This special issue serves as a powerful reminder that European integration is not all about the EC/EU. It documents in detail that many policy ideas originated in various ROs and IOs such as the Council of Europe, the OECD or the UN rather than the EC/EU, which only took them up in later stages of the policy-diffusion process. At the same time, the editors (Kaiser and Patel, this special issue) do not deny that EC power mattered in the end and that the EC ultimately came to dominate many of the various policy fields discussed in the articles.

As I tried to argue in this comment, the special issue also speaks directly to various theoretical debates in the social sciences. In particular, I have tried to interpret the findings within a framework emphasizing policy diffusion and have attempted to show how a diffusion perspective might be helpful to theorize the empirical data. What does this tell us about interdisciplinary or transdisciplinary research involving historians and social scientists?

At first glance, my argument could be read as confirming each other's stereotypes: Historians dig deep into the archives and come up with interesting empirical stories and data, while social scientists then theorize these findings by relating them to broader debates in their field. As if historical research were a-theoretical!

This is definitely not my point. Rather, this special issue documents a particular theoretical contribution of historians to the study of diffusion processes, which is very fruitful for the dialogue across disciplines. The approach chosen in the various articles is decidedly agency-centric and rejects the emphasis on structure in many social-science studies of diffusion. Moreover, the historical work shows the multi-directional nature of diffusion processes rather than the oftentimes uni-directional analysis of diffusion from a sender of policy ideas to various recipients. Of course, both arguments are not completely alien to the social sciences and have been made before. But this special issue documents that historians and political scientists have been engaging in a transdisciplinary dialogue for quite some time. In this case, historians have taken up theoretical arguments on diffusion originally developed in the social sciences – and then have criticized them thereby pushing the theoretical frontiers further. In the end, theory development is not and cannot be the domain of one particular discipline, but we are all in this together. This is what one can learn from this special issue on the general interdisciplinary dialogue between history and the social sciences.

Notes

1. Moravcsik, *The Choice for Europe*. For a similar approach by a historian see Milward, *The European Rescue of the Nation-State*.
2. Haas, *The Uniting of Europe*; Haas, *Beyond the Nation-State*.
3. In the following, I mostly use the term EC, as the special issue deals with the time period from 1967 to 1992. Is use the term EC/EU when I mean the European Union in general.
4. Patel, 'Provincialising the European Union'; Kaiser and Schot, *Writing the Rules for Europe*.
5. E.g. Fawcett and Hurrell, *Regionalism in World Politics*; Katzenstein, *A World of Regions*; Börzel and Risse, *The Oxford Handbook of Comparative Regionalism*.
6. For the distinction between 'scope' and 'level' of regional cooperation see Börzel and Risse, *Introduction*, 7–8.
7. For the following see Risse, *The Diffusion of Regionalism*.
8. Strang, 'Adding Social Structure to Diffusion Models', 325. See also Strang and Meyer, 'Institutional Conditions for Diffusion'; Gilardi, *Transnational Diffusion*; Solingen, 'Of Dominoes and Firewalls'; Simmons et al., *The Global Diffusion of Markets and Democracy*.
9. Convergence as a diffusion outcome is usually identified with the Stanford School of sociological institutionalism; see, for example, Thomas et al., *Institutional Structure*; Meyer et al., 'World Society and the Nation-State'. On policy convergence in particular see Holzinger et al., *Environmental Policy Convergence in Europe*.
10. Details in Risse, *The Diffusion of Regionalism*.
11. For a similar criticism see Solingen, 'Of Dominoes and Firewalls'; see also Solingen and Börzel, *The Politics of International Diffusion*.
12. The translation perspective in cultural studies has made this point for quite some time. See, for example, Bachmann-Medick, 'Introduction: The Translational Turn'; Bachmann-Medick, *The Trans/National Study of Culture*; Freeman, 'What Is "Translation?"'; Venuti, *Rethinking Translation*. For an application to European studies see, for example, Mörth, *Europeanization as Interpretation, Translation, and Editing of Public Policies*.
13. Overview in Ribeiro Hoffmann, *Inter- and Transregionalism*. See also Baert et al., *Intersecting Interregionalism*; Hänggi et al., *Interregionalism and International Relations*.
14. See Panke and Stapel, 'Exploring Overlapping Regionalism'; Chacha, 'Regional Integration and the Challenge of Overlapping Memberships on Trade'; Gomez-Mera and Molinari, 'Overlapping Institutions, Learning, and Dispute Initiation in Regional Trade Agreements'.
15. See Hofmann, 'Overlapping Institutions in the Realm of International Security'; Hofmann, 'Why Institutional Overlap Matters'.
16. On Sub-Saharan Africa see Hartmann, *Sub-Saharan Africa*. On Latin America see Bianculli, *Latin America*.
17. *Transnational* networks are dense patterns of interactions among actors whereby at least one non-state actor is involved (see Keohane and Nye, *Introduction*), while *transgovernmental* networks encompass subunits of national governments and of international/regional

MULTIPLE CONNECTIONS IN EUROPEAN COOPERATION

organizations (see Keohane and Nye, 'Transgovernmental Relations and International Organizations').

18. On epistemic communities in general see Haas, *Knowledge, Power and International Policy Coordination*; Haas, *Epistemic Communities, Constructivism, and International Environmental Politics*. On epistemic communities with regard to regional environmental governance see Haas, *Regional Environmental Governance*.
19. On TAN in general see Keck and Sikkink, *Activists Beyond Borders*.
20. On the various roles of parliaments in regionalism see Rittberger and Schroeder, *The Legitimacy of Regional Institutions*; Lenz, *The Politics of Institutional Symbolism*; Rüland and Bechle, 'Defending State-Centric Regionalism Through Mimicry and Localisation'; Dri, 'Limits of the Institutional Mimesis of the European Union'.
21. For similar transgovernmental networks in the transatlantic area see Newman, 'Building Transnational Civil Liberties'.
22. Overview in Simmons et al., 'Introduction: The International Diffusion of Liberalism'; Gilardi, *Transnational Diffusion*.
23. None of the three handbooks on European (Union) politics covers the Council of Europe in a separate chapter; see Magone, *Routledge Handbook of European Politics*; Jorgensen et al., *The Sage Handbook of European Union Politics*; Jones et al., *The Oxford Handbook of the European Union*. See, however, Checkel, 'Why Comply? Social Learning and European Identity Change'; Schimmelfennig, *Europe*.
24. On the evolution of the EPC in general see Smith, *Europe's Foreign and Security Policy*; Howorth, *Security and Defense Policy in the European Union*.
25. This resembles the role of the EPC throughout the Helsinki Process; see Thomas, *The Helsinki Effect*. For a discussion of the larger European influence on American foreign policy during the Cold War era see Risse-Kappen, *Cooperation among Democracies*.
26. On policy cycles in general see Jann and Wegrich, *Theories of the Policy Cycle*.
27. For social-constructivist approaches on European integration see Christiansen et al., *The Social Construction of Europe*.
28. For a general discussion see Risse, *A Community of Europeans?*
29. On this point see Börzel and Risse, *Three Cheers for Comparative Regionalism*.
30. For different dimensions of power see Barnett and Duvall, 'Power in International Politics'.

Acknowledgement

This special issue originated from activities directed by Wolfram Kaiser and Kiran Patel at the Research College 'Transformative Power of Europe?' at the Freie Universität Berlin, which Tanja Börzel and I have been co-directing since 2008 and which is funded by the German Research Foundation (DFG). I am very grateful to Wolfram and Kiran for inviting me to contribute to this special issue.

Disclosure statement

No potential conflict of interest was reported by the author.

Funding

This work was supported by the Deutsche Forschungsgemeinschaft [grant number FOR 1026].

Bibliography

Bachmann-Medick, D. "Introduction: The Translational Turn." *Translation Studies* 2, no. 1 (2009): 2–16.

Bachmann-Medick, D., ed. *The Trans/National Study of Culture. A Translational Perspective.* Berlin: De Gruyter, 2014

Baert, F., T. Scaramagli, and F. Söderbaum, eds. *Intersecting Interregionalism. Regions, Global Governance, and the EU.* Heidelberg: Springer Dordrecht, 2014.

Barnett, M., and R. Duvall. "Power in International Politics." *International Organization* 59, no. 1 (2005): 39–75.

Bianculli, A. "Latin America." In *The Oxford Handbook of Comparative Regionalism*, edited by T. A. Börzel and T. Risse, 154–177. Oxford: Oxford University Press, 2016.

Börzel, T. A., and T. Risse. "Introduction: Framework of the Handbook and Conceptual Clarifications." In *The Oxford Handbook of Comparative Regionalism*, edited by T. A. Börzel and T. Risse, 3–15. Oxford: Oxford University Press, 2016.

Börzel, T. A., and T. Risse, eds. *The Oxford Handbook of Comparative Regionalism.* Oxford: Oxford University Press, 2016.

Börzel, T. A., and T. Risse. "Three Cheers for Comparative Regionalism." In *The Oxford Handbook of Comparative Regionalism*, edited by T. A. Börzel and T. Risse, 621–647. Oxford: Oxford University Press, 2016.

Chacha, M. "Regional Integration and the Challenge of Overlapping Memberships on Trade." *Journal of International Relations and Development* 17, no. 4 (2014): 522–544.

Checkel, J. T. "Why Comply? Social Learning and European Identity Change." *International Organization* 55, no. 3 (2001): 553–588.

Christiansen, T., K. E. Jørgensen, and A. Wiener, eds. *The Social Construction of Europe.* London et al.: Sage, 2001.

Dri, C. F. "Limits of the Institutional Mimesis of the European Union: The Case of the Mercosur Parliament." *Latin American Policy* 1, no. 1 (2010): 52–74.

Fawcett, L., and A. Hurrell, eds. *Regionalism in World Politics: Regional Organization and International Order.* Oxford: Oxford University Press, 1995.

Freeman, R. "What Is 'Translation?'" *Evidence & Policy* 5, no. 4 (2009): 429–447.

Gilardi, F. "Transnational Diffusion: Norms, Ideas, and Policies." In *Handbook of International Relations.* 2nd ed, edited by W. Carlsnaes, T. Risse and B. Simmons, 453–477. London: Sage, 2013.

Gomez-Mera, L., and A. Molinari. "Overlapping Institutions, Learning, and Dispute Initiation in Regional Trade Agreements: Evidence from South America." *International Studies Quarterly* 58, no. 2 (2014): 269–281.

Haas, E. B. *The Uniting of Europe: Political, Social, and Economic Forces 1950–57.* Stanford, CA: Stanford University Press, 1958.

Haas, E. B. *Beyond the Nation-State. Functionalism and International Organization.* Stanford CA: Stanford University Press, 1964.

Haas, P. M., ed. *Knowledge, Power and International Policy Coordination,' International Organization, Special Issue*, 46, no. 1 (1992).

Haas, P. M. *Epistemic Communities, Constructivism, and International Environmental Politics.* London - New York: Routledge, 2016.

MULTIPLE CONNECTIONS IN EUROPEAN COOPERATION

Haas, P. M. "Regional Environmental Governance." In *The Oxford Handbook of Comparative Regionalism*, edited by T. A. Börzel and T. Risse, 430-456. Oxford: Oxford University Press, 2016.

Hänggi, H., R. Roloff, and J. Rüland, eds. *Interregionalism and International Relations. A Stepping Stone to Global Governance?* London-New York: Routledge, 2006.

Hartmann, C. "Sub-Saharan Africa." In *The Oxford Handbook of Comparative Regionalism*, edited by T. A. Börzel and T. Risse, 271–294. Oxford: Oxford University Press, 2016.

Hofmann, S. C. "Overlapping Institutions in the Realm of International Security: The Case of NATO and ESDP." *Perspectives on Politics* 7, no. 1 (2009): 45–52.

Hofmann, S. C. "Why Institutional Overlap Matters: CSDP in the European Security Architecture." *Journal of Common Market Studies* 49, no. 1 (2011): 101–120.

Holzinger, K., C. Knill, and B. Arts, eds. *Environmental Policy Convergence in Europe. The Impact of International Institutions and Trade.* Cambridge UK: Cambridge University Press, 2008.

Howorth, J. *Security and Defense Policy in the European Union.* Houndmills, Basingstoke: Palgrave - Macmillan, 2007.

Jann, W., and K. Wegrich. "Theories of the Policy Cycle." In *Handbook of Public Policy Analysis*, edited by F. Fischer, G. J. Miller and M. S. Sidney, 43–62. Boca Raton, FL: CRC Press, 2007.

Jones, E., A. Menon, and S. Weatherill, eds. *The Oxford Handbook of the European Union.* Oxford: Oxford University Press, 2012.

Jorgensen, K. E., M. Pollack, and B. Rosamond, eds. *The Sage Handbook of European Union Politics.* London - New York: Sage, 2007.

Kaiser, W., and K. K. Patel. "Multiple connections in European Cooperation: Interantional Organizations, Policy Ideas, Parctices, and Transfers 1967–1992." *European Review of History* 24, no. 3 (2017): 337–357.

Kaiser, W., and J. Schot. *Writing the Rules for Europe: Experts, Cartels, and International Organizations.* Houndmills, Basingstoke: Palgrave Macmillan, 2014.

Katzenstein, P. J. *A World of Regions. Asia and Europe in the American Imperium.* Ithaca NY: Cornell University Press, 2005.

Keck, M. E., and K. Sikkink. *Activists Beyond Borders. Advocacy Networks in International Politics.* Ithaca NY: Cornell University Press, 1998.

Keohane, R., and J. S. Nye, Jr. "Introduction." In *Transnational Relations and World Politics*, edited by Keohane and Nye, XII-XVI. Cambridge, MA: Harvard University Press, 1971.

Keohane, R. O., and J. S. Nye, Jr. "Transgovernmental Relations and International Organizations." *World Politics* 27: (1974): 39-62.

Lenz, T., "The Politics of Institutional Symbolism: Parliamentarization in Regional Economic Organizations," unpubl. manuscript, Amsterdam: Free University Amsterdam, 2013.

Magone, J. M., ed. *Routledge Handbook of European Politics.* London - New York: Routledge, 2014.

Meyer, J.-H. "Who Should Pay for Pollution? The OECD, the European Communities and the Emergence of Environmental Policy in the Early 1970s." *European Review of History* 24, no. 3 (2017): 377–398.

Meyer, J. W., J. Boli, G. M. Thomas, and F. O. Ramirez. "World Society and the Nation-State." *American Journal of Sociology* 103, no. 1 (1997): 144–181.

Milward, A. S. *The European Rescue of the Nation-State.* Berkeley, Ca: University of California Press, 1992.

Moravcsik, A. *The Choice for Europe: Social Purpose and State Power From Rome to Maastricht.* Ithaca NY: Cornell University Press, 1998.

Mörth, U. "Europeanization as Interpretation, Translation, and Editing of Public Policies." In *The Politics of Europeanization*, edited by K Featherstone and C Radaelli, 159–178. Oxford: Oxford University Press, 2003.

Newman, A. L. "Building Transnational Civil Liberties: Transgovernmental Entrepreneurs and the European Data Privacy Directive." *International Organization* 62, no. 1 (2008): 103–130.

Panke, D., and S. Stapel. "Exploring overlapping regionalism." *Journal of International Relations and Development* (2016): 1–28. doi: 10.1057/s41268-016-0081-x.

Patel, K. K. "Provincialising the European Union: Co-operation and Integration in Europe in Historical Perspective." *Contemporary European History* 22, no. 4 (2013): 649–673.

Patel, K. K., and O. Calligaro. "The True 'EURESCO'? The Council of Europe, Transnational Networking, and the Emergence of EC Cultural Policies, 1970–1990." *Review of European History* 24, no. 3 (2017): 399–422.

Ribeiro Hoffmann, A. "Inter- and Transregionalism." In *The Oxford Handbook of Comparative Regionalism*, edited by T. A. Börzel and T. Risse, 600–618. Oxford: Oxford University Press, 2016.

Risse-Kappen, T. *Cooperation among Democracies. The European Influence on U.S. Foreign Policy.* Princeton, NJ: Princeton University Press, 1995.

Risse, T. *A Community of Europeans? Transnational Identities and Public Spheres.* Ithaca NY: Cornell University Press, 2010.

Risse, T. "The Diffusion of Regionalism." In *The Oxford Handbook of Comparative Regionalism*, edited by T. A. Börzel and T. Risse, 87–108. Oxford: Oxford University Press, 2016.

Rittberger, B., and P. Schroeder. "The Legitimacy of Regional Institutions." In *The Oxford Handbook of Comparative Regionalism*, edited by T. A. Börzel and T. Risse, 579–599. Oxford: Oxford University Press, 2016.

Romano, A. "Re-designing Military Security in Europe: Cooperation and Competition Between the European Community and NATO During the Early 1980s." *Review of European History* 24, no. 3 (2017): 445–471.

Rüland, J., and K. Bechle. "Defending State-Centric Regionalism Through Mimicry and Localisation: Regional Parliamentary Bodies in the Association of Southeast Asian Nations (ASEAN) and Mercosur." *Journal of International Relations and Development* 17, no. 1 (2014): 61–88.

Schimmelfennig, F. "Europe." In *The Oxford Handbook of Comparative Regionalism*, edited by T. A. Börzel and T. Risse, 178–201. Oxford: Oxford University Press, 2016.

Simmons, B., F. Dobbin, and G. Garrett. "Introduction: The International Diffusion of Liberalism." *International Organization* 60, no. 4 (2006): 781–810.

Simmons, B., F. Dobbin, and G. Garrett, eds. *The Global Diffusion of Markets and Democracy.* Cambridge UK: Cambridge University Press, 2008.

Smith, M. E. *Europe's Foreign and Security Policy: The Institutionalization of Cooperation.* Cambridge UK: Cambridge University Press, 2004.

Solingen, E. "Of Dominoes and Firewalls: The Domestic, Regional, and Global Politics of International Diffusion." *International Studies Quarterly* 56 (2012): 631–644.

Solingen, E., and T. A. Börzel, eds. "The Politics of International Diffusion." *Presidential Special Issue of "International Studies Review"* 22, no. 2 (2014).

Soriano, V. F. "Facing the Greek Junta: The European Community, the Council of Europe and the Rise of Human Rights Politics in Europe." *European Review of History* 24, no. 3 (2017): 358–376.

Strang, D. "Adding Social Structure to Diffusion Models. An Event History Framework." *Sociological Methods & Research* 19, no. 3 (1991): 324–353.

Strang, D., and J. W. Meyer. "Institutional Conditions for Diffusion." *Theory and Society* 22 (1993): 487–512.

Thomas, D. C. *The Helsinki Effect. International Norms, Human Rights, and the Demise of Communism.* Princeton, New Jersey: Princeton University Press, 2001.

Thomas, G. M., J. W. Meyer, F. Ramirez, and J. Boli, eds. *Institutional Structure: Constituting State, Society, and the Individual.* Newbury Park CA: Sage, 1987.

Venuti, L. *Rethinking translation: discourse, subjectivity, ideology.* London, New York: Routledge, 1992.

Wassenberg, B. "Between Co-operation and Competitive Bargaining: The Council of Europe, Local and Regional Networking, and the Shaping of the European Community's Regional Policies, 1970s–1990s." *Review of European History* 24, no. 3 (2017): 423–444.

Index

1954 European Cultural Convention 65
1970 press communiqué criticizing Greek junta 33
1972 Paris Summit: community action in cultural field 68
1972 World Heritage Convention 67
1973 Environmental Action Programme 13, 42, 46
1974 Recommendation on the Implementation of the Polluter-Pays Principle 50
1983 Solemn Declaration on European Union 73

activism: *see* environment
actors: as vector for cooperation, competition and transfers 11–12
AEBR (Association of European Border Regions) 93; border regions interests lobbying 93–95; Interreg Initiative 98–99; Linkage Assistance for European Border Regions 99
Afghanistan invasion by Soviets 117
Ahrens, Karl: border regions interests lobbying 94
Alter, Karen: forum shopping 7
architectural heritage preservation and restoration 67
Association of European Border Regions (AEBR) 93
Atlantic Council 44–45
audio-visual policies: broadcasting emergence 72; broadcasting market integration 73; CoE and EC rivalry 72–75; CoE preliminary initiatives 71–72; EC emulation of CoE 72; transborder television regulatory race between CoE and EC 73–75
Austria: European Ministerial Conference on mass-media policies initiative 74; support of Greece's expulsion from the CoE 26

Batelle Institute 45
Becket, James 32
Biermann, Rafael: inter-organizational networking as a response to organizations' (states') inability to master transnational challenges 7

Blin, Bernard: transborder television regulation cooperation 74–75
border regions interests lobbying *see* AEBR
bounded rationality: actor strategies operating across a variety of IOs 7
Britain: cultural heritage conservation 69
broadcasting: emergence 72; market integration 73; transborder television regulatory race between CoE and EC 73–75

Canada: opposition to CSCE 117
Carpentier, Michel 48
Carter, President Jimmy: SALT 2 115
CCC (Council for Cultural Co-operation) 66
CCMS (Committee for the Challenges of Modern Society) 44
CDE (Conference on Confidence-and Security-Building Measures and Disarmament in Europe) 109, 140–141; defusing tensions and preserving détente initiatives 115–117; formation 109–110; French origin 114; geographical area of application 119–120; human rights inclusion proposal 119–121; transatlantic cooperation on CDE proposal 124–126
Centre for Nuclear Research in Karlsruhe on PPP in water-pollution control conference 51
Chaban-Delmas, Jacques: Committee on Local and Regional Affairs 88
CIMAB (Communauté d'intérêt moyen Alsace-Breisgau) 98
CIP (Community Initiative Policy): Interreg programme 98–99
Civic Trust in Great Britain 69
CLRAE (Conference of Local and Regional Authorities in Europe) 93
CoE (Council of Europe) 140; 1950s cultural policies 66; AEBR border regions interests lobbying 93–95; asymmetry of cultural resources with EC 68–69; audio-visual initiatives exploratory work 71–72; cultural cooperation 9–10; culture competition with EC in 1980s 71–76; demanding human

149

INDEX

rights respect in Greece 25–26; Eastern bloc cooperation 97; EC disengagement with on regional affairs 92; EC emulation of audio-visual policies 72; EC interplay influence in NATO 34; EC limiting dialogue with 10; EC prominence over in culture 64; European Architectural Heritage Year (EAHY) 67–68; 'European cultural policy' 66; financial resources for culture 70; Greek junta 25–27, 31; Greek membership 24, 32; inter-organizational cooperation with EC on culture 66; lack of regional policy institutional framework with EC 89–90; local/regional cooperation 10; origins 4; overlapping membership with NATO, EC, and OECD 54; pan-European cultural heritage endeavour 70; parliamentarian networks 141; pioneering environmental issues and principles 44; PPP (polluter-pays-principle) 47; punitive measures against Greece 23; regional policy cooperation with EC 90–91; regional representations 93; rivalry with EC on audio-visual policies 72–75; Steering Committee on Mass Media (SCMM) 72; *see also* Consultative Assembly of CoE

Cold War: East-West tensions impact on security concerns 115; Greek case 34

Committee for the Challenges of Modern Society (CCMS) 44

Committee of Six 89–90

Committee on Local and Regional Affairs: establishment 88

Common Security and Defence Policy 110

Communauté d'intérêt moyen Alsace-Breisgau (CIMAB) 98

'Communication on the Community Action in the Cultural Sector' 71

Community Initiative Policy (CIP) 98–99

Conference of European Ministers of Spatial Planning 91

Conference of Local and Regional Authorities in Europe (CLRAE) 93

Conference of Regional Peripheral Maritime Regions (CRPM) 93–96

Conference on Confidence-and Security-Building Measures and Disarmament in Europe *see* CDE

Conference on Disarmament 9

Conference on Security and Cooperation in Europe *see* CSCE

confidence-and security-building measures (CSBMs) 110

Consultative Assembly of CoE: coordinated initiatives against Greek junta with EC 31; demanding human rights 25–26; directive against Greek junta 26; investigation on Greece 23, 31–32

Consultative Committee in Brussels 96

Copenhagen Declaration on European identity 68

costs of pollution: harm to humans and nature versus pollution-control programmes 42–43; internalized into cost of production 46–47

Council for Cultural Co-operation (CCC) 66

Council of Europe *see* CoE

cross-border air and water pollution 44

cross-border cooperation lobbying 93–95

CRPM (Conference of Regional Peripheral Maritime Regions) 93–96

CSBMs (confidence-and security-building measures) 110

CSCE (Conference on Security and Cooperation in Europe): defusing tensions and preserving détente initiatives 115–117; human rights proposal for inclusion 119–121; MBFR link 112–113; transatlantic cooperation on CDE proposal 124–126; US CDE proposal support 117–118

Cuban Missile Crisis 112

culture: architectural heritage preservation and restoration 67–68; CoE's 1950s policies 66; competition between EC and CoE in 1980s 71–76; cooperation 9–10; cultural heritage conservation 67–70; EC prominence over CoE 64; European Architectural Heritage Year (EAHY) 67–70; identity politics 142; inter-organizational cooperation between CoE and EC 66; interpretations 64; media regulation to achieve cultural objectives 73–74; member-states identities 65; pan-European cultural heritage endeavour 70; post-Cold War cooperation 10; safeguarding Greek cultural heritage 71; transnational networking 69–70; Treaty of Rome 65; *see also* audio-visual policies

Dales, John 46–47

Davignon Report 33

de-centering EC/EU 137; agenda-setting phase of new policy ideas 141

Dehousse, Fernand 31; maritime funding 95

Denmark: lodging complaints with European Commission of Human Rights against Greek junta 26–27, 31

Département du Bas-Rhin 98

developing countries: EC political conditionality 33–34

diffusion 6; geographic contiguity 139–140; human agency 138; new policy ideas based on real policy problems 141–142; policy convergence 138; power 142; as processes 137–138; regionalism and regional governance 139

Directive 256 26–27

disarmament: 1970s 112–114; broadening EPC to include security and defence 118–119;

INDEX

CDE geographical area of application 119–120; CDE mandate 110; CDE proposal 115–117; CSCE-MBFR link 112–113; defusing tensions and preserving détente initiatives 115–117; domestic concerns 118; EC 9; government confidence-building measures 113; governments working with EPC 115; multilateral discussions push from France 115–116; Mutual and Balanced Force Reduction in Europe (MBFR) 112; transatlantic cooperation 120–126; unitary action nourished by European Union discussions 118; US support 117–118; US-Soviet agreement of limitation of strategic arms 113
dispute resolution 7–8
dual track decision of NATO 118
duplication of IOs 4

EAHY (European Architectural Heritage Year) 64, 67–70
East-West relations: CoE fostering cooperation with Eastern block 97; Cold War tensions 115; cultural heritage preservation 70; East- West cooperation funding 99; television broadcasting regulations 75
EC (European Communities) 2; 1950s marginal touches on culture 65; addressing environmental issues with economic experts 50–52; asymmetry of cultural resources with CoE 68–69; audio-visual policies 72–75; CoE influence on Greek junta approach 31; CoE interplay influence in NATO 34; copying ideas and policy solutions from member- states and other IOs 3; cost of pollution 42–43; crowding out other ROs 141; cultural cooperation post-Cold War 10; cultural expansion in 1970s 71; cultural heritage preservation initiatives 68; culture competition with CoE in 1980s 71–76; de-centering 137; defining PPP 49; disarmament policies 9; disengagement with CoE on regional affairs 92; Environmental Action Programme 13, 42, 46; environmental policies 9, 41, 45; European Political Cooperation (EPC) 33, 112; External Relations 30; financial resources 14; freezing its association agreement with Greece 30–31; Greek junta 23–28, 33; Hallstein's retirement 30–31; Helsinki Final Act 33; human rights 8–9, 30–33; institutional connections with OECD 45; inter-organizational cooperation with CoE on culture 66; lack of regional policy institutional framework with EC 89–90; legal integration 13–14; limiting dialogue with Council of Europe 10; lobbying target for financial resources 97–99; local/regional co-operation 10; maritime funding lobbying 95–96; market integration 13;

overlapping membership with NATO, Council of Europe, and OECD 54; parliamentarian networks 141; participation in Washington D.C. conference 46; political conditionality for developing countries 33–34; power capacities 141; PPP proposal 52–53; prominence over CoE in culture 64; regional policy cooperation with CoE 90–91; relationship strengths with other IOs 13; safeguarding Greek cultural heritage 71; security policy ideas 9; strengthening internal relations from 1987–1990 97; views on polluter-pays-principle (PPP) 42; see also EP
EC-Greece 27
ECHR (European Court of Human Rights) 24, 141
ECSC (European Coal and Steel Community) 4–5
Eden Plan of 1952 90
education 1
EEC (European Economic Community) 5 see also EC
EFTA (European Free Trade Association) 5
EIB (European Investment Bank): financial aid to Greece 31
Elles, Lady: artistic treasures report 67–68
emissions trading 46
environment 9; addressing issues with economic experts 49–52; costs of pollution 42–43, 46–47; Council of Europe's pioneering role 44; EC emergence 45; emergence as new political concern 41–44; Environmental Action Programme 13, 42, 46; Environmental Committee established 45; EP agenda-setting actions 49; exemptions 50–52; NATO's pioneering role 44; OECD route to environmental policies 44–45; OECD versus EC PPP recommendations 53; OECD versus EC views on cost of pollution 42–43; pollution control 42; references 45–46; trade implications of environmental policies 45–46; UN Stockholm Conference on the Human Environment 44; Washington D.C. conference 46; widespread awareness and social mobilization 142; see also PPP
Environmental Action Programme 13, 42, 46
Environmental Committee 41–42; established 45; Subcommittee of Economic Experts 50
environmental economics: addressing environmental issues with economic experts 49–52; costs of pollution internalized into cost of production 46–47; formation 46
EP (European Parliament): Committee on the Association with Greece 27; cross-border lobbying 94–95; culture 66; emulation of CoE audio-visual policies 72; environment presented as new policy objective 41; environmental agenda-setting 49; Greek junta 23, 27–31

INDEX

EPC (European Political Cooperation) 33, 110, 140–141; broadening to include security and defence 118–119; competition with NATO 115–122; EC connection 112; emphasis on security 115; formation 111–112; London Report 119; NATO cooperation 122–126; overlapping membership with NATO 110–111

ERDF (European Regional Development Fund) 91

EU (European Union) 1; Common Security and Defence Policy 110; de-centering 137; education cooperation programmes 1; inter-institutional dynamics 3; Maastricht Treaty 11; public image of environmental leader 43; role in international legal co-operation 7

Europa Nostra: European Architectural Heritage Year (EAHY) 67–70, 69

'Europe of regions' 92

European (Economic) Community 114–115

European Architectural Heritage Year (EAHY) 64, 67–70

European audio-visual policy 76

European Capital of Culture programme 73

European Coal and Steel Community (ECSC) 4–5

European Commission of Human Rights 24

European Communities *see* EC

European Conference of Local Authorities: European Architectural Heritage Year (EAHY) 67–70

European Conservation Year 44

European Convention on Human Rights 26

European Court of Human Rights (ECHR) 24, 141

European Cultural Convention of 1954 65

'European cultural policy' 66

European Economic Community (EEC) 5 *see also* EC

European Free Trade Association (EFTA) 5

European integration 5, 136 *see also* diffusion

European Investment Bank (EIB): financial aid to Greece 27

European Ministerial Conference on mass-media policies initiative 74

European Parliament *see* EP

European Political Cooperation *see* EPC

European Recovery Programme: OECD administration 44–45

European Regional Development Fund (ERDF) 91

European Union *see* EU

European Water Charter 44

exemptions: PPP proposal 48–52

External Relations 30–31

Faller, Walter 28

Fernández, Victor: human rights policies 8–9

Final Communiqué of the North Atlantic Council of December 1983 126

financial aid: stopping to Greece 31

financial resources: EC 14

'First Communication…about the Community's Policy on the Environment' 41

forum-shopping 7

Framework Convention on Cross-Border Cooperation 94

France: CDE origin 114; independent defence policy 112; multilateral disarmament discussions push 115–116; Television without Frontiers (TWF) Directive support 73

geographic contiguity 139–140

Gorbachev, Mikhail: CoE opening up to Eastern European countries 97

Greece: CoE membership 24–25; Cold War 34; coup d'état 22; EC suspension of its association agreement 25; safeguarding Greek cultural heritage 71

Greek junta: CoE and EC coordinated initiatives against 23, 31; complaints filed before European Commission of Human Rights 26–27, 31; Consultative Assembly of CoE investigation 31–32; demanding human rights respect 25–26; EC Commission 1970 press communiqué criticizing Greek junta 33; EC freezing its association agreement with Greece 30–31; EP communiqué against 27; EP hearing 28; EP resolution against 29; parliamentary assembly cooperation against 25–27; response to the European Commission of Human Rights complaints 27; Socialist Group actions against 28; stopping of EIB financial aid 31; Western states failure to take action 22; withdrawal from CoE 32

Grégoire, Robert 67–68

Habermas, Jürgen: Western European States legitimacy 92

Hallstein, Walter: retirement 30–31

Hannequart, Achille 51

Harmel Report 112

Harned, Joseph 45–46

Helsinki Final Act 33

historic monument restoration 67

historical legacies of IOs: safeguarding 6

historiography research 5–6

Holocaust education promotion IOs 1

human agency: diffusion 138

human rights 8–9; 1970 press communiqué criticizing Greek junta 33; CoE and EC coordinated initiatives against Greek junta 31; Consultative Assembly of CoE investigation of Greece 31–32; CSCE document inclusion 119–121; Directive 256 25–26; EC agenda expansion 33; EC freezing its association agreement with Greece 30–31;

INDEX

EP communiqué against Greek junta 27;
EP resolution against Greek junta 29; Greek
junta response to the European Commission
of Human Rights complaints 27; Greek
withdrawal from CoE 32; Helsinki Final
Act 33; lodging complaints with European
Commission of Human Rights against Greek
junta 26–27; political conditionality 34; post-
war European cooperation 24; rise of human
rights in international politics 24

ideas: as vector for co-operation, competition and
transfers 10
implementation: international agreements 7;
PPP 48
INGOs (international non-governmental
organizations) 2; European Architectural
Heritage Year (EAHY) 67–70; role in linking
IOs and advancing policy ideas across
institutional venues 7
institutions: pressures 11; as vector for
co-operation, competition and transfers 12–13
inter-institutional dynamics 3
inter-organizational networking: response to
organizations' (states') inability to master
transnational challenges 7
inter-regionalism 138–139
international agreements: implementation 7
International Holocaust Remembrance Alliance 1
international organizations *see* IOs
international regime complexity 2
International Relations research 6–7
Interreg Initiative 98–99
inventor of emissions trading 46
IOs (international organizations) 1; Eastern
European history 3; EC copying of ideas and
policy solutions 3; education co-operation 1;
identifying and addressing policy issues 10;
origins 4; overlap and duplication 4; post-
World War I co-operation and competition 4;
safeguarding own historical legacies 6
Italy: Television without Frontiers (TWF)
Directive support 73

Joint Parliamentary Commission EC-Greece 27
Jürgensen, Harald 51

Kampleman, Max: US CDE proposal support 118
Kneese, Allen V. 51
Kraft, Bjørn 66

The Last Utopia 24
legal cooperation: EU's role 7
legal diplomacy 24
legal integration: EC 13–14
Lennep, Emil van: costs of pollution 41–42
Levi-Sandri, Lionello 28

Liaison Bureau of European Regional
Organizations 96
Linkage Assistance for European Border
Regions 99
lobbying: border regions interests 93–95;
Consultative Committee in Brussels 96;
establishment of regional associations 93;
Interreg Initiative 98–99; Liaison Bureau
of European Regional Organizations 96;
maritime funding 95–96; regional interests
representation in CoE 93; regional policies 96;
shift towards EC for financial resources 97–99
local actors 12
local and regional affairs: border regions interests
lobbying 93–95; CoE and EC interactions 88;
CoE fostering cooperation with Eastern block
97; CoE *versus* EC treatment 88; Committee
of Six 89–90; Committee on Local and
Regional Affairs 88; Conference of European
Ministers of Spatial Planning 91; Conference
of Local and Regional Authorities in Europe
(CLRAE) 93; Consultative Committee
in Brussels 96; EC and CoE cooperation
90–91; EC disengagement with CoE 92; EC
objective to strengthen internal relations
from 1987–1990 97; 'Europe of regions'
92; European Regional Development Fund
(ERDF) 91; Interreg Initiative 98–99; lack
of institutional framework between CoE
and EC 89–90; Liaison Bureau of European
Regional Organizations formation 96; Linkage
Assistance for European Border Regions 99;
maritime funding lobbying 95–96; regional
interests representation in CoE 93; regional
lobbying associations establishment 93;
regional policies 96; shifting lobbying towards
EC for financial resources 97–99; subsidies to
disadvantaged regions 89; Western European
States legitimacy 92
local cooperation policies 10
London Report on European Political
Cooperation 119
Lummaux, Michel: transborder television
regulation cooperation 74–75

Maastricht Treaty: institutional pressure 11
Madrid Framework Convention on Cross-Border
Cooperation 94
Madsen, Mikael Rask: legal diplomacy 24
Malfatti, Franco Maria: presenting environment
as new policy objective 41
Malmgren, Harald: trade implications of
environmental policies 45–46
maritime funding lobbying 95–96
market integration 141; broadcasting 73; EC 13
Marreco, Anthony 32
Martino, Edoardo 30–31

INDEX

MBFR (Mutual and Balanced Force Reduction in Europe) 112–114
Meunier: forum-shopping 7
Meyer, Jan-Henrik: Polluter Pays Principle (PPP) 9
military détente' 116
military security: CDE 109–110; Common Security and Defence Policy 110
Monnet, Jean: European Coal and Steel Community (ECSC) 4
movement of ideas and policies: diffusion 6
Moyn, Samuel: *The Last Utopia* 24
Mozer, Alfred 94
Mutual and Balanced Force Reduction in Europe (MBFR) 112

NATO (North Atlantic Council) 111; CDE geographical area of application agreement 119–120; CDE proposal support 115–117; CoE and EC interplay 34; CSCE-MBFR link 112–113; defusing tensions and preserving détente initiatives 115–117; disarmament's competition and co-operation 9; dual track decision 118; EPC competition 115–122; EPC cooperation 122–126; formation 111; French push for multilateral disarmament discussions 115–116; Harmel Report 112; MBFR talks 112; overlapping membership 54, 110–111; pioneering role in international environmental policies 44; transatlantic cooperation on CDE proposal 124–126; US CDE proposal support 117–118
Netherlands: lodging complaints with European Commission of Human Rights against Greek junta 26–27, 31
NGOs (non-governmental organizations) 44
the Nine 112
Noël, Émile: cooperation with CoE on audio-visual field 72–73
North America: opposition to CDE 117–118
North Atlantic Council *see* NATO
North-South integration: safeguarding Greek cultural heritage 71
Northern Franco-German Region Pfalz-Mittlerer Oberrhein Nord Alsace (PAMINA) 98
Norway: lodging complaints with European Commission of Human Rights against Greek junta 26–27, 31
Nott, John 119

OECD (Organization for Economic Co-operation and Development) 1; addressing environmental issues with economic experts 49–50; administration of European Recovery Programme from 1948 onwards 44–45; cost of pollution differences 42–43; EC PPP recommendation differences 53;

Environmental Committee 41–42, 45; environmental exemptions 50; institutional connections with EC 45; neoliberal economic growth policies after oil crisis 43; overlapping membership with NATO, Council of Europe, and EC 54; Polluter Pays Principle (PPP) 9, 42, 47–51; route to environmental policies 45
OEEC (Organization for European Economic Co-operation) 4
Oele, Adriaan Pieter 49
Oreja, Marcelino 72–73
Organization for Economic Co-operation and Development *see* OECD
overlapping memberships 138–139; EC, NATO, Council of Europe, and OECD 54; EPC and NATO 110–111
overlapping regionalism 138–139

PAMINA (Region Pfalz-Mittlerer Oberrhein Nord Alsace) 98
pan-European Council of Europe: education co-operation programmes 1
Paris Summit of 1972: community action in cultural field 68
parliamentarians 141; as actors 12; cooperation on Greek case 25–27; vectors of exchange in the Greek case 23
Parliamentary Assembly of the CoE *see* EP
policy convergence 138
Polish crisis 121
political conditionality: developing countries 34
political negotiations: environmental exemptions 50
Polluter Pays Principle *see* PPP
pollution control 42; addressing issues with economic experts 49–52; costs 42–43, 46–47; Council of Europe's pioneering role 44; polluter-pays-principle (PPP) 42, 47–49
Pollution, Property and Prices 46–47
post-Cold War cultural co-operation 10
post-war European cooperation: human rights 24
power: capacities of EC 141; diffusion of policy ideas 142
PPP (polluter-pays-principle) 9, 42, 47–49; 1974 Recommendation on the Implementation of the Polluter-Pays Principle 50; Council of Europe inclusion 47; defining with economic implications 49–52; EC definition 49; EP agenda-setting 49; exemptions 48; fair competition 47; John Dales' *Pollution, Property, and Prices* 46–47; OECD defining 47–48; OECD *versus* EC recommendations 53; political stakes and commitment levels of member-states 52; solution efficiency 47
Premoli, Augusto 68
press communiqué criticizing Greek junta in 1970 33

154

INDEX

pressures on policy issues 10–11
'Problems of Environmental Economic' seminar 50
public debate 10
public pressure 10–11

Radius, René 89
Raustiala, Kal: international regime complexity 2
realist epistemological perspective of European
  integration literature 5
Recommendation on the Implementation of the
  Polluter-Pays Principle if 1974 50
Region Pfalz-Mittlerer Oberrhein Nord Alsace
  (PAMINA) 98
regional actors 12
regional cooperation policies 10
regional lobbying: border regions interests
  93–95; Consultative Committee in Brussels 96;
  establishment of new associations 93; Interreg
  Initiative 98–99; Liaison Bureau of European
  Regional Organizations 96; maritime funding
  95–96; regional interests representation in CoE
  93; regional policies 96; shift towards EC for
  financial resources 97–99
'Report on the Future Tasks of the Alliance' 112
Resolution on Air Pollution Control 44
Rey, Jean 29
Rougemont, Denis de: regionalist views 93

SALT (US-Soviet agreement of limitation of
  strategic arms) 113
SALT 2 115
Sàndys, Duncan 12; EAHY spiritus rector 69
Santero, Natale 90
Schmidt, Helmut: support of Greece's expulsion
  from the CoE 26
Schultz, Klaus Peter 93
Schwartz, Ivo: TWF 74
SCMM (Steering Committee on Mass Media) 72
security: 1970s 112–114; broadening EPC to
  include security and defence 118–119; CDE
  geographical area of application 119–120;
  CDE proposal 115–117; CSCE-MBFR link
  112–113; defusing tensions and preserving
  détente initiatives 115–117; domestic concerns
  118; East-West Cold War tensions 115; EC
  9; European governments' deterioration
  of confidence in US administration 113;
  France's independent defence policy 112;
  government confidence-building measures
  113; governments working with EPC 115;
  human rights inclusion stance from US
  119–121; MBFR talks 112; transatlantic
  cooperation 120–126; unitary action
  nourished by European Union discussions 118;
  US CDE proposal support 117–118; US-Soviet
  agreement of limitation of strategic arms
  (SALT) 113

'Senate of Regions' 95
SEPC (Service for the Environment and
  Consumer Protection) 48, 51
Single European Act of 1987 42
social science research 7–8
Socialist Group: actions against Greek junta 28
Solemn Declaration on European Union of 1983 73
Soviet Union: invasion of Afghanistan 117; US
  sanctions against after Polish crisis 121
SPD (Sozialdemokratische Partei Deutschlands):
  support of Greece's expulsion from the CoE 26
Spénale, Georges 29
Spinelli, Altiero 46
Stanford School: diffusion 6
states: as vector for co-operation, competition
  and transfers 11
Steering Committee on Mass Media (SCMM) 72
strategic arms-limitation see SALT
'Stronger Community Action in the Cultural
  Sector' 71
Sub Commission on Prevention of
  Discrimination and Protection of Minorities:
  Greek case 24
Subcommittee of Economic Experts: OECD
  Environmental Committee 50
Sweden: lodging complaints with European
  Commission of Human Rights against Greek
  junta 26–27, 31

television regulation competition and
  cooperation between CoE and EC 73–75
Television without Frontiers (TWF) Directive
  73–74
the Ten 112
Thornberry, Cedric 32
Toulemon, Robert 46
trade implications: environmental policies 45–46
transatlantic cooperation on CDE proposal
  124–126
transatlantic relations: security 120–122
transfrontier television convention 1972
transnational and transgovernmental
  networks 139
transnational networking: cultural heritage 69–70
Treaty of Maastricht: cultural competences 76
Treaty of Rome 65; European (Economic)
  Community 114–115
TWF (Television without Frontiers) Directive
  73–74

UN (United Nations): Greek case 24; Stockholm
  Conference on the Human Environment 44
UNESCO (United Nations Education, Scientific,
  and Cultural Organization): 1, 67–70
United Europe movement: Duncan Sandys 12
United States: CDE proposal support 117–118;
  European governments' deterioration of

INDEX

confidence in US administration 113; human rights inclusion in CSCE document 120–121; sanctions against Soviet Union after Polish crisis 121; stance on East-West relations and human rights as source of tension in Western Europe 124; transatlantic cooperation on CDE proposal 124–126

US-Soviet agreement of limitation of strategic arms (SALT) 113

van der Stoel, Max 32

vectors for co-operation, competition and transfers 10–13

Victor, David G.: international regime complexity 2

von Malchus, Viktor 94

Warsaw Pact: European security conference 112

Washington D.C. environmental conference 46

Weber, Pierre: border regions support 94

Western European States: legitimacy 92

Western European Union (WEU) 4

Western governments cohesion: broadening EPC to include security and defence 118–119; CDE geographical area of application 119–120; confidence-building measures on security 113; defusing tensions and preserving détente initiatives 115–117; domestic concerns 118; seeking transatlantic cooperation on CDE proposal 124–126; unitary action nourished by European Union discussions 118; US stance on East-West relations and human rights as source of tension 124; as vector for co-operation, competition and transfers 11; working with EPC on security 115

WEU (Western European Union) 4

World Heritage Convention of 1972 67

Yerokostopoulos, Achille 26

Zighdis, Ioannis 26